# Crisis in Teaching

SUNY Series

# FRONTIERS IN EDUCATION
*Philip G. Altbach, Editor*

The Frontiers in Education Series features and draws upon a range of disciplines and approaches in the analysis of educational issues and concerns, helping to reinterpret established fields of scholarship in education by encouraging the latest synthesis and research.

Other books in this series include:

*Class, Race, and Gender in American Education*
—Lois Weis (ed.)

*Excellence and Equality: A Qualitatively Different Perspective on Gifted and Talented Education*
—David M. Fetterman

*Change and Effectiveness in Schools: A Cultural Perspective*
—Gretchen B. Rossman, H. Dickson Corbett, and William A. Firestone

*The Curriculum: Problems, Politics, and Possibilities*
—Landon E. Beyer and Michael W. Apple (eds.)

# Crisis
## in
# Teaching

## Perspectives on Current Reforms

*Edited by*
Lois Weis
Philip G. Altbach
Gail P. Kelly
Hugh G. Petrie
Sheila Slaughter

*State University of New York Press*

Some of these chapters have appeared in *Educational Policy*, Volume 1, Number 1 (1987). They have been reprinted with the permission of the publisher. The chapter by Andrew Gitlin and Robert Bullough Jr. appeared in a slightly different form in *Educational Policy*, Volume 1, Number 2 (1987).

Published by
State University of New York Press, Albany

© 1989 State University of New York

For information, address State University of New York
Press, State University Plaza, Albany, N.Y., 12246

**Library of Congress Cataloging-in-Publication Data**

Crisis in teaching.
    (SUNY series in frontiers in education)
    Includes bibliographies and index.
    1. Teachers—United States.    2. Teaching.
3. Teachers—Training of—United States.    4. Education—
United States—Aims and objectives.    I. Weis, Lois.
II. Series.
LB1775.C76      1988                    371.1′02        87-33634
ISBN 0-88706-819-7
ISBN 0-88706-820-0 (pbk.)


10 9 8 7 6 5 4 3 2 1

# Contents

# Acknowledgments

Numerous people have helped to shape this volume. Special thanks are due to Edith Hoshino and John Truax, who copyedited the manuscripts; and Caroline Gaynor, Pat Glinski, and Carol Norris who provided much needed help in other ways.

Thanks also to Lois Patton of SUNY Press, who supported this project from the beginning, and Gerald Dorfman, publisher of Geron-X who kindly permitted some of the chapters to be reprinted from *Educational Policy*.

# Introduction

\There is, according to many, a "crisis in teaching." The "best and the brightest" do not elect to enter teaching; teaching practices are said to be dreary and ineffective; and prospective teachers learn little in mediocre teacher education programs. Little wonder, so the argument goes, that America is falling behind in the global competitive market-place.\Our schools are failing, and the failure is due largely to teachers. By implication, it is also due to faculties of education in colleges and universities\

This volume examines the crisis. We seek to explore the definition of *crisis*, the evidence for its existence, reforms proposed to "solve" it, and possible effects of proposed reforms. We do not claim to present answers to all questions raised here. Rather, it is our attempt to unravel the current rhetoric of crisis and focus on proposed solutions. We provide varying points of view as we question simplistic solutions. Such solutions, we will suggest in this volume, often mask complex problems.

## THE CRISIS: WHAT IS IT?

\Within recent years, a spate of national reports have focused on the nation's schools. All the reports are critical of current practices, but no consensus exists as to what the crisis in education actually is.[1] The Gardner Commission ties the crisis to the fact that student scores on the SAT and other tests of ability have declined during the 1970s.[2] The Carnegie report, on the other hand, focuses on the fact that high schools "have been weakened by reduced support, declining public confidence and confusion over goals."[3] The National Science Board (NSB) faults the high school for not teaching enough science, mathe-

1

matics, and technology.[4] The Paideia Proposal argues that students
need to be exposed to a broad liberal arts curriculum and sees the crisis
as too much specialization.[5] The point is that no consensus exists as to
what the broader crisis in education is, and, therefore, no consensus as
to appropriate solutions.

There may be a lack of consensus as to what the general crisis in
education is, but there tends to be agreement on the fact that teachers,
and, by implication, teacher training programs, are largely responsible
for it. Just as schools historically have been expected to solve a range
of social, economic, and political problems not necessarily of their
making, teachers are, in turn, expected to solve all the problems of
schools. From the then Secretary of Education Terrell H. Bell's *A Nation
at Risk* to the Education Commission for the States' *Action for Excellence,* and the Twentieth Century Fund's *Making the Grade,* most
reports place blame for the current condition of schools almost entirely
on teachers.[6] Most important is the fact that it is the teachers themselves
in the first round of reports, rather than the conditions under which
they work, who are taken to task. Almost none of the original reports,
with the clear exception of Theodore Sizer's *Horace's Compromise,* focus
on the working conditions of classrooms and schools that might encourage mediocrity.[7]

In point of fact, the language of crisis is, as Catherine Cornbleth
argues in the first chapter of this volume, used as a rallying point, and
no sustained analysis is found in any of the reports of the extent to
which the quality of teaching has gone down, or whether teachers are
responsible for the alleged decline in SAT scores or any other indicator
of crisis. It is asserted that there is a crisis in teaching based on the notion that there is a crisis in education. The assumption is that if a crisis
in education does exist (however *crisis* is defined), teachers *must* be responsible for it and that, they, therefore, can solve it. If we address the
crisis in teaching, presumably all will be well with the schools. By extension, this means, in some of the reports, that all will be well with the
nation's economy.[8]

While this is certainly an unfair burden to place upon teachers,
and there is a need for a clear analysis of what the crisis in teaching actually is, few would argue with the point that teachers and teaching
could be better. A number of proposals have been put forth within the
last two years which have built upon the initial round of reports. Most
notably, the Holmes Group report *Tomorrow's Teachers* and the Carnegie study *Teachers for the 21st Century* have taken on the task of proposing reform in teaching.[9] We will, in this volume, examine a number
of their specific proposals.

## PROPOSED REFORMS

Proposed reforms tend to fall into two categories: those associated with teacher education and those associated with the teaching profession. Both the Holmes Group report and the Carnegie study take seriously the challenge to reform both teacher education and teaching. As such, they move far beyond proposals regarding teachers in earlier reports.

One of the major goals of the Holmes Group is to make the education of teachers intellectually sound, with the assumption being that it has not been so in the past. *Competent teaching*, as defined by Holmes, "is a compound of knowledge of four elements: (1) a broad general and liberal education; (2) the subject matter of the teaching field; (3) pedagogy and educational literature; and (4) reflective practical experience."[10]

In line with a "broad general and liberal education," Holmes recommends an extended teacher education program, encompassing the perspectives of the liberal arts. In an attempt to upgrade teacher education, students would receive a bachelor's degree in a discipline, with a stress on the liberal arts, and obtain a master's in teaching only after completing the bachelor's degree. The stress on the liberal arts is coupled with the notion that the undergraduate curriculum would itself be changed in order to produce more educated teachers. Thus, according to a summary of Holmes, "[r]eform of teacher education obviously must be coupled to changes in arts and science undergraduate education that center on the development of courses in core subjects that elaborate the structure of the disciplines and the disciplines' most powerful and generative ideas."[11]

Hugh G. Petrie and Alan R. Tom take up this debate here. Petrie takes a position supporting the extension of teacher education programs along the lines of the Holmes Group report, and Tom raises questions about this position. The possible long-term effects of extending the teacher education program to five years, thereby reducing the role of traditional four-year teacher training colleges in the preparation of teachers, needs to be considered carefully here. Some of the points raised by Gary Sykes in this volume relate to this point.

Robert Calfee also calls for reform in teacher education. He focuses specifically on pedagogy, stressing the importance of teaching teachers to articulate the principles underlying lessons. He argues for pedagogical improvements that would encourage an emphasis on explicitness, explanation, and the ability to articulate what is important. Although he does not tie his proposals to the Holmes Group directly, his ideas serve to elaborate proposed improvements in pedagogical training, offering a perspective supplied by no one else in this volume.

A second set of proposed reforms addresses the teaching profession itself. One proposal involves standards of entry into the profession. The Holmes Group commits itself to develop and administer a series of Professional Teacher Examinations that can provide the basis for teaching credentials and licenses. The development of local examinations throughout the country and the current use of the National Teacher Examination in some states reflects concern over standards despite time spent in teacher preparation programs.

Although the Carnegie and Holmes reports are generally supportive of each other in the sense that both stress the liberal arts, graduate-level professional preparation, internships beyond student teaching, closer school-community connections, change in the structure of the teaching profession itself, and strong assessment procedures, Carnegie has recently emphasized almost wholly the development of a National Teachers' Board with a stress on the testing of teachers. Holmes, on the other hand, focuses on a tripartite approach; that is, graduation from an approved program, passing a set of tests and involvement in an approved internship. Given the Carnegie push for testing, it is important that we look carefully at tests and at claims that increased testing will automatically result in a resolution of the crisis.[12] A number of the authors in this volume touch upon this issue, but we do not address it at great length here.

A further reform is linked to teacher salaries. Some of the early national reports did stress this issue and assumed that raising teacher salaries will automatically serve to attract brighter people into the profession. The Education Commission for the States argues that those going into teaching are the least intelligent among college students, and few studies take issue with this point. The notion is that if teacher salaries are more competitive, we will attract brighter students, thereby altering the nature of the profession.

One of the most controversial of the proposals surrounding pay is that of merit pay, and the leaders of the National Education Association (NEA) and the American Federation of Teachers (AFT) differed in their response to it.[13] Steven Jacobson addresses the merit pay issue here. He suggests that merit pay plans have become a catch-all and that little is likely to result until some of this conceptual confusion is worked out.

There have, in addition, been a number of proposals for differentiated staffing, also as an incentive for attracting and retaining brighter people into teaching. Both Holmes and Carnegie endorse this concept. The idea behind differentiated staffing is that the best and the brightest will enter teaching only if the rewards and, most importantly, opportunities for professional advancement, are increased dramatically. This means not only raising salaries but offering quasi-administrative positions and increased autonomy to those at the top of the profession. Thus, Holmes put forth a three-tiered system to be comprised of the Career Professional Teacher, the Professional Teacher, and Instructor. The Career Professional Teacher will be capable of assuming responsibility for not only the classroom, but aspects of the school, and even the university. The Professional Teacher would be an autonomous classroom teacher, and the Instructor would teach only under the supervision of a Career Professional Teacher. Carnegie offers a similar proposal.

The proposed reforms regarding differentiated staffing are far-reaching in their potential effects and may serve to polarize even further administrators and teachers. In fact, a group of administrators in Rochester have taken the district to court because they argue that teachers are now assuming administrative functions—functions not properly within their realm. As more and more districts attempt a differentiated staffing model, these cleavages are likely to be even greater and potential benefits and/or costs are as yet not known. In this volume, R. Jerrald Shive and Charles W. Case offer their idea of differentiated staffing. Susan Moore Johnson and Niall C. W. Nelson raise questions about such an idea in practice and discuss the conditions under which teachers will or will not support them.

The varied proposals for reform are controversial and we have attempted to capture some of this controversy here. Among educators themselves the response is not uniform. Albert Shanker, AFT President, points to some of the areas of reform in this volume and suggests alternative reforms. Hendrik D. Gideonse offers an overview of the negative responses and, from his point of view, misunderstandings, regarding the Holmes report. This is a time of ferment in education as Shanker and Gideonse make clear.

Andrew Gitlin and Robert Bullough, Linda M. McNeil, Mary Haywood Metz, Michael W. Apple, and Gary Sykes in this volume raise criticisms from a broader perspective. Gitlin and Bullough discuss the negative implications of traditional evaluation procedures for teachers and McNeil argues that too much control over teachers in the form of state-mandated testing, in particular, may cause the most creative teachers to leave the profession. Top-down reform, she argues, may result in outcomes exactly opposite to what are intended.

Metz points to the semiautonomous nature of teacher culture. She argues, based on ethnographic work in the "Heartland" schools, that teacher culture takes its shape and form for a variety of reasons, none of which are directly amenable to external control. She suggests that reforms must pay attention to teachers' need for pride in craft and the way in which this pride can shape teacher culture. Any reform ignoring this need is doomed to failure. Apple responds to the notion that technology will somehow solve the current crisis. Numerous reports, including *A Nation at Risk,* suggest that this is the case. Apple specifically looks at the use of computers in school and the way in which computers are linked to teacher work. Gary Sykes offers a look at the positive and negative points of professionalism, suggesting that professionalism as an ideology has worked for the benefit of the few rather than the many. He offers ways in which teaching may possibly escape some of the negative aspects because schools are state institutions.

Authors in this volume raise questions about proposed reforms. A coherent message in this volume is that no simple answer is found to the problems that beset teaching. We cannot go out and find a "quick fix" if we are to engage seriously in reform. We must think through what the problems actually are, the solutions proposed, and the possible effects of these solutions. Just as schools cannot solve all of society's problems, teachers cannot solve all of schools' problems. This should not deter us from taking reform seriously in teaching and teacher education, however. All this means is that easy solutions will necessarily mask complex problems and that we should look carefully at possible unanticipated consequences of our proposals. We must be ever watchful of the actual effects of proposed solutions if we are ever to move beyond the short-term effects of the "language of crisis."

## NOTES

1. Gail Kelly raises this point in "Setting the Boundaries of Debate About Education," in *Excellence in Education: Perspectives on Policy and Practice,* Philip Altbach, Gail Kelly, and Lois Weis, eds. (Buffalo, N. Y. : Prometheus Press, 1985), pp. 31–42.

2. National Commission on Excellence in Education, *A Nation at Risk: The Imperative for Educational Reform* (Washington, D. C.: U. S. Government Printing Office, 1983).

3. Ernest Boyer, *High School: A Report on Secondary Education in America* (New York: Harper and Row, 1983).

4. National Science Board, Commission on Precollege Education in Mathematics, Science and Technology, *Educating Americans for the 21st Century: A Plan of Action for Improving Mathematics, Science and Technology Education for All American Elementary and Secondary Students so That Their Achievement Is the Best in the World by 1995* (Washington, D. C. National Science Foundation, 1983).

5. Mortimer Adler, *The Paideia Proposal* (New York: Macmillan, 1982).

6. *A Nation at Risk; Making the Grade: Report of the Twentieth Century Fund Task Force on Federal Elementary and Secondary Education Policy* (New York: Twentieth Century Fund, 1983). Education Commission of the States, *Action for Excellence: Task Force on Education for Economic Growth* (1983).

7. Theodore Sizer, *Horace's Compromise: The Dilemma of the American High School* (Boston: Houghton Mifflin, 1984).

8. The most obvious example of this position is that in *A Nation at Risk.*

9. A Report of the Holmes Group, *Tomorrow's Teachers* (1986); and the Report of the Task Force on Teaching as a Profession of the Carnegie Forum on Education and the Economy, *A Nation Prepared: Teachers for the 21st Century* (1986).

10. Frank Murray, "Summary of the Holmes Group Recommendation," mimeographed p. 5.

11. Frank Murray, p. 6.

12. See *Educational Policy,* vol. 1, no. 2 (1987) for a special issue devoted to testing and evaluation.

13. See Joel Spring, "Political and Economic Analysis," in Philip Altbach, Gail Kelly and Lois Weis, eds. *Excellence in Education* (Buffalo, N. Y. : Prometheus Press, 1985), pp. 75–89.

CATHERINE CORNBLETH

Chapter One

# *Cries of Crisis, Calls for Reform, and Challenges of Change*

In the fifth year of the current cycle of education reform activity, as some people are wearying of the effort and others are claiming a more far-reaching second phase, we would do well to reexamine the situation in an attempt to determine what has been accomplished, where we are heading, and what the apparent effects are. Even a cursory review of the reports calling for education reform reveals widespread agreement that teachers and teaching are a major source of both the problems of schooling and their solution. A crisis in teaching has been proclaimed, recommendations have been offered for its resolution, and some action has been taken on those recommendations—with the promise of more to come.

My purpose here is to review critically the cries of crisis and calls for reform of teaching and then to consider challenges of change. Following a brief exploration of the crisis approach characteristic of social reform efforts in the United States, I examine two purported problems of teaching—the projected shortages of qualified teachers and the poor quality of teaching—and proposed solutions. The questions of interest include: What is the problem? Why is that a problem? For whom is it a problem? What is the likelihood that the proposed solutions will resolve the identified problems or the larger crisis? Who benefits from the proposed solutions? In considering challenges of change, I suggest that several major problems of teaching and reform have yet to be addressed.

## CRIES OF CRISIS[1]

The ritual and rhetoric of reform are a way of life in the United States. Out of the larger context of U. S. schooling and society, the current cries of crisis and calls for education reform are easily misunderstood. Given the complexity, change, and uncertainty of our culture, a crisis is needed to capture our attention. Crisis language has become an integral part of our everyday political and social life. Cries of crisis and their accompanying calls for reform signify dissatisfaction, impatience, and optimism. Whatever the perceived threat to life, liberty, property, and/or happiness, typically it is seen to stem from forces beyond our immediate control but to be resolvable if we are willing to make the necessary sacrifices.[2]

Striking similarities are found in the language employed, problems identified, and solutions recommended in the education reform reports. Crisis and urgency, exhortation and hope are dramatically communicated in language intended to shape belief and mobilize action. In addition to the "rising tide of mediocrity" and "act of unthinking, unilateral disarmament" of *A Nation at Risk,* we are told by the National Commission for Excellence in Teacher Education that"At stake is not the present status of teachers but the future of the nation" while the Carnegie Task Force tells us that although

> concern over the quality of education in this country has been expressed in repeated warnings . . . most Americans still do not fully understand the gravity of the situation . . . We do not believe that the educational system needs repairing; we believe it must be rebuilt to match the drastic change needed in our economy if we are to prepare our children for productive lives in the twenty-first century.

Schools and teachers are simultaneously seen as a national disgrace and as a prime source of national salvation.

Education, including teacher education, like other U.S. institutions, is seemingly decentralized. No formal integration is found across organizational levels, nor is an operational central authority found.[3] Would-be reformers must gain the attention and support of a range of audiences. Historically, nationwide efforts to change have occurred as reform movements with evangelical religious characters rather than as less flamboyant legislative and administrative or bureaucratic efforts to improve.[4]

Task force or commission activities leading to brief reports that receive wide media exposure and generate public discussion are to be expected in this context. Commissions, however, typically operate under constraints that make it difficult for them to do more than dramatize perceived problems, give the appearance of national consensus regarding their solution, and reassure the public that the problems are being thoughtfully considered by sincere, knowledgeable people.[5] Therefore, it is important to reform that the reports be taken as a starting, not an end, point in the consideration of problems and possible responses. They are helpful in arousing awareness but should not be allowed to limit debate or action.

In the school reform reports, for example, the identified problems of schooling and recommended solutions direct attention to curriculum and standards, school leadership and management, and teaching and teacher education. The proposed remedies call for more requirements and higher standards. Many assume that higher standards somehow enhance both teaching and learning, that more is better, and that quantity becomes quality. Given these assumptions, no apparent need exists to consider reforming the structural arrangements of schooling. Following the school reform reports, current organizational patterns would remain intact while changes are made within and around them. As Peterson observed, "A crisis is discovered and various reforms are proposed, but in the end no institutional change is deemed necessary to push back the rising tide of mediocrity."[6] Subsequent reform reports and other observers have recommended structural changes such as differentiated staffing, which would expand the responsibilities of the highest level of teachers at the expense of current administrators. Master, lead, or career professional teachers would play a major role in curricular, staff development, and teacher evaluation decisionmaking, perhaps eliminating the need for some administrative positions as well as realigning relationships among teachers and between teachers and administrators.

Before examining purported problems of teaching and proposed solutions, speculating why teachers and teacher education have become a primary target of criticism and reform is advisable. Several strands of explanation seem plausible. Teachers are highly visible and as yet have been unable to claim special (i. e., professional) expertise; having attended school, most presume to be knowledgeable about schools and teaching. Teacher education programs are few in number (approximately 1200) relative to school districts (more than 18,000), and teacher educators have little status and few resources that might translate into political clout within their colleges or universities let alone within the larger political arena. Targeting teacher education rather than the performance of current teachers avoids attacking an organized occupation with more than two million members and considerable political influence. Furthermore, because schooling is a state responsibility, both teachers and teacher education are subject to state control.[7] It would not be unreasonable to suggest that teachers and teacher education have been targeted because of their visibility and/or vulnerability and, further, that preoccupation with teaching deflects attention from other problems of schooling and groups with vested interests in the present educational system.[8] The focus on teachers and teaching also can be seen as reflecting a widespread inclination toward psychological reductionism where problem causes and cures are assumed to reside in the person rather than in the situation. This is not to say that teaching and teacher education are without problems but to question the centrality of the identified problems and the adequacy of the proposed solutions.

## CALLS FOR REFORM

The two problems of teaching examined here were highlighted in most of the education reform reports. Both are seen as negatively affecting the quality of teaching in the nation's elementary and secondary schools and thus contributing to the crisis in teaching. They have received widespread attention, generated considerable professional and public debate, and reached policymaking agendas. Although interrelated, they represent different kinds of problems that seem to call for different kinds of response. One is the projected shortage of qualified teachers—an estimated 400,000 to 900,000 shortfall by 1992 if current trends continue.[9] This problem has been defined as attracting and retaining qualified teachers. The second is the poor quality of teaching, resulting in the declining competitiveness of the United States in global markets, and imperiled national security, as well as students' poor showing on various achievement tests. This problem has been defined primarily in terms of inadequate teacher education, specifically low standards, too little academic coursework, inadequate field experience, and failure to use the growing base for teaching.[10] Although other factors affecting the quality of teaching have been cited as problems in need of solution (e.g., the conditions of teachers' work, the criteria of teacher evaluation), they have received relatively little attention to date from education policymakers.

### Teacher Shortages

On the projected teacher shortage, Darling-Hammond has offered the most thorough and thoughtful analyses I have encountered.[11] She points out that there is no agreement as to what constitutes a "real" shortage of teachers, i.e., one of crisis proportions, and that

> issues of teacher shortage are ultimately political .... If teacher shortages exist, then inducements to teaching must be found .... Essentially, the competing claims about teacher shortages are arguments over the desirability of raising standards and salaries, on the one hand, or maintaining current conditions, on the other.[12]

Current conditions include more than 30,000 "teachers" with emergency or temporary certificates during the 1985–86 school year. "With changes in certfication and hiring standards," Darling-Hammond notes, "the supply of teachers can be altered at will so that, based on body counts at least, supply can always equal demand."[13] In addition, class sizes can be increased and course offerings reduced. "We are left," she concludes,

> with indications of shortages in some teaching fields [particularly science, mathematics, foreign languages, and special education] and locations [particularly large cities]; upswings in demand; signs that the shrinking supply of new teachers may have bottomed out; and a volatile policy environment that will complicate projections.[14]

The problem of teacher shortages has been defined as attracting and retaining qualified teachers, particularly in those subject areas and locations where shortages currently exist. The current and projected teacher shortages constitute a problem for several reasons. One is that the absence or overburdening (e.g., with more or larger classes) of qualified teachers reduces learning opportunities for affected students, most likely those already least advantaged, and impedes school reform efforts. A second assumes that shortages will be remedied by hiring underqualified recruits with negative effects not only on student learning opportunities and school reform efforts but also on the professionalization of teaching. A related third reason is that the pool of qualified but currently nonteaching teachers who might be called upon appears to be shrinking. Other reasons involve the costs in dollars and relative status (e.g., of teachers in relation to other school personnel) to make teaching more attractive to qualified young people.

Shortages of qualified teachers present a problem for several constituencies, particularly the students and their families in districts hardest hit. Also affected are school personnel, state agencies that certify teachers, and society at large if increasing numbers of students are poorly served by their teachers. Schools, colleges, and departments of education (SCDEs) that prepare teachers are affected insofar as they are expected to prepare more teachers while maintaining or raising quality.

The importance of problem setting is that what is identified as a problem and how it is defined shape solution efforts. Problem definition, in effect, determines what solutions are considered plausible, thus highlighting some options and masking others. In this case, distinguishing between the problem of teacher shortages and the problem of shortages of qualified teachers is important. The former can be resolved in large part by lowering certification standards, by offering temporary or emergency certification, and sometimes by providing alternative certification routes (e.g., on-the-job supervision and after-school seminars). The latter cannot.

As policymaking moves from agenda setting to policy formulation, problems may be redefined in ways that make them more manageable and their resolution less likely to offend important constituencies.[15] If the public, policymakers, and educators are serious about avoiding the projected shortages of qualified teachers, monitoring problem definition so as to avoid attempts to reduce the problem to one of body counts is necessary.

A related issue concerns the declining proportion of minority teachers vis-à-vis the increasing proportion of minority students in public elementary and secondary schools. If having minority teachers as role models is valued, then their dwindling numbers constitutes a problem. Given that more and more attractive opportunities are available to minority as well as female college graduates now than one or two decades ago, the problem becomes one of making teaching more accessible and attractive to minorities.

The solutions to the problems of teacher shortages proposed by the school and teacher education reform reports differ in several important respects. The school reform reports recommended "flexible" or non-traditional means of teacher certification as well as financial incentives such as grants and loans to prospective teachers in subject areas facing shortages. To improve teacher quality as well as attract and retain sufficient numbers of qualified teachers, they recommend differentiated staffing (e.g., master teacher recognition, career ladders) and salaries based at least in part on measured effectiveness.[16]

While the teacher education reform reports endorse financial incentives and higher salaries linked to accountability and differentiated staffing, they are more cautious about flexible certification routes. For example, the Holmes Group report *Tomorrow's Teachers* clearly points to the dangers of repeating the experiences of the 1950s and 1960s when many underqualified individuals were certified as teachers *via* non-traditional routes and then tenured. Instead, Holmes strongly recommends differentiated staffing, which

> would make it possible for communities to respond to disequilibrium in the supply of and demand for teachers. To meet past shortages, standards were lowered across the board and individuals with spurious preparation were able to achieve full professional status as teachers. The concept of differentiated staffing would permit responsibile expansion and contraction of a pool of teachers [at the entry, instructor, level], while protecting the integrity of the professional teaching force.[17]

Differentiated staffing also is seen as a way of rewarding and retaining superior experienced teachers and of making use of their expertise, for example, in curriculum change and the induction of new teachers.

A second difference between the recommendations of the school and teacher education reform reports with respect to attracting and retaining sufficient numbers of qualified teachers is the education reform reports' emphasis on improved working conditions and increased teacher autonomy and responsibility. The bottom line of this argument, which is supported by existing research, is that good teachers will not be attracted to or remain in teaching unless they are treated as professionals.[18] A third difference is the teacher education reform reports' emphasis on widespread, active recruitment, especially of minority teachers, supported by special programs, scholarships, and forgiveable loans. Overall, the teacher education reform reports' recommendations are more comprehensive and sensitive to equity concerns. They eschew lowered standards and look to improved teaching conditions and recruitment as well as financial incentives to attract and retain qualified teachers representative of the diversity of the population.

The likelihood that the proposed solutions will resolve the identified problem or contribute to the resolution of the larger crisis depends on at least three factors: scale, integration, and competition. *Scale* refers to the size or scope of the efforts. Token recruitment or financial assistance programs, for example, will be just that. They will give the appearance of reform but have little effect. *Integration* refers to the coordination of various changes in mutually supportive ways. It seems unlikely, for example, that even massive recruitment efforts will have much effect unless the conditions and financial rewards of teaching are substantially improved. Piecemeal changes, like token programs, will have little effect. *Competition* refers to what occurs in other occupational sectors that serves to make teaching more or less attractive, regardless of what reforms are obtained in teaching and schooling. Clearly, teaching as an occupation, professional or other, does not exist in isolation. Its attractiveness is in part a function of the relative attractiveness of other occupations. A declining economy with diminishing opportunities elsewhere, for example, would increase the appeal of teaching even as it currently exists.

To have a reasonable chance of success, the proposed reforms must be coordinated and massive. In the forseeable future, incremental improvements are highly unlikely to provide sufficient numbers of qualified teachers for all students.

## *Teacher Quality and Teacher Education*

According to the various commentators, the quality of teaching in the nation's schools ranges from mediocre to dismal. While the presence of outstanding teachers is recognized, the vast majority of the teachers typically are portrayed in unflattering terms. In the school reform reports, blame is placed on teacher education programs. The teacher education reform reports acknowledge the need for strengthening teacher preparation programs and call for changing teaching conditions in the schools in order to improve the quality of teaching and student learning. Under current conditions, they argue, teachers are discouraged from practicing what they know and are able to do. Better educated teachers will not have much impact on students learning until the conditions of teaching are changed to facilitate rather than impede quality teaching.

Consensus is apparent that the quality of teaching and teacher education can and should be improved. The problem has been defined largely as one of reforming preservice or initial teacher education. The major problems with preservice teacher education have been specified as low standards for program admission and completion, insufficient academic coursework, inadequate field experience, and neglect of the growing knowledge base for professional practice. Although the Holmes Group and the AFT and NEA continue to call for reform of the conditions of teaching as well as teacher education, little action has occurred to date in this arena. The de facto definition of the teacher quality problem in terms of the weakness or irrelevance of preservice teacher education programs, despite questionable supporting evidence (see Note 10), seems to be a function of teacher education's previously noted vulnerability vis-à-vis other possible targets of blame and reform.[19]

In any event, teacher quality is perceived as a problem because too many students are not learning as much (or as easily or as rapidly) as desired, the assumption being that better teaching will yield improvements in learning. The learning of interest is primarily that measured by standardized tests, which is assumed to contribute to national economic strength and security. Teacher quality is not only a problem for sudents and society in general, but also for school administrators and education policymakers under pressure from parents to porovide an education that will enable their children to compete successfully in tomorrow's world, for teachers seeking professional recognition, and for SCDEs struggling for status and, in some cases, survival.

The solution to the problem of teacher quality-education proposed by the school reform reports is to establish high standards for program admission and completion, including competence in an academic discipline and demonstration of effective teaching performance. These standards are to be established jointly by SCDEs and state certifying agencies who will administer the required tests. Mandated testing is to ensure undefined quality. How the standards are to be met and maintained is not addressed.

The teacher education reform reports, especially Holmes and Carnegie, move considerably beyond the call for higher standards and competency testing. Although standards are prominent among their recommendations, attention is directed not only to controls but to structural change and substansive improvement. Most noteworthy are their proposals for strengthening undergraduate liberal arts studies and academic majors, for graduate professional study consistent with the growing research generated and craft derived knowledge base for teaching, and for supervised internship or induction experiences in cooperating schools akin to teaching hospitals.

The intent is to prepare teachers to be reflective practitioners who continue to learn and improve their teaching, in contrast to competent technicians who implement others' prescriptions. In order to accomplish ths goal, changes in the conditions of teachers' work are recommended including provision of time, space, materials and technology, support services, and autonomy (i.e., greater participation in decision-making) commensurate with their responsibilities. Teachers are to be treated as professionals and held accountable for student learning. Finally, in support of their proposals for teacher education reform and the professionalization of teaching, Holmes and Carnegie advocate restructuring teaching by differentiating teacher roles (i.e., distinguishing

novice instructors from experienced professional teachers and lead or
career professional teachers). Such restructuring requires changes in
the current division of authority between teachers and administrators
and reallocation of resources from "administrative overhead" to instruction. The Holmes and Carnegie reports point to the interdepen-
dence of higher education, teacher education, and teaching and the
resulting need for coordinated reform strategies.[20]

The teacher quality-education problem presents substantially
greater challenges than does the problem of teacher shortages. Whereas
the latter is a well-structured problem (i.e., the goal and means to its attainment are known or knowable), the teacher quality-education problem is ill-structured. In addition to complexity, it is characterized by an
ill-defined, and perhaps nonconsensually definable, goal and by uncertainty regarding means of goal attainment and their attendant costs
and benefits. What is relatively certain is that the teacher quality-
education problem will be much more costly to remedy. The costs ac-
crue both in resources and in more far-reaching changes that threaten
established structural arrangements and role incumbents. What would
happen, for example, to the roles of principals and assistant principals
(and assistant superintendents for instruction and curriculum coordinators) in school districts that instituted differentiated teacher roles
along the lines suggested by Holmes and Carnegie? Also, compared
to the problem of teacher shortages, resolution of the teacher quality-
education problem seems to require more attention to integration of
change efforts than to scale and competition factors. A danger here is
that the narrow definition of the teacher quality problem primarily in
terms of preservice teacher education serves to divert attention from
school site reforms necessary to enhanced teaching and learning. The
likelihood that any or all of the proposed solutions will resolve the
identified problem of teacher quality-education or contribute to the
resolution of the larger crisis is thus problematic.


## CHALLENGES OF CHANGE

Reform that would enhance the quality of teaching poses multiple
challenges. Underlying the identification of particular problems and
solutions, and the enactment of those solutions, are conceptual and
structural issues. In this section, I first explore apparent conceptual or
theoretical weaknesses in the education reform proposals with the intent of stimulating reconsideration and strengthening of the conceptual
framework that might guide the form and substance of change efforts.

Then I conclude by considering structural aspects of education reform.

## Conceptual Challenges

Our language, conceptions, and style of discourse are important because they both reflect and shape how we see, think about, study, and act on matters of teaching and their reform. The language with which situations, problems, and solutions are framed is necessarily selective. Regardless of how rational or scientific our language and discourse might appear, they are not neutral. They are social constructions that convey and sustain selected values that benefit some interests at the expense of others. My concern is to reduce the possibility of squandering opportunities for education reform on poorly constructed or ill-fitting ideas.

Conceptually, the reform reports reflect and help perpetuate a technocratic rationality that is at odds with the goals of quality teaching and teachers as reflective practitioners. By technocratic rationality, I mean a mode of reasoning, investigation, or planning that gives priority to considerations of procedure or technique. While technocratic rationality may be productive in other arenas (e.g., engineering), it is inherently antithetical to social—including educational—change because questions of purpose and substance, of value and interest, tend to be ignored. They are either reduced to procedural questions (e.g., means of assessment) or assumed to be unimportant, beyond the parameters of rationality, or already resolved. The irony of technocratic rationality in social affairs is that, by deflecting attention from questions of purpose and substance and their social and political implications, it precludes the institutional reforms that it purports to foster. Consequently, that enactment of the proposed reforms would have the desired result is highly unlikely unless, of course, the desired result is the appearance rather than the actuality of reform.

Technocratic rationality and its consequences are especially evident in the school reform reports' emphasis on standards and standardization and in the teacher education reform reports' assumptions regarding the nature and use of a knowledge base for teaching and teacher education. The school reports are nearly silent on questions of purpose and do not significantly challenge the status quo within or without the schools and teacher education programs. Purposes are taken for granted, and attention is given to means of accomplishing presumably consensually derived goals. in the name of undefined quality and excellence, the emphasis is on standards and efficiency.

Coherence is obtained by establishing a common curriculum, and effectiveness is to follow from more frequent and rigorous testing. In effect, improving schooling and teacher education is mandated by moral exhortation and legislation or by administrative decree.[21]

*Knowledge Base.* With respect to the nature and use of a knowledge base for teaching and teacher education, Holmes and Carnegie take the position that knowledge is cumulative and accumulating and that it can and should be directly applied in classroom practice. Holmes emphasizes research generated knowledge while Carnegie recognizes both research generated and craft derived knowledge. The latter refers to the experiential knowledge of exceptional teachers. While Holmes provides a few clues as to the presumed nature and intended use of the growing knowledge base, Carnegie leaves particulars to be determined by a National Board of Professional Teaching Standards, which will "define what teachers need to know and be able to do."[22]

In *Tomorrow's Teachers,* we are told that "scholarship and empirical research in education has matured, providing a solid base for an intellectually vital program of professional studies,"[23] that this knowledge base must be articulated and means developed "by which it can be imparted" to prospective teachers,[24] and that "formal knowledge must be used as a guide to practical action."[25] Illustrations of such formal, research-generated knowledge in action include using "advanced organizers," asking "higher-order questions," and waiting "more than a few seconds" for a student's response to one's questions.[26] Less specific reference is made to research on teacher thinking and decisionmaking and to recent cognitive research on how student misconceptions interfere with their learning of science concepts.

Holmes thus offers a narrow, technocratic conception of knowledge and its use that ends to be ahistorical and decontextualized. It is ahistorical and decontextualized insofar as findings are taken out of the settings in which they were found and assumed to be widely generalizable—if not universal. Furthermore, the initial purposes for which knowledge was sought and used and the underlying assumptions tend to be ignored or unknown, although not without continuing effect. Individualized instruction, for example, derives historically from efforts to control rather than promote personal development.[27] Ironically, the effectiveness of contemporary forms of individualization is measured by standardized tests.

The ahistoricism and decontextualization of technocratic conceptions of knowledge and its use also tend to separate understanding and practice. Research findings, usually correlations between teacher behaviors and student learning as measured by standardized achievement tests, are taken out of their context in time, place, and purpose. Then they are presented as broadly generalizable prescriptions (or guidelines) for teacher behavior, regardless of subject area, grade level, student group, or desired student outcome. Teachers are to incorporate these findings into their classroom practice, not necessarily understanding them (e.g., why an observed correlation was obtained) or their limitations.

Furthermore, knowledge seems to be construed as discrete, empirically grounded findings or "facts" with instrumental utility, i.e., direct applicability to classroom practice. The underlying assumptions are (1) that research-generated knowledge provides widely applicable guidelines (if not prescriptions) for practice that experts should make available to teachers for application in their classrooms, and (2) that the findings and accompanying guidelines eventually will add up to productive teaching and learning. How this accumulation and application might be accomplished is not addressed in *Tomorrow's Teachers*.

Nor is consideration given to interpretive as well as instrumental uses of research-generated and other knowledge. By interpretive use, I mean using knowledge to test one's beliefs, to generate hypotheses that are tested in one's own practice, and to create conceptual frameworks for giving meaning to classroom events. In contrast to the instrumental position, which relies on experts to interpret research findings and experience, casting the teacher as compliant technician, the interpretive position encourages active, reflective, and responsible teacher roles. If tomorrow's teachers are to be reflective practitioners, we ought not to rely on "imparting" research findings with the expectation that they be instrumentally applied.

The technocratic rationality implicit in the Holmes and Carnegie reports, like that of the earlier school reform reports, is inadequate to the task of reform. It also fosters expert control and demeans teachers. School teaching and learning are social activities, not technical ones; even if they could be made technical, we do not know enough to prepare teachers as competent technicians. Reform requires coherent conceptions of knowledge and its use in teaching and teacher education that are consistent with the reflective practitioner ideal and sensitive to the conditions of teaching.

One alternative to technocratic rationality and knowledge use is a constructivist conception of knowledge and its use informed by a critical rationality. By constructivist, I mean a conception of knowledge as socially constructed rather than given or revealed (divinely or scientifically), tentative rather than fixed or certain, personal as well as public or formalized, and integrated rather than fragmented. An important implication of this view is that knowledge can be reconstructed.[28] Critical rationality is characterized by wide-ranging skepticism as well as grounding in logical argument and empirical data. It entails probing beneath surface appearances, and questioning claims, evidence, and proposals. Technical concerns are not ends in themselves; instead, they serve both debunking and generative purposes, for example, in questioning the data on projected teacher shortages. Critical rationality can further understanding and reform by illuminating contradictions that point to tensions or strains which might become loci for change such as the contradiction between reflective practice and instrumental knowledge use.[29]

Combining critical rationality with a constructivist conception of knowledge would generate a reconstruction of the knowledge components of teacher education along the following lines. Teacher education programs would integrate social and contextual with technical knowledge. The contextual knowledge would include institutional dynamics and historical perspective that would enable teachers to take a critical stance.[30] The organization and treatment of this knowledge by teacher educators and prospective teachers would demonstrate its tentativeness and patterns and relationships, including links to prospective teachers' experience and personal knowledge—not lists or prescriptions to follow—and the dialectic—not dichotomy—between theory and practice. Knowledge use would be for purposes of understanding, interrogation, and informed action. Thus, its use would be interpretive and emancipatory as well as instrumental.

Such a constructivist conception of knowledge and its use, informed by a critical rationality, represents an alternative language and style of discourse that might guide education reform efforts. It holds the potential for redistribution of educational benefits to more individuals and groups than does technocratic rationality, which tends to benefit established interests and contributing experts by buttressing the status quo. What might happen if, for example, prevailing notions of individualization were questioned, classroom practices were individualized to foster rather than standardize student learning, and as a result achievement differentials among students were reduced drastically? The value of the reform reports lies in the attention they have drawn to education and possibilities for reform rather than in the particular changes they propose. To take advantage of the opportunity for reform without being constrained by technocratic rationality is a major challenge facing would-be reformers.

*Teaching without Instruction.* In reviewing the reform reports, I found that, while addressing the quality of teaching, they ignored instruction. Apparently, instruction was assumed to be nonproblematic or to be taken care of by use of the emerging knowledge base for teaching. Personally, I am not that sanguine. Instruction is crucial to the purposes of schooling and to equity concerns and, therefore, ought not to be left to chance.

Influenced by recent cognitive process theory and research, I define instruction as assisting students' learning by actively mediating between students and what is to be learned in ways that further meaningful student elaboration (i.e., processing) of information. Such mediation can involve demonstrating or telling students *how to do it* (e.g., identify the main idea(s) of a paragraph, determine the credibility of an argument) or asking a series of questions so that students can *figure it out* for themselves.[31] In addition to what and how, cognitive instruction is also specific and explicit regarding when or where and why to do it. Instruction would not include presenting information *per se*, giving directions (*to do* a task as opposed to *how* to do it), or offering evaluative feedback. Nor would it involve imposing a particular strategy by insisting that students "do it my way" instead of employing feasible alternatives.

Although this and similar conceptions of instruction have gained the attention of some researchers, the more common conception among educators seems to be what has been popularized as "direct instruction" on the basis of process-product studies of teacher effectiveness. Direct instruction refers to

> academically focused, teacher-directed classrooms using sequenced and structured materials ... teaching activities where goals are clear to students, time allocated for instruction is sufficient and continuous, coverage of content is extensive, the performance of students is monitored, questions are at a low cognitive level so that students can produce many correct responses, and feedback to students is immediate and academically oriented. ... [T]he goal is to move the students through a sequenced set of materials or tasks. Such materials are common across classrooms and have a relatively strong congruence with the tasks on achievement tests.[32]

Missing from "direct instruction" is any sense of instruction as described above in terms of active mediation. Direct instruction seems not to be instruction at all but a management system that provides opportunity to learn. Increasing students' opportunity to learn is, of course, desirable, but it is no substitute for instruction. Given opportunity to learn, students who have the requisite knowledge and skills can take advantage of the opportunity while students who do not cannot and, without instruction, they are likely to fall further and further behind. Evidence available from classroom studies suggests that instruction as defined here occurs infrequently.[33]

The problem, then, is that we have mistaken opportunity to learn for instruction and have encouraged teaching without instruction. It is a problem because students are not learning as much (or as easily or rapidly) as possible and desired. It is a particular problem for students who could benefit most from assistance in learning. The problem of teaching without instruction cannot be resolved by mandate; standards and testing of either teachers or students cannot change classroom practice. Problem resolution seems to require research into effective means of instruction, teacher education or reeducation, and modification of the conventional wisdom and practice of classroom teaching. The latter is likely to be especially difficult as it requires behavioral as well as conceptual changes in the culture of schooling.

## Structural Challenges

What is needed to significantly improve the quality of teaching is a much different way of thinking about and acting on problems of teaching and schooling than has been followed in the past. The Carnegie report, *A Nation Prepared: Teachers for the 21st Century,* acknowledges the need for "far-reaching changes in our schools and in education policy" and "a growing awareness that further progress is unlikely without fundamental changes in structure . . . that the biggest impediment to progress is the nature of the system itself."[34]

Consistent with the Carnegie position, the preceding analysis suggests that the problems of teaching and education reform more generally cannot be resolved without changes in the structure of the educational system in the United States. Structure here refers to established roles and relationships, including operating procedures, shared beliefs, and norms (i.e., tradition, culture).[35] Because the structure of an educational system conditions participants' interaction within it,[36] changing the practice of teaching requires structural changes in the educational system. By themselves, changes within the teacher education subsystem will not be sufficient to reform classroom teaching.

As previously noted, the school reform reports eschew structural change. The problems of teaching are seen as being in the teacher, not in the teaching situation or in the interaction of person and situation. Improved teaching is to be obtained by the stick of higher standards

and the carrot of higher pay.[37] Structural changes, although not identified as such, are recommended by the Holmes and Carnegie reports,
which address problems of quality teaching beyond initial teacher
education and standards of occupational entry. Both the proposed improvements in the conditions of teachers' work in schools and differentiated staffing would rearrange roles and relationships, modify operating procedures, and reorient beliefs and norms. How this is to be
accomplished is not at all clear. It is clear that the task is a complex and
formidable one that will not yield to slogans or simplistic solutions.

Historically, in the United States, formal organizational control
within the educational system has become increasingly rationalized
and centralized while control of actual classroom practice has remained relatively diffuse and resistant to centralization. Consequently,
nationwide change efforts tend to focus on organizational matters and
to be largely technical or procedural (e.g., credentialling, testing).[38] Sustained, substantive changes in the content and daily practice of teaching and teacher education are less likely to be effectively mandated by
upper echelons or external agencies. It follows that national education
reform efforts are likely to be technical, at least in part because that is
the kind of change over government agencies and educational organizations such as school districts and SCDEs have the most control. It is
also the kind of change that least threatens existing structures, their role
incumbents, and external groups with an interest existing arrangements (e.g., business corporations, upper-middle-class parents). If more
far-reaching changes are to be made, the initiative will most likely come
from other sources such as local groups of "progressive" educators, professional associations, and special purpose coalitions such as the Carnegie Task Force and the Holmes Group.

Curiously, perhaps, grounds for optimism regarding structural
changes supportive of quality teaching can be found within the apparent contradictions among the reform proposals, and in the in-
terrelations among structural factors. One contradiction already noted
is that between the teacher as reflective practitioner and the teacher as
compliant technician.[39] Teachers prepared as reflective practitioners
are less likely to accept the compliant technician role than their pre-
decessors. It is not beyond the realm of possibility that groups of reflective practitioners, with external support, could successfully challenge
conditions of work that mitigate quality teaching. Change in one area is
likely to impact others.

Differentiated staffing along the lines proposed by Holmes and
Carnegie seems to offer considerable possibility for the kinds of structural changes needed to foster quality teaching. The creation of a cadre

or lead or career professional teachers would alter existing roles and relationships, which could, in turn, lead to modification of shared beliefs and norms as well as school operating procedures. If teacher leaders do not simply emulate prevailing administrator role models, the tension between schools' control and educative functions might be resolved in favor of the latter.[40]

Granted, these kinds of changes are not the ones now attracting the most attention from the public, policymakers, or educators. Teacher educators, for example, seem to be preoccupied with the question of whether initial teacher preparation should be a four-, five-, or six-year program while policymakers are dealing with certification standards and testing mechanisms. If we want reform that promises substantial improvement in the quality of teaching—and student learning—then we need to focus on proposals such as those offered by Holmes and Carnegie that are likely to have more leverage for structural changes in schooling. And we should not give up easily. In a recent commentary, Boyd refers to research suggesting that "despite initial resistance and setbacks, reforms nevertheless may succeed over the long haul, *if* advocates persist and manage to gradually gain legitimacy and acceptance for such ideas."[41] Otherwise, crises of teaching will continue to be a way of life.

## NOTES

1. An earlier version of this section appeared in my "Ritual and Rationality in Teacher Education Reform," *Educational Researcher* 15 (April 1986): 5–14.

2. Murray Edelman, *Political Language: Words that Succeed and Politics that Fail* (New York: Academic Press, 1977). C.f. Sacvan Bercovitch, *The American Jeremiad* (Madison: University of Wisconsin Press, 1978). Bercovitch illustrates the continuing use and influence of the jeremiad (the Puritan political sermon) as a rhetorical form. The language of educational crisis and reform does resemble the jeremiad's peculiar combination of castigation and affirmation, i.e., the charge that we have fallen from grace because of our weaknesses (i.e., sins) but that salvation can be reclaimed by hard work and sacrifice as directed by our ministers. As a result, the secular or sacred mission is revitalized.

3. In the 1980s, compared to the previous two decades, the states (especially some governors and legislators) have taken a more active role in education, including teacher education, policymaking. See Michael W. Kirst, "State Policy in an Era of Transition," *Education and Urban Society* 16 (February 1984):225–237.

4. John W. Meyer, "Reform and Change," *IGF Policy Notes* 5 (Fall 1984): 1–2.

5. Paul Peterson, "Did the Education Commissions Say Anything?" *The Brookings Review* 2 (Winter 1983):3–11.

6. Peterson, p. 8.

7. For an analysis of how and why teacher education has become an issue on state policy agendas, see Catherine Cornbleth and Don Adams, "The Drunkard's Streetlamp? Contexts of Policy Change in U. S. Teacher Education" (paper presented at the Ontario Institute for Studies in Education/Higher Education Group Conference, "Governments and Higher Education, The Legitimacy of Intervention," OISE, Toronto, October 1986).

8. It also might be argued that the present focus on education diverts attention from serious national economic and political problems and efforts to bring about reform in these areas. See Ira Shor, *Culture Wars: School and Society in the Conservative Restoration 1969–1984* (Boston: Routledge and Kegan Paul, 1986).

9. Linda Darling-Hammond, "What Constitutes a 'Real' Shortage of Teachers?" *Education Week* 6 (January 14, 1987): 29.

10. Even if one accepts the charge of poor teaching, its attribution to teacher education programs is questionable inasmuch as practicing teachers average more than twelve years' experience; many, if not most, are not "products" of current teacher education programs. Furthermore, those years of classroom experience probably have had considerably more impact on what teachers do or do not do than the one or two years of teacher education they experienced more than a decade ago.

11. Darling-Hammond, "What Constitutes"; Linda Darling-Hammond, *Beyond the Commission Reports: The Coming Crisis in Teaching,* Rand Report R-3177-RC (Santa Monica, Calif.: The Rand Corporation, July 1984). Two recent reports projecting no teacher shortage are highly suspect. In *Teacher Crisis: Myth or Reality?* (Washington, D. C: National Center for Education Information, 1986), Emily C. Feistritzer presents conclusions at odds with her data. The Bureau of Labor Statistics' prediction of no teacher shortage is based on the 1969 teacher turnover rate of 6 percent, not the 1984 rate of 9 percent, and optimism that more people will enter or reenter teaching in the next few years; see Daniel Hecker in the Winter 1986 issue of *Occupational Outlook Quarterly* (cited in Darling-Hammond, "What Constitutes," p. 29).

12. Darling-Hammond, "What Constitutes," p. 29.

13. Darling-Hammond, "What Constitutes," p. 29.

14. Darling-Hammond, "What Constitutes," p. 29.

15. On agenda setting and policy formation with respect to state-level teacher education policy, see Cornbleth and Adams, pp. 24–32.

16. For a summary of the major school reform reports, see Lawrence C. Stedman and Marshall S. Smith, "Recent Reform Proposals for American Education," *Contemporary Education Review* 2 (Fall 1983):85–104.

17. The Holmes Group, *Tomorrow's Teachers* (East Lansing, Mich: The Holmes Group, 1986).

18. Susan J. Rosenholtz, "Political Myths about Education Reform: Lessons from Research on Teaching,"Phi Delta Kappan 66 (January 1985): 349–355.

19. On the predicament of teacher education, see Cornbleth, "Ritual and Rationality," p. 7.

20. Improving teacher quality-education would not necessarily exacerbate the problem of teacher shortages according to a recent Rand Corporation study. Instead, enactment of proposed reforms may make teaching more appealing and attract individuals who would have pursued other careers. Michael Sedlack and Steven Schlossman, *Who Will Teach? Historical Perspectives on the Changing Appeal of Teaching as a Profession* (Santa Monica, Calif: The Rand Corporation, 1987).

21. The sterility and destructiveness of the increasing "hyperrationalization" of schooling has been cogently demonstrated by Arthur E. Wise, *Legislated Learning* (Berkeley: University of California Press, 1979). Hyperrationalization occurs when procedures presumed to facilitate goal attainment take precedence and a life of their own. Preoccupation with management and accountability techniques is accompanied by neglect of purpose, substance, and value. The technocratic rationality of hyperrationalization typically results in further bureaucratization in lieu of reform.

22. Carnegie Task Force on Teaching as a Profession, p. 50.

23. The Holmes Group. p. 50.

24. The Holmes Group. p. 63.

25. The Holmes Group. p. 51.

26. The Holmes Group. p. 52.

27. On the nature and consequences of ahistoricism and decontextualization in education and research, see Thomas S. Popkewitz, "History in Educational Science: Educational Science as History" (Madison: University of Wisconsin Press, September 1986). On individualization in historical perspective, see Thomas S. Popkewitz, "The Sociological Bases for Individual Differences: The Relation of Solitude to the Crowd," in *Individual Differences and the Common Curriculum,* 82nd Yearbook of the National Society for the Study of Educa-

tion, Part I, G. D. Fenstermacher and J. J. Goodlad, eds. (Chicago: University of Chicago Press, 1983).

28. Jonas F. Soltis, "Education and the Concept of Knowledge," in *Philosophy and Education,* 80th Yearbook of the National Society for the Study of Education, Part I, J. F. Soltis, ed. (Chicago: University of Chicago Press, 1981).

29. This example is elaborated in Cornbleth, "Ritual and Rationality," pp. 10–12.

30. Henry A. Giroux and Peter McLaren, "Teacher Education and the Politics of Engagement: The Case for Democratic Schooling," *Harvard Educational Review* 56 (August 1986):213–238.

31. Willard Korth and Catherine Cornbleth, "In Search of Academic Instruction," *Educational Researcher* 9 (May 1980):9; Catherine Cornbleth and Willard Korth, "If Remembering, Understanding, and Reasoning Are Important...," *Social Education* 45 (April 1981):276, 278–280.

32. Barak V. Rosenshine, "Content, Time, and Direct Instruction," in *Research on Teaching: Concepts, Findings, and Implications,* P. L. Peterson and H. J. Walberg, eds. (Berkeley: McCutchan, 1979), p. 38. For a subsequent refinement, which does not substantially alter the conception of instruction, see Barak V. Rosenshine and Robert Stevens, "Teaching Functions," in *Handbook of Research on Teaching* (3rd ed.), M. C. Wittrock, ed. (New York: Macmillan, 1986).

33. For a review, see Catherine Cornbleth, "Critical Thinking and Cognitive Process" in *Review of Research in Social Studies Education: 1976–1983,* W. B. Stanley, ed (Boulder, Col.: Social Science Education Consortium, 1985).

34. Carnegie Task Force on Teaching as a Profession, *A Nation Prepared: Teachers for the 21st Century* (Washington, D. C.: Carnegie Forum on Education and the Economy, 1986), in *Chronicle of Higher Education* (May 21, 1986):47.

35. Don Adams and Catherine Cornbleth, "Contexts of Educational Planning" (Pittsburgh: University of Pittsburgh Press, February 1987).

36. Margaret S. Archer, *Social Origins of Educational Systems* (London: Sage, 1984).

37. Interestingly, the proposals for increasing the quality of teaching do not include monitoring teachers' performance after the prospective teachers have passed the entry tests and probationary screening. In effect, the costs of higher standards are borne by outsiders.

38. John W. Meyer and Brian Rowan, "The Structure of Educational Organizations," in *Organizational Environments,* J. W. Meyer and W. R. Scott, eds. (Beverly Hills, Calif: Sage, 1983).

39. See, e.g., Donald A. Schön, *The Reflective Practitioner* (New York: Basic Books, 1983).

40. On the ways in which the organization and administration of secondary schools favors control at the expense of education, see Linda M. McNeil, *Contradictions of Control* (London: Routledge and Kegan Paul, 1986).

41. William L. Boyd, "Rhetoric and Symbolic Politics: President Reagan's School-Reform Agenda," *Education Week* 6 (March 18, 1987):28,121.

# Part I

## *Teacher Education Reform*

ROBERT C. CALFEE

Chapter Two

# Those Who Can Explain, Teach...

When I entered graduate school in the late 1950s, the "teacher-proof" curriculum was in ascendance. This approach called for careful task analysis, precise specification of instructional objectives, and a tight linkage between teaching and testing—proper engineering was the key—, and the teacher's role was to manage the system. A quarter century later, many observers are beginning to question the validity of the "assembly line" view of education. Some criticisms take shape as "It ain't right!" Others, reflecting American pragmatism, claim "It don't work!"

In this article, I suggest that both criticisms have merit. My major themes are that (1) the capacity to explain is a vital facet of communication and problem solving in modern life, and (2) the school is the primary vehicle for promoting the knowledge and skill needed to be articulate. My bottom line is a variation on the old saw: THOSE WHO CAN, DO: THOSE WHO CAN'T, TEACH.

Lee S. Schulman[1] has suggested a variation on the theme: THOSE WHO CAN, DO: THOSE WHO UNDERSTAND, TEACH.

My proposal goes a step beyond Schulman by rephrasing a point made a while ago by Nathaniel L. Gage and others:[2] THOSE WHO CAN, DO: THOSE WHO CAN EXPLAIN, TEACH.

The essay begins with three anecdotes illustrating the consequences when communication breaks down in a complex setting, when a group fails to be explicit, when a "mindless"routine is followed. Next is a definition of articulateness for teaching; I use *explain, articulate* and *explicate* more or less interchangeably. The conclusion presents some thoughts about teacher training and professionalization at the local school site. The essay includes references, but the purpose is to lay out a hypothesis rather than to "review the literature."

## THREE ANECDOTES

### The Portland Flight

Late in 1978,[3] an airliner bound for Portland was directed by Ground Control to slow its approach to the airfield; traffic was heavy. Ground Control also asked for a fuel check. The flight engineer reported to the captain that the fuel remaining was marginal given the estimated landing time. The captain decided that the fuel load was adequate and so reported to Ground Control. The crew was preoccupied with a faulty "gear warning" light. As the airliner made its way to the anticipated touchdown, the flight crew's conversation, as recorded by the "black box," touched occasionally on the fuel situation. Only toward the end did the flight engineer and the first officer question the captain's assessment of the fuel supply. Just short of the runway the airliner "flamed out" and crashed, killing ten passengers and severely injuring another 23.

### A Death in Miami

The March 10, 1985 *New York Times*[4] gave a graphic report of the death of Bob East, a popular Miami newspaper photographer. East was undergoing a routine operation for removal of a cancerous eye. During the operation, the surgeon removed 50 *ccs* of cerebrospinal fluid (CSF) to reduce pressure in the brain cavity. After the eye was removed, the fluid was reinjected. A second vial marked "CSF" was also injected. Within minutes, vital signs indicated trauma. The patient was brain-dead.

During the operation, a resident left an unmarked vial of preservative on an operating tray. The vial was picked up by a nurse who asked about the contents; a member of the surgical team glanced up and said, "CSF." It was marked accordingly. An hour following the emergency, the resident returned—"Where's my glutaraldehyde?" The surgeon froze. "At that moment I realized what had happened, and I just screamed: 'Oh my God! Oh my God!'" East's lawyer said afterward, "I don't see what happened to Bob East as an isolated case. Time and time again I see instances of poor communication between doctors and nurses result in horrible tragedy."

*The Reading Lesson*

The next anecdote may seem unrelated to the first two. It has little drama, nor is it immediately apparent that anyone is being harmed. Yet an argument can be made that there is a parallel.

Visit a typical American elementary classroom during reading instruction, and you are likely to see the teacher with a group of students, the basal reading manual spread across her lap, directing the youngsters through a routine typical of virtually every series on the market. The other students in the classroom will be at their seats completing worksheets.

The routine goes as follows.[5] At the beginning of the lesson, the teacher prints a list of words on the board—the *vocabulary*. Youngsters volunteer meanings, look up each word in the glossary, or make a sentence using the word. The process takes only a few minutes. Next the teacher *prepares* the students for the daily passage by asking questions on the topic of the story-to-come. The discussion is brief. *Round-robin reading* then ensues; each child reads aloud a paragraph or two from the story, generally to the end of the page. The teacher asks a *few questions* about the material. At the end of the story, the teacher raises summary questions. At the end of the entire exercise, generally about twenty minutes, students return to their seats for *worksheet activities.*

The routine is predictable because the teacher is scripted by the manual. Questions are laid out verbatim, and manuals provide the answers; the teacher may occasionally be informed that "answers may vary," but otherwise there is little need for the teacher to improvise.

## WHERE IS THE TRAGEDY?

*Dangers in the Reading Lesson*

In the first two anecdotes, it is clear that a breakdown in communication led to severe consequences for those involved. What is the problem in the reading lesson? The parallels are twofold. First, the reading lesson is highly implicit; teacher and students move through a highly routinized procedure without any clear articulation of the meaning and purpose of the activities.

Second, the results are disastrous for the students and for the teachers as well. Several reports[6] show that the schools are failing to teach youngsters the essential skills in thinking and communication essential to success in modern society. To be sure, recent years have seen steady progress in low-level routines assessed by standardized tests; children from disadvantaged backgrounds are moving closer on those tasks to the achievement of those from middle-class settings. But the abilities that matter most are *not* improving, and the standing of at-risk youngsters (who increasingly comprise a greater segment of the school population) remains at an intolerably low level.[7]

### What Alternatives Exist?

Let me stay with the reading lesson for a while longer, in order to illustrate what I mean by *explanation* in the school setting. Some might argue that the design of the basal lesson is very "explicit"—the teacher is told exactly what to do. True enough, but the writers of the lesson materials make no effort to articulate the principles underlying the lesson, the teacher is not prepared to be critical of the materials, and students are seldom led to an explanation of what is going on.

And so what are the alternatives? I propose two answers to this question. First, the basic design of the basal reading lesson is badly flawed, and should be changed. (Incidentally, my focus in this article is literacy—reading and writing. Similar problems afflict virtually every subject matter.) Second, whatever shape the lesson takes, the role of the teacher needs to move toward an emphasis on *explicitness, explanation,* and the ability to *articulate* what is happening and what is important.

On the first point, I have discussed elsewhere shortcomings in present textbook design.[8] Briefly, the problem is a lack of coherence. Students encounter too many facts, too few organizing structures, and too few transferable procedures for comprehending text. Existing textbooks lack coherence, and they do not challenge students to think.

These criticisms hold for textbooks in general; they are directly applicable to the basal reader. A dash of vocabulary, a little "background," decoding practice, low-level factual questions. The routine becomes familiar, and it has the intellectual challenge of taking a shower. A more adequate design, in my opinion, would lead the teacher to concentrate during a given lesson on one of the major domains of reading (decoding, vocabulary development, or comprehension), and would lead the youngster to an appreciation of processes and structures that transcend specific lesson content. For instance, one can imagine a lesson in which the teacher begins by stating that the primary goal is to *analyze* a story, adding that *character* and *plot* are important tools for this task. Next the teacher reads the story to youngsters (ensuring that all students have a common exposure to the text, regardless of their decoding skills). The teacher then engages the students in a discussion of character and plot, leading them to reconstruct the narrative. The lesson ends with a review of the techniques for understanding story structure. The emphasis throughout is on *text comprehension,* rather than a mishmash of bits and pieces.

Now to the second point—embedded in the preceding lesson redesign are several features related to *explicitness.* The lesson begins with a *clearly stated purpose.* The purpose is *reviewed at the conclusion* of the lesson, with examples of how to apply the methods in other settings. The lessson uses *technical language* throughout (e.g., *plot* and *character).* The emphasis is less on "getting the correct answers" and more on constructing and justifying an interpretation of the story. Virtually any answer may be acceptable if it can be explained.

## WHY DO TEACHERS DO WHAT THEY DO?

This question is critical to the thesis of the present chapter. The answer is that teachers have a tough time explaining why they do what they do. The description of a reading lesson sketched above permits me to make two points and to suggest a conclusion. The point of the examples is not only that the materials are flawed, but that the teachers accept and use them uncritically. Why?

### Who Me? Think?

The first point is that existing materials relieve teachers of the need to think about what they are doing. Everything is laid out in complete detail. Arthur Woodward reports classroom observations showing that "many of the teachers . . . (both experienced and less experienced) followed their textbooks almost word for word."[9] This reference is noteworthy because it is recent, because it is in a journal sympathetic to the teacher's situation, and because it includes references to other supporting studies. Studies at Michigan State's Institute for Research on Teaching [IRT] report that student teachers are given scant advice about thoughtful use of textbooks and manuals and that novices experience problems in making their way through the materials.[10] As a consequence, new teachers tend to "follow the teachers' guides rather mechanically, moving through the activities and managing to 'get through', without really understanding what they were doing"—this at an institution attempting major reform in teacher education.

Susan Ohanian speaks as a practicing teacher about routinization.[11] In readable prose, she argues that the reliance of teachers on manuals is due only partly to shortcomings in preservice training. She finds education courses generally dissatisfying as an intellectual diet, but suggests that "the blame for worthless courses lies as much with the teachers who take them as with the professors who teach them. As a group, we teachers are intransigently anti-intellectual. We demand from our professors carry-out formulae, materials with the immediate applicability of scratch-and-sniff stickers."

## The "Quiet" Profession

The second point is that teachers are indeed inarticulate when asked to justify their work as professionals.[12] Kathryn M. Anderson-Levitt reports the musings of an elementary teacher in France, whose interpretations of student performance were "contradictory ..., ambiguous ..., varied ..., uniquely tailored to a particular student."[13] Magdalene Lampert describes the "dilemma-managing" teacher, who more or less explicitly juggles the conflicting demands, expectations, and realities of the task—equality or excellence, student interest or subject matter, creativity or standards.[14] Such individuals are rare (though her description of the "small-town" teacher[15] is engaging and familiar); more typical is the "teacher as technical-production manager," with "responsibility for monitoring the efficiency with which learning is being accomplished."[16] The manager is not asked to explain what is happening, only to ensure that it proceeds effectively. The IRT studies support this generalization and also demonstrate the enhanced effectiveness of teachers to explain concepts to students when they themselves are helped to become more articulate. A key element in the process of "self-explanation" is the development of concepts and of labels for those concepts. Philip W. Jackson noted some time ago "the absence of a technical vocabulary unique to teaching ..., and little use of jargon from related fields."[17]

## Does it Matter?

The conclusion is that the lack of clearly explicated professional concepts is a serious impediment to efforts to improve the quality of schooling in this country. What is the basis for this conclusion? Why might it be important for a teacher to be articulate? One hypothesis is that the teacher who gives a rationale for his or her actions will be more effective with students. The empirical research on teacher explanation lends weak support to the thesis; students taught by teachers who are better at explaining may do little better on standardized tests.[18] The students may be more aware of the purposes of the lesson and better able to explain the purposes to others.[19] Attitudes may also be positively affected.[20]

One can argue also that the essence of schooling is explication. Several scholars, drawing a contrast between spoken and written language, have observed the importance of explicitness in written language.[21] Informal speech tends to be interactive, idiosyncratic, and egocentric—"Ya' know what I mean." Technical writing, in contrast, is much more complete; less remains to be read between the lines. Written text tends to be less dependent on context and less subject to misinterpretation. The *medium*, however, is not the message. Writing can be implicit and personal; a letter between lovers leaves much unsaid. A formal speech, in contrast, has many of the characteristics of a written message. It is the *style* of communication—*natural* versus *formal*—that is important for this contrast.[22] Exchanges between literate people are constantly moving back and forth along the continuum, sometimes easy-going, sometimes rhetorical. Nor is *value* the issue; both styles are needed in modern society.

Literacy, then, provides a mechanism for promoting explicitness. The formal style associated with literacy fosters efficiency and clarity in communication, outcomes essential to survival in modern times. It is easy to reduce "reading" to the basics—little more than translation of a minimal vocabulary from print to sound. In fact, this area of the curriculum is more appropriately viewed as the entree to the real "basic skills"—thinking, problem-solving, and communication.

### Explaining and Teaching

The primary task of the teacher, if this argument has validity, is to aid the student to become more articulate. The principle has a broad reach. To have mastered a subject matter does not mean you can explain it, nor does it mean that you can help others to understand it.

Some months ago I watched two world-class flutists conduct a master class. Their students were skilled and motivated, eager to improve. The masters were excellent at diagnosis; teaching was another matter. Having identified a shortcoming, they were hard put to articulate it. They talked around the point, they modelled, they recounted previous experiences, they told jokes—but both had trouble pinning down the issue in explicit detail. I do not question their musical expertise, to the contrary—but they were not effective as teachers.

An emerging literature supports the proposition that good teaching is good explaining. Much of the work is from IRT, including studies by Duffy referenced above. Roehler and Duffy, after proposing that "as teacher educators, there is little we can tell our prospective teachers about how to be good explainers" (a strange disclaimer), proceed to describe several characteristics of effective explanation in classroom settings.[23] These characteristics are: plentiful "teacher talk" at the beginning of the lesson, reference to thinking processes useful in the task, gradual transfer of responsibility from teacher to student, active engagement of students ("Why?" "Explain your answer"), and explicit opportunities for students to transfer the skill.

Students whose teachers practice these strategies were more aware of the purpose of the lesson, and more likely to transfer what they learned to new situations. The IRT program fits the view of teaching envisaged in the Holmes report: "Teachers must lead a life of the mind. They must be reflective and thoughtful: persons who seek to understand so that they may clarify for others, persons who can go to the heart of the matter."[24] It is, however, at variance with present practice as portrayed, for instance by Edwin Susskind and Seymour Sarason:[25] teachers talk a lot; most of their questions require straight recall and brief factual responses; students seldom have much chance to raise questions of their own.

## THE CONCEPT OF EXPLICITNESS

What does it mean to be explicit? I have relied on the reader's intuitions; let me try to be explicit about *explicitness*. The Latin root entails an *unfolding*, a laying bare of the inner workings of something that is otherwise hidden. The concept is closely akin to *explaining*, or "spreading out," and to *articulating*, which means to "divide at the joints." I have suggested elsewhere that planning a coherent curriculum is much like carving a turkey; you must know where the joints are located.[26] In order to explicate a concept, an individual must be able to *step outside* the topic; if you are totally involved in the content, then you may be good at "doing" but not necessarily at explicating. Effective explication also requires command of a *technical language* for describing the subject matter, a *structural framework* for organizing the details of the topic and a *grounded set of experiences* related to the topic.

### Stepping Outside

In order to explain something, a person often needs to step aside and think about the phenomenon. Psychologists speak of *metacogni-*

*tion,* going *beyond* thinking.[27] The person who reflects on his or her actions, who adopts a strategic posture toward a problem, who consciously thinks about thinking, is said to be engaging in metacognition. Sometimes described as a developmental process, metacognition may actually result from instructional activities designed to promote the enterprise. A parallel concept is Piaget's notion of *formal operational thought,* the ability to operate on physical objects with abstract concepts and tools.[28] Piaget may actually have been investigating the effects of Swiss schools.

Reflection, time to think, discussion with colleges—observers of American education have noted that such activities are rare for teachers and administrators. The observers also tend to remark on the "complexity" of the educational enterprise. Education as a field of practice had had little success in *standing aside* from itself.[29] Academic kibitzers on the sidelines offer advice to the troops, but teacher surveys reveal little opportunity for reflection. For administrators the situation is even worse;[30] a business acquaintance recently spent a couple of days with two principals from our local school district, and his remark at the end told it all: "Those poor guys don't have a minute to think during the entire day!"

The lack of reflection arises from several sources, I suspect: the lack of a broadly accepted "theory of education," the absence of a professional vocabulary, and inherent complexity of the phenomenon. Elsewhere I have drawn a contrast between *transparent* versus *opaque* technologies—a fly swatter with a personal computer, for instance.[31] Direct observation may suffice to understand (and explain) the first device; it's not enough in the second instance. Gaining insight into a first-grade classroom or a science textbook is not a trivial task; the "technologies" of the modern classroom can be difficult to comprehend. "Stepping outside" is rewarding only when it yields a clearer picture.

Time is also a problem. In a survey of working conditions, teachers report little communication with colleagues.[32] They do not talk with principals about much and are not consulted concerning decisions about curriculum and instruction. Samuel B. Bacharach concludes that "... schools are some of the least supportive organizations that I have ever seen." This account contrasts sharply with Lee S. Shulman's ideal: "[The teacher] is capable of reflection leading to self-knowledge, the metacognitive awareness that distinguishes draftsman from architect, bookkeeper from auditor. A professional is not only capable of practicing and understanding his or her craft, but of explaining why, of communicating the reasons for professional decisions and actions to others."[33]

The absence of reflection has several side effects, three of which are worthy of note. First, school people tend to be reduced from professionals to mechanics. Students move down the assembly line and objectives are bolted on. If an activity makes little sense, no one has time and energy to question it. Second, teachers and administrators do not communicate with one another, leading to isolation and loneliness. Third, there is no coordinated response to the increasing number of "emergencies." State and district leaders demand higher standards; financing declines; test scores go down; students drop out. With neither time, tools, nor traditions to buttress thoughtful reflection, schools appear as bucket brigades fighting an old-fashioned barn fire.

## TECHNICAL LANGUAGE, STRUCTURAL FRAMEWORK, BASIS IN EXPERIENCE

To be articulate about a complex domain, knowledge is essential—you have to know the territory; you have to know where the joints are located. The more complicated the phenomenon, the more important for knowledge to be organized, coherent, comprehensive, and grounded in practical experiences. I propose the three categories heading this section as a base for articulate knowledge—they may not be perfect, but they are a start.

### An Example

Rather than an abstract description, I will work from a concrete example: the comprehension of expository prose. For practical purposes, you may thnk of this domain as covering everything except "stories"—technical writing.[34] The point of the example is to review the manner in which expository prose is *explicated* in present-day reading instruction. I will consider in turn the role of technical language, structural frameworks, and opportunities for practice.

Beginning about the third grade, students experience increasing amounts of exposition. Science and social studies are major sources, but other areas of life inside and outside school fall under the same rubric. For instance, the newspaper and telecasts are largely expository, as are instructions for completing 1040A form assembling a bicycle. Most of this material is unfamiliar and complicated. How is exposition presented in current reading series? How do teachers handle the domain? What is the level of student achievement? The answers are short but not very sweet: (1) The contrast between narration and exposition is seldom emphasized. (2) Elementary teachers are generally unaware of the contrast; they may draw a distinction between fact and fiction, but their focus is on content rather then structure. (3) Student performance on tasks that require expository comprehension is generally poor.

What might be the curriculum for expository comprehension? Does a *technical language* exist? The answer is a definite "yes." Almost any good college text on composition provides the basic elements. These labels may vary slightly, but core ideas can be identified.[35]

Does a *structural framework* exist? Clearly so. Most texts discuss three basic forms—*description, sequence,* and *argument/persuasion.* Each form includes a number of distinctive styles, forming a hierarchical network.[36] Less well presented is the notion of *recursion*—writers often address a topic in one dominant style (e.g., legends about mermaids are illustrated by a series of examples), but incorporate other genre along the way (e.g., an anecdote about a phony mermaid ends the text to enliven it).

Experience—can one find *examples* of expository writing appropriate for children of different ages? I think the answer is again "yes." I found no difficulty in locating materials when my children were growing up. To be sure, it is less easy to identify examples covering a given structure or topic, and therein hangs the tale. The "market" is weak. The English coordinator at a fairly prestigious high school, when asked why no" essays" were included in a reading list for gifted high school students, replied that such collections were "hard to find!"

Technical language, a structural framework, opportunities for experience—all three should be readily available for instruction in expository comprehension. What is the practical reality? Neither the technical language nor the basic categories are emphasized in the materials for instruction, the scope-and-sequence charts, or the training (preservice and inservice) of the typical elementary teacher. Opportunities for practice are quite limited. Expository prose is relatively scarce in most basal series; most of the "stories" are really stories! When exposition appears, the focus is on the content ("This piece is about beaver dams.") When strategies are introduced, they tend to be quite general.[37] The most demanding subject matters—science and social studies—give little attention to procedures for handling the basic structures. The assumption seems to be that *doing* will lead to *knowing.* This theory may eventually work for some individuals, but it is inefficient and many students fall through the cracks. Laura R. Rochler and Gerald G. Duffy provide vivid contrasts between situations in which students are left to their own devices within a lesson sequence and those in which the teacher provides a supportive scaffold.[38]

*Isn't It Boring?*

My comments may portend a draconian view of schooling—such need not be the case. One can identify instances where teachers provide students with explicit, well-articulated introductions to powerful concepts in ways that are not only humane but exciting.[39] The "magic" of experience is not dispelled because one works within a clear and comprehensible context. Instead, the context may provide an environment within which the magic becomes more likely. Explicitness and conscious articulation are not required at all times and places. Practice leads most routines to become automatic, so that under normal conditions a person is unaware of the origins of a skill. If you understand the principle, however, then you can return to a metacognitive level "in case of emergency."

## IMPROVING THE PROFESSION OF TEACHING

What is the potential for public education in the United States? What is the most that we can expect from our institutions of schooling? Several observers have identified the teacher as the most critical in assessing this issue, and I agree. Implicit in the analysis thus far is a higher standard for teachers (and administrators). I think that they must know what they are about, and that the level of their knowledge must be such that they can readily explicate what they know. Moreover, I believe that it is possible to achieve this goal with existing resources—not easy, but possible.

*The Bad News*

Some colleagues will disagree with my argument, with both the identification of articulateness as a key element for improving practice, and with my optimism about what can be achieved. A few years ago Gary Sykes sketched a dire picture of the teaching profession, "a growing conviction that teaching is an imperiled profession and that efforts now under way to improve matters are insufficient, misguided, or both."[40] Sykes based his argument on three contradictions:

*1. The Teaching Force.* The country wants our teachers to be talented individuals who are effective with students from a broad range of home backgrounds; it also needs a lot of "bodies" [for caretaking functions, inter alia] who are relatively cheap.

*2. "Education" and the University.* Schools of education serve a vital role for improving public education, and their students compromise a significant proportion of the university's clients; but schools of education are at the bottom of the pile when it comes to allocation of university resources, including respect.

*3. Science and Art in Teaching.* The prevailing trend is to guide teaching practice by a "positivist epistemology," largely behaviorist in origin; the folks in the trenches are all too often overwhelmed by the unscientific "uncertainty, instability, and uniqueness of teaching."

How can one respond to Syke's analysis? I do not question his tenets, which seem on target. Certain "easy" resolutions have been proposed:

*1. Higher Standards.* Let's develop tests (at least for the basics of reading, writing, and mathematics), and bar from the profession anyone who cannot pass acceptable standards. I have spoken elsewhere on this general topic;[41] Albert Shanker is persuasive about the silliness of teacher testing in its present manifestations.[42]

*2. More Money.* Let's increase teacher salaries substantially, at least for entry level teachers. From the large influx of candidates, we can then select the cream of the crop. Unfortunately, the money is not there, and the current batch of college students is unlikely to be attracted to the profession by modest changes in entry-level salaries.

*3. Improved Preservice Training.* Eliminate undergraduate education programs. Improve the rest of the undergraduate program in America's universities and colleges. Ensure that college professors not only do a better job of teaching their specialty, but also ground tomorrow's teachers in the fundamental principles of the structure of knowledge and pedagogy. These recommendations from the Holmes and Carnegie reports strike me as lacking in feasibility.[43] The ideas are attractive, and address the issues with which I an concerned. I do not see the motivation or machinery for promoting a fundamental change in undergraduate education by college faculties, however,

Is the task of improving public schooling in America therefore impossible? I don't think so. As a colleague commented recently. "That answer is unacceptable!" It is unacceptable for a couple of reasons. First, the success of public schooling for all our children is a long-standing American ideal, one that merits continued attention. Second, contemporary demographics pose an interesting "human capital" problem. As I write these words, the *San Francisco Chronicle* headlines *Shortage of Teenagers.* Local Burger King restaurants cannot find enough qualified youngsters to handle the counter.[44] John W. Gardner states the matter at a more profound level:

> The importance of education is not limited to the higher orders of talent. A complex society is dependent every hour of every day upon the capacity of its people at every level to read and write, to make difficult judgments, and to act in light of extensive information. The manager of a chemical plant said to me recently, "We can't even have an errand boy who isn't literate. Everything in this plant has to be handled with care [memories of Bhopal].[45]

## Some Possible Solutions

And so what is the answer? What strategy might prevail over the inarticulateness endemic in the teaching profession at present? The challenge (and I would argue, the opportunity) is greatest in the elementary grades. Here the teacher is expected to be master (or mistress) of several subject matters—language, math, science, social studies, the arts, and physical education.

I propose two approaches. First, the local school has a great deal of autonomy, more than policymakers might desire. Relatively small elementary schools, in particular, are capable of fashioning an articulate community of professionals—"on the sly" perhaps. Second, providing administrators at the school and district level with clearly articulated knowledge about the "beef" of curriculum and instruction should have substantial payoff. A few words about each possibility.

## The School as the Center

The local school provides a workable foundation for establishing a professional community. One of the early proposals in this spirit was advanced by Robert J. Schaefer in *The School as a Center of Inquiry.* This small and neglected treatise is a rich source of ideas:

> We can no longer afford to conceive of the schools simply as distribution centers for dispensing cultural orientations, information, and knowledge developed by other social units. . . . It must also be a center of inquiry—a producer as well as a transmitter of knowledge . . . . Educational literature unduly concentrates . . . on the problem of recruiting "good" teachers to the relative neglect of analysis of the nuturing qualities of the institutions for which recruits are

sought.... [We] have the economic resources, the manpower..., and the preliminary knowledge to make that vision [of the school as a center of inquiry] a reality.[46]

Schaefer's remarks, especially the last sentence, may seem farfetched today. I think not. Examples that approximate this "vision" can be found in present practice. Some programs are "teacher-oriented," in the sense that the individual teacher is the focus of the program (e.g., the Bay Area/National Writing Project at Berkeley, Duffy's program at Michigan State, the Teacher Center Consortium of the New York AFT), but appear to have induced school-level effects. None of these programs emphasizes the coherent view of curriculum presented earlier in this paper, but they do provide technical language and a structured view of one or more domains.

An example of a difficult sort is the certification program for novice teachers developed by the New Jersey Department of Education. The program builds upon the notion that professional knowledge exists in the field of teaching, that training beyond the undergraduate program is necessary, and that the local district and school are a feasible locus for professional development. "During the ... training program, each candidate will have the support of a four-person team made up of the school administrator, an experienced peer teacher, a college faculty member (or an individual with comparable expertise), and a curriculum specialist."[47] I do not know how this experiment is proving out, nor does the description make completely clear the substance of the training experience. But the resource package and the general philosophy is consistent with my analysis.

Finally, for the past several years, my colleagues and I have been experimenting with a school-based staff development program, which has the explicit goal of developing a set of concepts and terms in the area of literacy. The project is grounded in a clearly articulated curriculum for literacy. Small-group discussion techniques support the teachers in explicating the processes and structures for handling textual materials.[48] Our program builds upon a thorough examination of the curriculum of reading. Explicitness *per se* is not the only issue— *what* is being explicated matters a lot. Over the past few decades, schools and classrooms seem to have lost their curricular foundations. As Shulman noted, subject matter domains must regain a place of prominence: "The [present] emphasis is upon how teachers manage their classrooms, organize its activities, allocate time and turns, structure assignments, ascribe praise and blame, formulate the levels of their questions, plan lessons, and judge student understanding. What we miss are questions about the *content* of the lessons taught, the questions asked, and the explanations offered."[49]

The issue is not "truth," but a workable representation of a domain. In English rhetoric—the basis for reading, composition, and literature—concepts like the contrast between narration and exposition are widely accepted by experts. In science, the areas of physics and biology evoke ideas and procedures of fundamental importance. In social studies, the historian, the geographer, the economist, and the socologist bring perspectives that illuminate human affairs. The conceptual foundations for the subject matters are of preeminent importance. It is not enough for the teacher to have been "exposed" to these areas; knowing what you know requires more than exposure. "To think properly about content knowledge requires going beyond the facts or concepts of a domain. It requires understanding the structures of the subject matter . . . ."[50] The materials of instruction build on this conceptual base, as do the pedagogical methods and assessment techniques appropriate to a given subject matter.

## *The Articulate Administrator*

The critical role of the principal has been highlighted by a number of studies, most noticeably in the Effective Schools literature.[51] The nature of this leadership is less clearly defined. *Vision* is frequently mentioned, along with a panoply of management skills, but the character of the vision is seldom all that clear. When it does take shape, its form concentrates on specific outcome measures (most often standardized tests) and closely correlated instructional activities. This list does not seem to touch on the "beef" of education.

At least two efforts stand somewhat apart from this trend. One is an initiative by California Superintendent Bill Honig, who has initiated a Principals' Academy grounded in the notion that principals should have a clearly articulated conception of curriculum and instruction. Honig posed the challenge at the first meeting of the Academy's advisory committee: "If you ask a manager for General Motors, 'What's your job?', the answer will be, 'Building cars!'" Honig's point was that school administrators need a comparable vision of their job—educating children. The Association of Teacher Educators in *Mirrors of Excellence* puts the matter more concretely: Principals should be the best teachers in the school.[52]

In another initiative, Ramon Cortines, superintendent of the San Jose Unified District, is leading an effort in collaboration with me and my colleagues at Stanford University to achieve a similar effect. In this project, administrators from all levels of the District are developing case studies of the role of language in a wide variety of activities—a bilingual summer school, analysis of the changes in classroom discussion resulting from a recent desegregation settlement, examination of a newly adopted science series, and review of memoranda and other methods of communication between administrators in the district, among others.

## HOW WILL THE STORY END?

The agenda that I have sketched is ambiguous, and it flies in the face of increasing pressures for regimentation; state tests direct the curriculum in the classroom, and teachers and administrators have only marginal control. Continuation of this strategy seems likely to fail us, and the failure will be more apparent as we look more deeply at writing and at student understanding of the content areas.

The essence of the argument is fairly simple—knowing what you know is critical to the educational experience. Instruction that leaves the student inarticulate misses the point, even if we go through the motions. The curriculum domains are the key; it is not enough to "know" about a subject matter area, but to understand it in a fashion that allows you to explain it. Management, the focus of educational preparaton today, is important but not sufficient. Imagine that doctors were judged solely on following procedures, and it did not matter if most of their patients died. We need a happier ending for education . . . .

## NOTES

1. Lee S. Shulman, "Those Who Understand: Knowledge Growth in Teaching." *Educational Researcher* 15 (1986):4–14.

2. Nathaniel L. Gage, Maria Belgard, Daryl Del, Jack E. Hiller, Barak Rosenshine, and Waldemar R. Unruh, "Explorations of the Teacher's Effectiveness in Explaining" (Technical Report No. 4, Stanford University School of Education, 1968).

3. National Transportation Safety Board (NTSB), *Annual Review of Aircraft Accident Data* (Washington, D.C., 1978).

4. "One Death, Many Questions in Miami," *The New York Times,* March 10, 1985, p. 12.

5. Delores Durkin, "What Classroom Observations Reveal about Reading Comprehension Instruction," *Reading Research Quarterly* 14 (1984):481–533.

6. NAEP, *The Reading Report Card: Progress toward Excellence in our Schools* (Princeton, N. J.: Educational Testing Service, 1985); NAEP, *Writing Trends across the Decade:* 1974–1984 (Princeton, N. J.: Educational Testing Service, 1986); Commission on Reading, *Becoming a Nation of Readers* (Washington, D. C.: National Institute of Education, 1985).

7. Arthur N. Applebee and Judith A. Langer, "Moving towards Excellence: Writing and Learning in the Secondary School Curriculum" (Technical Report to NIE, Stanford University, 1984); NAEP, *Writing Trends across the Decade: 1974–1984.*

8. Robert C. Calfee, "The Design of Comprehensible Text," in *The Dynamics of Language Learning: Research in the Language Arts,* James R. Squire, ed. (NCTE/ERIC Center, forthcoming).

9. Arthur Woodward, "Over–programmed Materials: Taking the Teacher out of Teaching," *American Educator* 10 (1986):26–31, 26.

10. IRT, "Student Teaching: Putting It All Together," *News and Notes* 13 (April 11, 1986); IRT, "Student Teaching: Following the Book or Doing Your Own Thing," *News and Notes* 13 (April 25, 1986).

11. Susan Ohanian, "On Stir-and-Serve Recipes for Teaching," *Phi Delta Kappan* 66 (1985): 696–701, 697.

12. Philip W. Jackson, *Life in Classrooms* (New York: Holt, Rinehart and Winston, 1968), p. 143.

13. Kathryn M. Anderson-Leavitt, "Teacher Interpretation of Student Behavior: Cognitive and Social Processes," *Elementary School Journal* 84 (1984): 315–337, 322, 333.

14. Magdalene Lampert, "How Do Teachers Manage to Teach? Perspectives on Problems in Practice," *Harvard Educational Review* 55 (1985): 178–194.

15. Gertrude McPherson, *Small Town Teacher* (Cambridge, Mass. Harvard University Press, 1972).

16. Lampert, p. 191.

17. Jackson, p. 144; Gerald G. Duffy, Laura R. Roehler, Michael S. Meloth, Cassandra Book, Linda Vavrus, Joyce Putnam, and Roy Wesselman, "The Relationship between Explicit Verbal Explanations during Reading Skill Instruction and Student Awareness and Achievement: A Study of Reading Teacher Effects," *Reading Research Quarterly* (forthcoming).

18. Jere E. Brophy and Thomas L. Good, "Teacher Behavior and Student Achievement," in *Handbook of Research on Teaching,* 3rd ed. (New York: Macmillan, 1986), pp. 328–75.

19. Laura R. Roehler, Gerald G. Duffy, Joyce Putnam, Roy Wesselman, Eva Sivan, Gary Rackliffe, Cassandra Book, Michael Meloth,and Linda Vavrus, *The Effect of Direct Explanation of Reading Strategies on Low Group Third Graders' Awareness and Achievement* (Michigan State University, Institute for Research on Teaching, 1986).

20. Dale H. Schunk and Paula D. Cox, "Strategy Training and Attributional Feedback with Learning Disabled Students,"*Journal of Educational Psychology* 78 (1986):201–9.

21. John Goody, *The Domestication of the Savage Mind* (Cambridge: Cambridge University Press, 1977); David R. Olson, "From Utterance to Text: The Bias of Language in Speech and Writing," *Harvard Educational Review* 47 (1977), pp. 257–81; David R. Olsen, Nancy Torrance, and Angela Hildyard, *Language, Literacy, and Learning: The Consequences of Reading and Writing* (Cambridge: Cambridge University Press, 1985).

22. Sarah W. Freedman and Robert C. Calfee, "Understanding and Comprehending," *Written Communication* 1 (1984):459–90.

23. Laura R. Roehler and Gerald G. Duffy, "What Makes One Teacher a Better Explainer than Another?" *Journal of Education for Teaching* (forthcoming).

24. Judith Lanier, *Tomorrow's Teachers: The Holmes Report* (East Lansing, Mich.: Michigan State University, 1986), p. 52.

25. Edwin Susskind, "Encouraging Teachers to Encourage Children's Curiosity," *Journal of Clinical Child Psychology* XX (1979):101–6; Seymour Sarason, *Schooling in America: Scapegoat and Salvation* (New York: Free Press, 1983).

26. Robert C. Calfee, "The Mind of the Dyslexic," *Annals of Dyslexia* 33 (1983):9–28.

27. Ann L. Brown, "Knowing When, Where, and How to Remember: A Problem of Metacognition," in *Advances in Instructional Psychology* vol. 1, Robert Glaser, ed. (Hillsdale, N. J.: Ernbaum Associates, 1978). pp. 77–165.

28. Barbel Inhelder and Jean Piaget, *The Growth of Logical Thinking* (New York: Basic Books, 1958).

29. Jean Piaget, *Science of Education and Psychology of the Child* (New York: Viking Press, 1971).

30. Arthur Blumberg and William Greenfield, *The Effective Principal* (Boston: Allyn and Bacon, 1980).

31. Robert C. Calfee, "Computer Literacy and Book Literacy: Parallels and Contrasts," *Educational Researcher* 14 (1985):8–13.

32. Samuel B. Bacharach, *The Conditions and Resources of Teachers* (Washington, D. C.: National Education Association, 1986).

33. Shulman, p. 13.

34. Bruce K. Britton and John B. Black, *Understanding Expository Text* (Hillsdale N. J.: Erlbaum Associates, 1985).

35. Robert C. Calfee and Marilyn Chambliss, "Structural Design Features of Large Texts," *Educational Researcher* (forthcoming).

36. Robert C. Calfee and Robert G. Curley, "Structures of Prose in the Context Areas," in *Understanding Reading Comprehension,* James Flood, ed. (Newark, Del.: International Reading Association, 1984), pp. 161–80.

37. Peter Winograd and Vicki C. Hare, "Direct Instruction of Reading Comprehension Strategies," paper presented at the Conference on Learning and Study Strategies, University of Kentucky (1984).

38. Laura R. Roehler and Gerald G. Duffy, "Studying Qualitative Dimensions of Instructional Effectiveness," in *Effective Teaching of Reading: Research and Practice,* James V. Hoffman, ed. (Newark, Del.: International Reading Association, 1986), pp. 181–97.

39. Roehler and Duffy, "Studying Qualitative Dimensions of Instructional Effectiveness."

40. Gary Sykes, "Contradictions, Ironies, and Promises Unfulfilled: A Contemporary Account of the Status of Teaching," *Phi Delta Kappan* 64 (1983): 87–93, 87.

41. Robert C. Calfee, Edmund Lau, and Lynne Sutter, "Establishing Instructional Validity for Minimum Competency Programs," in *The Courts, Validity, and Minimum Competency,* George Madaus, ed. (Boston Kluwer-Nijhoff, 1983), pp. 95–113.

42. Albert Shanker, "Assessment of Teachers," address to National Evaluation Systems Symposium, American Educational Research (1986).

43. Lanier; Lewis Branscomb, *A Nation Prepared: Teachers for the 21st Century* (New York: Carnegie Forum on Education and the Economy, 1986).

44. "Shortage of Teenagers," *The San Francisco Chronicle, May 22, 1986, p. 1.*

45. John W. Gardner, *Excellence: Can We Be Equal and Excellent Too?* 2nd ed. (New York: W. W. Norton, 1984), p. 53.

46. Robert J. Schaefer, *The School as a Center of Inquiry* (New York: Harper and Row, 1967), p. 1, 7, 5.

47. Saul Cooperman and Leo Klagholz, "New Jersey's Alternate Route to Certification," *Phi Delta Kappan* 66 (1985): 591–95, 694.

48. Robert C. Calfee and Marcia K. Henry, "Project READ: An Inservice Model for Training Classroom Teachers in Effective Reading Instruction," in *The Effective Teaching of Reading: Research and Practice,* James V. Hoffman, ed. (Newark, Del.: International Reading Association, 1986), pp. 199–229.

49. Shulman, p. 8.

50. Shulman, p. 9.

51. Ronald Edmonds, "Characteristics of Effective Schools," in *Reading Education: Foundations for a Literate America,* Jean Osborn, Paul T. Wilson, and Richard C. Anderson, eds. (Lexington, MA: Lexington Books, 1985), pp. 123–30.

52. Association of Teacher Education, *Mirrors of Excellence* (Reston, Va.: ATE, 1986).

ALAN R. TOM

Chapter Three

# A Critique of the Rationale
# for Extended Teacher Preparation

For more than one-half century, teacher educators and policy analysts have discussed the relative merits of four-year teacher preparation and of various forms of extended teacher preparation.[1] Now, as we enter the latter half of the 1980s, arguments for moving to extended teacher preparation are more widespread than ever, although many of these arguments have roots which go back fifty or more years. This paper delineates the core arguments used by contemporary proponents of extended teacher preparation, identifies the historical origins of these arguments, and questions the validity of these arguments.[2]

Before addressing the arguments underlying the rationale for extended teacher preparation, we need to be clear about what constitutes extended preparation. Unfortunately, extended preparation comes in many forms. For example, most extended preparation programs entail a master's degree,[3] but a few programs award only partial credit toward a master's degree.[4] Some extended programs entail considerable professional work during the initial four years of study,[5] while other designs assume that the applicant does little or no professional study until the graduate program commences.[6] Internships sometimes play a prominent role in extended programs,[7] while in other cases clinical work does not involve internships[8] and may even include the first year of teaching.[9] Thus, we are much less sure what structure is involved when we refer to extended teacher preparation than when we speak of four-year teacher preparation.

Rationales for extended programs, however, are less varied than are the structural arrangements of these programs. Thus, we can identify and assess these rationales without too much concern whether internships are involved, whether a degree results from a particular program, or whether professional work is largely restricted to the graduate portion of the program. In those instances when it is important to discuss the structure of an extended program, I will assume that an internship is present, that professional work is heavily concentrated at the graduate level, and that a master's degree is granted at the conclusion of the program. I am specifying the structure of an extended program in this way because these features increasingly appear to be the norm among proponents of extended teacher preparation. But I will not be making many references to the structure of extended programs, because the focus of this analysis is on the arguments for extended programs, their persistence over time, and the extent to which these arguments are compelling.

While many specific arguments are made to defend the superiority of extended programs over four-year ones, these arguments tend to fall into two broad categories. One category of argument can be characterized as the "inadequate time" hypothesis while the second category entails making an analogy between teacher education and the postbaccalaureate professional schools.

## THE INADEQUATE TIME HYPOTHESIS

A typical example of this argument is enunciated by Denemark and Nutter:

> This chapter deals with one of the main obstacles—inadequate resources for teacher education—and, in particular, with the inadequate time available for effective teacher education within the existing institutional patterns.[10]

Looking for a variety of rationales for extended teacher preparation, Schwanke concludes:

> Those supporting extended programs thus emphasize that preservice programs are artificially constrained within four years and cannot produce fully competent teachers within these limits.[11]

While Schwanke was summarizing recent rationales for extended preparation, he could just as easily have been speaking of earlier discussions. One-half century ago, Counts argued for extended preparation on the basis that the dramatic social and economic changes of his day required better educated teachers to interpret these developments to students.[12]

Reviewing the extended preparation rationales promulgated in the first half of the twentieth century, Von Schlichten concludes:

> The dominant reason offered in justification of the proposals which have been made is that the needed skills, knowledge, and understanding now require five years for their acquisition or development.[13]

Clearly, the inadequate time hypothesis has long been a major element in the case for extended teacher preparation.

But at various points in the twentieth century, differing areas of skill and knowledge have been viewed as inadequately developed through the conventional four-year program. These potential areas of deficiency coincide with the three types of expertise typically associated with teacher preparation: general education, subject matter preparation, and professional education. In turn, I examine each type of expertise, focusing on how significant the deficiency is currently viewed as being and on how persuasive the case for this purported deficiency is.

In the case of general education, proponents of extended teacher preparation often recommend a general education similar to that obtained by other college graduates. Typical of this position is Atkin, who argues that teachers cannot claim authority if the level of the general public's education is perceived as stronger than that received by teachers. Taking into account the relatively high college-attendance rate of the American public, Atkin concludes that "teachers should have a bachelor's degree that is considered as rigorous as anyone else's. That is, their general education should be just as strong as that required of other college graduates.[14]

The appropriateness and validity of Atkin's argument is hard to evaluate. First, in those cases in which prospective teachers are housed in the college of arts and sciences, there is no difference between the general education received by teachers and that received by other arts and science students. Second, Atkin's appeal is partly to the status a stronger general education allegedly would bestow upon teachers, and it is difficult to know whether increased status for teachers is indeed correlated with increased general education requirements for prospective teachers.

But Atkin also claims that an equivalent education requirement for teachers and other students is desirable if we want the public to view teaching as "an occupation demanding intellectual skills."[15] This claim presumes the general education in today's higher education institutions is a substantial academic experience that prepares teachers for the dimension of their work which is "intellectual, moral, social, and cultural" in origin.[16] Yet Atkin explicitly states that in making the case for the strengthening of general education requirements for teachers he is making "no defense of what passes for general education at most universities."[17] Atkin's restiveness about the current condition of liberal arts education is widely shared and has recently been the subject of a major national report sponsored by the Association of American Colleges.[18] This report suggests that all students receive a minimum required program of study, focusing on nine objectives or criteria; the emphasis ought not be on expanding so-called distribution requirements but rather on intellectual experiences directly addressing the nine criteria.

If we merely require more liberal arts courses of prospective teachers, the value of such work is dubious. A recent study of course selection suggests that students tend to choose their electives on the grounds of how undemanding these courses are.[19] Such a finding, though not unexpected, is nevertheless disturbing. Now, as in the past, a major difference between many four-year and extended teacher preparation programs is the increased number of general education electives available to the prospective teacher in extended programs. Thus Conant's cautions about the value of general education electives in the teacher curricula of the 1960s bears repeating today:

> The issue between four-year and five-year continuous programs turns on the value one attaches to free electives. And if a parent feels that an extra year to enable the future teacher to wander about and sample academic courses is worth the cost, I should not be the person to condemn this use of money. But I would, as a taxpayer, *vigorously protest the use of tax money* for a fifth year of what I consider dubious value.[20]

We must ask ourselves whether more general education electives are really in the best interests of prospective teachers or whether a more important undertaking is the rethinking and regeneration of that general education undertaken by undergraduates in teacher education.

A second area where advocates of extended teacher preparation recommend increased work is in the subject matter(s) to be taught. Most often these recommendations are made for elementary teachers, most of whom currently major in education. Proposals vary, but frequently elementary teachers are expected to major as an undergraduate in an "academic" subject (preferably one taught in the elementary school) and to do substantial course work in other subjects typically in the curriculum of self-contained elementary classroom. Prospective secondary teachers not only are expected to complete an academic un-dergraduate major but often also to engage in graduate study in this area.

The common thread running through these recommendations is the assumption that prospective teachers need more subject matter study than is possible in the typical four-year program. Generally, this increased study is defended on the basis that subject matter com-petence is essential to the conduct of the intellectual operations at the core of teaching. However, Atkin also makes a status-based argument for more subject matter study to ensure that teachers obtain the respect of the general public.[21] In looking at the recommendation for added subject matter study, I focus not so much on the status such added study might give to teachers but rather on the intellectual value of this supplemental subject matter preparation.

On the surface, that added subject matter study would be of sub-stantial value to the prospective teacher seems self-evident. There is evidence, however, that added subject matter study does not contribute to more effective teaching, unless this coursework is in advanced courses.[22] Hawley atempts to interpret this puzzling finding:

> This last point seems counterintuitive but it may suggest that once one has a dozen courses or so in one's field, it is not the number of courses, nor the grades one gets in them that are important, but whether one un-derstands fundamental principles and the structure of the discipline or body of knowledge involved.[23]

Might it be possible that only in advanced academic work is the student exposed to the fundamental principles and structure(s) of a discipline? Atkin recounts his own experience as as undergraduate chemistry major to illustrate the intellectual deficiencies introductory course work:

> I proceeded in my chemistry course-sequence on faith, without feeling particularly knowledgeable about the subject as it was conceived by those who knew it best. That is, I had no clear idea of which concepts were most fundamental, which had the most explanatory power, which were relatively transient, which were most likely to offer a foundation for future developments ... Like many other undergraduate majors, I didn't see the forest for the trees. It was not until my 24th semester hour of chemistry, when I took physical chemistry, that the field began to reveal some coherence to me, and I began to understand which knowl-edge within chemistry was of the most worth.[24]

My own undergraduate experience is similar to that of Atkin, except that I never felt I had much insight into the nature of history—

particularly into the methodology employed by historians—until I began graduate study in history. The Association of American Colleges report concludes that the problem with the American college curriculum is not that knowledge is ignored but rather that the curriculum "offers too much knowledge with too little attention to how that knowledge has been created and what methods and styles of inquiry have led to its creation."[25]

The typical undergraduate major is not so much intended to reveal the fundamental concepts and structure(s) of a field as to prepare the student for subsequent serious study of discipline at the graduate level. Generally, the assumption is made that considerable background material needs to be covered before the student, perhaps late in undergraduate study or more likely early in graduate school, can focus upon fundamental disciplinary ideas and can conduct inquiry in the style characteristic of that discipline. It is precisely this understanding of core ideas and of inquiry processes which the prospective teacher needs, if he or she is to be able to teach youngsters something more than bits and pieces of disconnected knowledge. In particular, the prospective teacher needs to understand how knowledge is verified in a discipline, both so that these epistemological processes can be introduced to elementary and secondary students and so that the teacher can place proper restrictions on the certainty of disciplinary knowledge.

Added subject matter study for teachers is thus of doubtful value, especially at the undergraduate level. This is precisely what would occur if extended teacher preparation involved the pursuit of a baccalaureate degree with little or no professional work during the first four years. Secondary teachers might profit somewhat if their undergraduate majors were supplemented by graduate-level study in the discipline. But prospective elementary teachers are unlikely to benefit from expanded undergraduate study, because this study will be composed primarily of introductory courses. All that such increased study is likely to do is to clutter the minds of prospective elementary teachers with strings of unrelated facts and theories. That this increased knowledge is going to yield better elementary teachers is questionable, although many elementary teachers could no doubt profit from additional subject matter study of the proper kind.

The third area in which four-year programs are seen as inadequate is professional education. Denemark and Nutter employ a widely accepted argument when they assert that the growing knowledge base in professional education justifies moving to extended teacher preparation programming:

> The adequacy of education's base of knowledge is central to the case for extended programs of teacher preparation. Is the base sufficient to sup-

port an extended, fully professional initial preparation program for teachers ... We believe the present base of knowledge justifies lengthening and reforming initial teacher-preparation programs.[26]

Typically this knowledge base is presumed to be most appropriately located at the graduate level,[27] but there are many who argue for integrating professional and academic study throughout five or six years of university study.[28]

In reality, the discussion of the professional education component of teacher preparation has little bearing on the rationale for extending teacher education beyond four years. For one thing, few, if any, argue that someone who is a postbaccalaureate student, and thus only one or two years older than the typical undergraduate, is prepared to study a professional curriculum which is considerably more sophisticated and demanding than that which an undergraduate can handle. Second, graduate courses in preservice teacher education are not likely to differ significantly in rigor and quality from undergraduate professional courses because the same faculty members would be responsible for both levels of instruction.[29] Third, even if a special graduate faculty in education existed and even if the postbaccalaureate student were able to tackle a very sophsticated professional curriculum, the application of this content to classroom settings is an extraordinarily complex process.[30] Finally, if unnecessary and redundant professional content were simply eliminated from the current undergraduate professional curriculum, this step by itself should make room for increasing the professional knowledge base within the current undergraduate curriculum.[31]

All of these considerations suggest that the knowledge base for professional education—which supposedly is growing rapidly—is not really key to the rationale for extended teacher preparaion. On the contrary, it is the increased emphasis on general education and subject matter preparation which is central to the case for expanding teacher education beyond the "inadequate time" provided by the four-year curriculum. It just happens that many advocates of extended teacher preparation choose to place the professional curriculum at the graduate level.

## THE PROFESSIONAL SCHOOL ANALOGY

The fundamental reason that many educators and policymakers place the professional curriculum at the graduate level is related to a second category of arguments for extended teacher preparation programming. This cluster of arguments can be characterized as the professional school analogy. Here are two instances of this reasoning:

It is now time in the evolution of teaching as a profession to insist that
the prerequisite for entry into a professional teacher-training program
be the successful completion of a sound undergraduate education cen-
tering on the liberal arts. Schools of medicine, law, and veterinary
medicine require their applicants to be educated persons before they
begin their professional studies. Should education ask less?[32]

The five-year program may also be seen as a necessary element in win-
ning recognition of professional status for the practicing teacher—and
professional school status for the beleaguered education college. The
professions of law, medicine, dentistry, and pharmacy have all expanded beyond an undergraduate education of four years.[33]

Von Schlichten has traced similar reasoning back as far as 1905
when Dexter argued that our high school teachers cannot "attain the
status of professional respectability which should be theirs, until they
have invested at least four years' time in the academic side of college
work, with at least one year's graduate work directed largely to a
theoretical and practical study of school problems."[34]

Would having autonomous professional schools of education help
establish elementary and secondary school teaching as a profession?
Would such a development bring increased status to colleges of education by removing them from the stigma of being associated with undergraduate education? Probably not. Attaining the status of a profession is a complex affair related only in part to the organizational
structure of the training institutions or to the educational level of the
trainee.[35] Societal attitudes toward the value of the service provided by
the teacher, public doubt about the effectiveness of schooling, severe
limitations on the professional autonomy of teachers, disagreeable
working conditions for teachers—all these factors affect the prestige
associated with elementary and secondary teachers.[36] Thus, even if a
college of education were to augment its status by disconnecting itself
from undergraduate education and becoming solely a professional
school, the effect of this structural change on the status of teachers
is problematic.

At the same time, the movement of the college of education to
autonomous professional school standing disassociates professional
teacher training from the undergraduate college of arts and sciences.
This break is undesirable because the general education and specialized subject matter preparation of teachers is—or ought to be—much
more closely connected to their professional training than is the case
for other professions."The knowledge base needed for the study of
education,"notes Hatfield, "ranges across the entire university curri-

culum to a much greater extent than is the case in preparation programs for law and medicine." Hatfield proceeds to argue that the preparation of teachers must be seen as representing "an all-university responsibility far beyond the control of an autonomous school of education."[37] The inevitable interconnection of the professional and academic in teacher preparation has long been argued. An eloquent statement of this position was made more than one-half century ago by Judd:

> The situation in which education finds itself is unique, because it is at one and the same time a professional subject and an academic subject. The meaning of this statement will be clear if one contrasts education with such a purely professional subject as law. Law has a body of subject matter peculiar to itself. The line can be drawn between courses in torts and courses in political science or political economy without involving any serious overlapping. On the other hand, when education is administered to a prospective teacher it is very difficult, if not impossible, to make a sharp distinction between the subject which the teacher is going to teach and the professional courses which he pursues in preparing himself for his work. For example, a person who is going to teach history must study history first of all, and he must be competent in the subject matter of that department or he will not be professionally equipped. In a very proper sense of the word history is a professional subject.[38]

Judd concludes that "education must be defined as only quasi-professional in character. It is much more closely related to the whole range of subjects taught in the schools than these subjects are to one another."[39]

Thus, the established professional schools can more easily disconnect themselves from the undergraduate college of arts and sciences than can the department or college of education. All the established professional schools need to do is specify a few prerequisites that are seen as necessary to subsequent professional study, while the college of education cannot do its work unless the entire college of arts and sciences experience—general education as well as disciplinary study—is of the highest quality. Indeed, it is the college of education that ought to be in the forefront of the call for the reform of the general education curriculum and that ought to be insistent that undergraduate arts and science majors ground students in the fundamental ideas and inquiry processes of each discipline.

All of these arguments for coordination between the college of education and the college of arts and sciences—or for that matter with such other colleges as art, home economics, or music—may strike the reader as obvious but also as politically naive. Attempts at university-wide coordination of undergraduate teacher preparation have not been notably successful, and attempts to arrive at mechanisms for such coordination seem cumbersome and not likely to succeed in the highly fragmented environment of the typical university.[40] Clark characterizes the hope that we will ever get a meaningful universitywide commitment to teacher education as a "pipe dream" that ignores the organizational realities of the university. To support his argument, he cites a variety of factors, including the low prestige associated with both undergraduate studies and professional training, with teacher education in particular, and with the teaching of "service courses" for another segment of the university. Clark presents a convincing case for the difficulty of developing a good working arrangement between the college of arts and sciences and the college of education.[41] This difficulty is further exacerbated by the widely held belief among college professors that there is nothing much to learn about teaching than cannot be acquired on the job.

Thus, I am not sanguine that cooperation between the college of education and the college of arts and sciences will come about easily. Extraordinary effort is required, but such effort seems justified. The argument that education ought to be a professional school similar to law, medicine, dentistry and others is, at root, a false analogy. Education , as Judd argued fifty-five years ago, is a quasi-professional field, at once both professional and academic. While political realities on university campuses may make the realization of this hybrid very dfficult, we need to make the effort to maintain a dual commitment to the academic and professional heritage of teacher preparation.

## PLURALISM IN STRUCTURES

In this paper, no ringing endorsement of four-year teacher preparation is found. In fact, I believe that a number of problems exist with present-day teacher education, problems which ought to be identified, delineated, and addressed. Doing so, however, goes beyond the scope of this paper.[42]

What I have attempted to do is penetrate beyond the surface arguments about the virtues of extended teacher preparation and to challenge its fundamental rationale. Thus, considerable attention is directed to the inadequate time hypothesis, especially to whether lengthening the study of general education, academic subjects, and professional education is an important reform. Particular attention is given to general education and subject matter preparation, as these two areas are widely viewed as being too small in scope. On the contrary, I have argued, the problem with general education is its quality and coherence, not its length. Further, additional academic study is not as important as reorganizing this study so its focus is more on core disciplinary ideas and inquiry processes. Thus, a reasonable case can be made that the rethinking of general education and subject matter preparation is a far more significant reform than the expansion of either of these areas of study. Similarly, the present size of the professional curriculum may well be sufficient for the pedagogical knowledge that has been developed in recent years, providing the current professional curriculum.

At the same time, there is no reason to believe that housing professional education in an autonomous postbaccalaureate professional school is a wise idea. Establishing an autonomous professional school structure is not likely to augment the status of the occupation of teaching. Moreover, such a professional school of education tends to artificially separate the academic and professional aspects of teaching. Instead of disassociating itself from undergraduate arts and sciences instruction, the department or school of education ought to support the reform of the arts and sciences curriculum and seek to regenerate the professional aspect of teacher preparation.

The proper policy to pursue is to work at improving the quality of teacher preparation. We ought to address the quality of general education and subject matter education, as well as the quality of professional education. Key questions concern the ends and purposes of teaching and teacher education—where we confront what Zeichner calls alternative paradigms[43]—as well as issues concerning the coherence of general education and the extent to which subject matter preparation entails the fundamental study of a discipline. Some may find it congenial to pursue reform of teacher education within an extended format; others may believe needed changes can be made within the traditional four-year structure.

While we can hope that research on the efficacy of four-year and extended formats might indicate which structure is superior, the relative value of these two structures has been at issue for many years. Which structure is better is likely to remain contested; both structures should be possible.

## NOTES

1. Morris Cogan, "'Master of Arts in Teaching' at Harvard University," *Journal of Teacher Education* 6 (June 1955): 135–42; George S. Counts, "Present-

day Reasons for Requiring a Longer Period of Preservice Preparation for Teachers," *National Education Association Proceedings* 73 (1935): 694–701; George Denemark and Norma Nutter, "The Case for Extended Programs of Initial Teacher Preparation," in *Advances in Teacher Education,* vol. 1, Lilian G. Katz and James D. Raths, eds. (Norwood, N. J.: Ablex Publishing, 1984), pp. 203–46; Henry Holmes, *Shall Teachers Be Scholars,* occasional pamphlet no. 1 (Cambridge Mass.: Graduate School of Education, Harvard University, 1937); John S. Murray, "The Extended Program for Teacher Training: A Procedural Critique," *Journal of Teacher Education* 33 (September–October 1982): 2–5; B. Othanel Smith, *A Design for a School of Pedagogy* (Washington, D. C.: U. S. Department of Education, 1980); Kenneth Winetrout, "In Defense of the Four-year Program in Teacher Education," *Phi Delta Kappan* 44 (January 1963): 183–84; Paul Woodring, *New Directions in Teacher Education* (New York: Fund for the Advancement of Education, 1957).

2. In addition to weaknesses in the arguments underlyng the rationale for extended teacher preparation, there are several hidden costs of instituting extended preparation. To mandate extended preparation is to encourage a focus on procedural issues, to narrow the talent pool for teachers, to reduce the diversity of colleges/universities offering teacher education, and to neglect the financial implications of adopting extended preparation. See Alan R. Tom, "The Case for Maintaining Teacher Education at the Undergraduate Level" (St. Louis: Washington University, Department of Education), pp. 1–38, 18–29. (ERIC Document Reproduction Service No. ED267067).

3. David C. Smith, Robert G. Carroll, and Bess Fry, "PROTEACH: Professional Teacher Preparation at the University of Florida," *Phi Delta Kappan* 66 (October 1984): 134–45; John E. White, "How We Arrived at Five-year Teacher Education," *Education Week,* (September 18, 1985), p. 24.

4. Jeffrey B. Dunbar, "Moving to a Five-Year Teacher Preparation Program: The Perspective of Experience," *Journal of Teacher Education* 32 (January–February 1981): 13–15; Dale P. Scannell and John E. Guenther, "The Development of an Extended Program," *Journal of Teacher Education* 32 (January–February 1981): 7–12.

5. Michael D. Andrew, "A Five-Year Teacher Education Program: Success and Challenges," *Journal of Teacher Education* 32 (May-June 1981): 40–43; Dunbar, pp. 13–15; White, p. 24.

6. Ernest L. Boyer, *High School* (New York: Harper and Row, 1983), pp. 174–78; Hendrik D. Gideonse, "A Future Role for Liberal Colleges in the Preparation of Teachers," in *Teacher Education in Liberal Arts Settings: Achievements, Realities, and Challenges,* Alan R. Tom, ed. (Washington, D. C.: American Association of Colleges for Teacher Education, 1984). pp. 1–11.

7. Andrew, pp. 40–43; White, p. 24.

8. Smith, Carroll, and Fry, pp. 134–35.

9. Dunbar, pp. 13–15.

10. Denemark and Nutter, p. 204.

11. Dean Schwanke, "Extended Preservice Programs: Assessing the Argument," *Journal of Teacher Education* 32 (January–February 1981): 54–55, 54.

12. Counts, pp. 694–701.

13. Erwin W. Von Schlichten, "Idea and Practice of a Fifth-Year Requirement for Teacher Certification," *Teachers College Record* 60 (October 1958): 41–53, 49.

14. J. Myron Atkin, "Preparing to Go to the Head of the Class," *The Wingspread Journal* (Special Section on Teacher Education), Summer 1985, pp. 1–3, p. 2.

15. Atkin, p. 2.

16. Gideonse, p. 3.

17. Atkin, p. 2.

18. Select Committee of the Association of American Colleges, *Integrity in the College Curriculum: A Report to the Academic Community* (Washington, D. C.: Association of American Colleges, 1985).

19. Eva C. Galambos, Lynn M. Cornett, and Hugh D. Spitler, *An Analysis of Transcripts of Teachers and Arts and Sciences Graduates* (Atlanta: Southern Regional Educational Board, 1985). Cited in Willis D. Hawley, *Breaking Away; The Risks and Inadequacy of Extended Teacher Preparation Programs* (Nashville, Tenn.: Vanderbilt University, Peabody Center for Effective Teaching, 1985).

20. James B. Conant, *The Education of American Teachers* (New York: McGraw Hill, 1963), p. 204.

21. Atkin, pp. 1–3.

22. Cynthia A. Druva and Ronald D. Anderson, Science Teacher Characteristics by Teacher Behavior and by Student Outcome: A Meta-Analysis of Research," *Journal of Research in Science Teaching* 20 (May 1983): 467–79.

23. Hawley, p. 16; Hawley cites Gaea Leinhardt and Donald A. Smith, "Expertise in Mathematics Instruction: Subject Matter Knowledge," *Journal of Educational Psychology* 77 (June 1985): 247–71.

24. Atkin, p. 3.

25. Select Committee, p. 24.

26. Denemark and Nutter, p. 213.

27. Atkin, pp. 1–3; Boyer, pp. 174–78; Gideonse, pp. 1–11.

28. Andrew, pp. 40–43; Dunbar, pp. 13–15; Scannell and Guenther, pp. 7–12.

29. Hawley, pp. 14–15.

30. Marilyn Cohn, "A New Supervision Model for Linking Theory to Practice," *Journal of Teacher Education* 32 (May–June 1981): 26–30.

31. Joseph M. Cronin, "State Regulation of Teacher Preparation," in *Handbook of Teaching and Policy,* Lee S. Shulman and Gary Sykes, eds. (New York: Longman, 1983), pp. 171–91; Arnold M. Gallegos, "The Dilemma of Extended/Five-Year Programs," *Journal of Teacher Education* 32 (January–February 1981): 4–6.

32. Jonas F. Soltis and Michael Timpane, "Cultivating a Community of Teaching," *Education Week* (May 2, 1984), pp. 24, 19, 24

33. Murray, p. 4.

34. Von Schlichten, p. 42.

35. Hawley, pp. 12–13.

36. Harry Judge, *American Graduate Schools of Education: A View from Abroad* (New York: Ford Foundation, 1982), p. 29–31.

37. Robert C. Hatfield, "Professional-School Approach Is Too Narrow for Teacher Preparation" (letter to the editor), *Education Week* (August 29, 1984), p. 13.

38. Charles H. Judd, "The School of Education," in *Higher Education in America,* Raymond A. Kent, ed. (Boston: Ginn, 1930), pp. 157–91, 174.

39. Judd, p. 174.

40. Allan Tucker and Robert B. Mautz, "Solving the Teacher Education Problem: A University-Wide Obligation," *Educational Record* 65 (Spring 1984): 34–37.

41. David C. Clark, "Transforming the Contexture for the Professional Preparation of Teachers." Forthcoming in *Advances in Teacher Education,* vol. 2, Lilian G. Katz and James D. Raths, eds. (Norwood, N. J.: Ablex Publishing).

42. See, for example, Kenneth M. Zeichner, "Preparation for Elementary School Teaching," in *Career-long Teacher Education,* Peter J. Burke and Robert G. Heideman, eds. (Springfield, Ill.: Charles C. Thomas, 1985), pp. 62–97.

43. Kenneth M. Zeichner, "Alternative Paradigms of Teacher Education," *Journal of Teacher Education* 34 (May–June 1983): 3–9.

Chapter Four

# Teacher Education, the Liberal Arts, and Extended Preparation Programs

What should be the role of liberal education in teacher education programs? Clearly, teachers must know what they teach. But how much biology should a high school biology teacher know? How much course work in English literature does an elementary school teacher need to be able to teach writing? What would an appropriate academic major be for an elementary teacher? Learning to read is one of the key goals of elementary education, yet no liberal arts department of reading exists. Nor do I know of a single college English or linguistics department that teaches the content of reading. Even in the area of content knowledge, such questions have no easy answers.

When one moves beyond subject matter competence, the questions become even more complex. Who is responsible for the misspelled words and poor grammar in the teacher's letter home to the parents—the college of education, the English department, or the teachers themselves? Is it the responsibility of the liberal education portion of a teacher education program to instill within a would-be teacher the inquiring, adaptive spirit needed for lifelong professional development?

To what extent *should* a teacher be educated in the liberal arts? My contention is that, among professions, teaching has perhaps the strongest connection to the liberal arts. Teachers have no less a responsibility than to induct young people into our society and culture. The disciplines associated with liberal education are strong reflections of that society and culture, and the teacher is, along with the family, the church, and the media, one of the most powerful transmitters of the values and norms of our society.

But the case for the liberal arts in teacher preparation extends beyond the fact that teachers are major transmitters of culture. The liberal arts also contribute to the professional qualifications of teaching. The issue here is not professional education versus liberal education. Rather, the issue is whether we want liberal-professional education that favors high levels of conceptual skills and application or technical-professional education that favors prescriptive knowledge and narrow skill performance.

If teachers are to be more than mere technicians, faithfully following a "teacher-proof" curriculum, then professional skills of problem-solving, analysis, and critical thought are needed. These are precisely the intended outcomes of a liberal education. How, if at all, can such liberal education goals be pursued in the context of professional teacher preparation? Is the sometimes meager general education background of other professionals such as doctors and engineers enough for teachers?

Contrary to the notion of teacher as technician, the image emerging in the literature of the 1980s portrays the teacher as a critical problem-solving professional. From B. O. Smith's *A Design for a School of Pedagogy* to David Berliner's work on teacher effectiveness; from Hendrik Gideonse's calls for a revolution in teacher education to Judy Lanier's research on teacher preparation, the teacher is conceived as a true professional. Recently, Lee Shulman has even argued that the teacher not only must know *that* something is the case, but also must understand *why* it is the case—a level of understanding not often attempted even in typical academic majors.[1]

If one accepts this concept of teacher as liberal-professional, some important consequences follow. A compelling case can be made for the wide-ranging contribution of liberal education to teacher preparation, a contribution that goes far beyond the simple notion of mastery of content. Even that most often criticized part of teacher preparation— the methods course—can be improved by appropriate contributions from the liberal arts and sciences.

In order to see how this is so, I need to set forth a working perspective on teaching. For me teaching involves: (1) the intentional use of a variety of communicative strategies; (2) to help render accessible to student inquiry and learning; and (3) a body of knowledge, set of skills, or group of character traits deemed valuable.

Doubtless, something is included in this definition that is objectionable to someone, and perhaps something is left out that should be included. Nevertheless, the components at least touch on most of what we have come to understand from our conceptual and empirical inquiries into the conditions and techniques of teaching and learning in complex social settings. This view of teaching suggests that liberal education may contribute to teacher preparation in four major areas: (1) general education; (2) higher order skills such as inquiry, critical analysis, and decision-making; (3) the traditional content areas; and (4) methods of teaching.

## GENERAL EDUCATION

The general education portion of a teacher preparation program serves four critical functions:(1) extension and expansion of the knowledge base formed in high school; (2) introduction to scientific and artistic modes of inquiry and expression; (3) refinement and extension of personal and societal values; and (4) cultivation of each student's ability to communicate in an informed and reflective manner—most particularly through writing. As is discussed later, the pedagogical portion of a teacher preparation program must include these same goals in its courses and fieldwork. More specifically, the general education of a teacher should include the following:

- *Effective communication.* All teachers should be able to read, write, listen, and express themselves in a coherent and intelligible manner.
- *Mathematics.* All teachers should be able to comprehend and use fundamental mathematical concepts and operations to be able to keep records, perform data analyses, and carry out testing and evaluation.
- *Scientific understanding.* All teachers should have a basic grasp of the major methods and results in the natural and social sciences and the technological implications of these results. Not all citizens need to be technical experts, but our technological society demands at least a general appreciation of science technology.
- *Historical and social consciousness.* All teachers should understand the ineluctable fact that both our individual and social experiences are historically grounded. To prepare students for a global perspective in the twenty-first century, teachers need a comprehensive background in the historical and cultural traditions shaping the societies of the world.
- *Humanities.* All teachers should appreciate the human condition as it is illuminated by language, literature, and philosophy so that they may encourage their students to live full, meaningful lives.

In principle, these skills are advertised as goals of many programs of general education. They appear to be minimally necessary for every

citizen, not just teachers. Nevertheless, such general education typically
has had one of the lowest priorities in our institutions of higher education. It is often ignored by senior professors and administrators, and
viewed with suspicion by students with narrowly vocational interests.
Worst of all, it is widely assumed that a simple collection of introductory courses in the major fields constitutes a general education. Introductory courses in any discipline are primarily designed for those
who will major in that field. The idea that such courses will at the same
time provide the basic skills for a genarally educated student—whether
prospective teacher or not—must be seriously questioned. The general
education curriculum in our colleges and universities is largely chaotic,
with the weak distribution requirements in place no substitute for a
coherent course of study.

A number of scholars are beginning to recognize the inadequacy
of general education as it is currently carried on in our nation's colleges
and universities. For example, in 1984 the NIE Study Group report, *Involvement in Learning*[2] calls for renewed attention to providing a
coherent general education for all students, whether they are prospective professionals or not. The 1985 report of the Association of
American Colleges, *Integrity in the College Curriculum: A Report to the
Academic Community*[3] indicates the sorry state to which general education has fallen and urges a rededication to a coherent view of liberal
learning with a revitalized general education core. Teachers must be no
less well educated in this sense than the average well-educated member
of our society.

## HIGHER-ORDER SKILLS AND COMPETENCIES

Competent teachers must be multi-talented and extremely adaptive professionals. From motivation and discipline of students, to
choice of curricular materials, instructional strategies, and organizational resources, the teacher must deal with an enormous array of con-
tingencies. Has Johnny learned fractions? How much review of yester-
day's lesson on geography is necessary? What items should be on the
unit test? What reading group should Jane join? How can I motivate
Susie to participate more? Are Richard's problems at home interfering
with his ability to concentrate? What are the most likely misunderstandings students will have of the physical concept of work? These and
a host of other questions must be answered by teachers each day. Can
the liberal arts and sciences help?

In order to make these types of decisions and choices, teachers
must be able to analyze a wide variety of situations in a way that leads

to satisfactory formulation and solution of problems. They must learn to be critical, creative, and integrative thinkers, to transcend the narrow boundaries of disciplinary thought and to see things as a whole.

In addition to the somewhat abstract reasoning competencies just described, the traditional human traits so often associated with elementary and secondary teaching must not be ignored. Character, compassion, caring, and concern must also be acquired by would-be teachers. Although sometimes slighted in overly rationalistic descriptions of liberal education, historically these characteristics have been thought to be appropriate outcomes of a truly liberal education. They are certainly necessary for those to whom we entrust our young.

The most basic of all human characteristics is that of making and acting on choices. While the knowledge of concepts and skills from general education studies can inform choice–making, it is the value system in both its affective and cognitive dimensions that provides the cultural and personal meanings and justification for making choices. Without imposing any specific set of values, the teacher must be able to help students come to appreciate the values that shape their choices and decisions. It is in such a way that teachers most appropriately transmit culture in a free society.

The cognitive, affective, and choice-making characteristics described above have long been espoused by advocates of liberal education. Typically, the assumption is made that these ends will be achieved almost as a by-product of taking the standard distribution requirements of an undergraduate degree. However, I do not believe these competencies will be achieved without explicit attention to their realization. For example, one of the key features in the modern mathematics curriculum is the attempt to get students to pay attention to the "reasonableness" of the answers they get by algorithmic procedures. The ability roughly to estimate answers is essential to understanding mathematics and is part of critical thought in mathematics. Yet one finds little if any attention paid to estimation in typical college mathematics programs. A variety of courses and integrative experiences must be developed to address the goals of problem formulation and solution, critical thinking, ethical and social development, lifelong learning, and human concern. New approaches are essential for all liberal arts graduates, but they must be given special focus and purpose in the context of professional teacher preparation.

To live is to adapt; to adapt is to learn. To instill a passion for learning is to instill a passion for living. This level of thought and action is not easily conveyed simply by more detailed work in the disciplines, for that only leads one further into the discipline. What is wanted is an examination of how the disciplines assist in developing the individual. Jan Blits puts it well when he says:

> Liberal education aims to prepare young people for an intelligent life. Its most important goal is to teach them to become thoughtful about themselves and the world, about their actions and their thoughts, about what they do, what they say, what they want, and what they think. It seeks to illuminate life, and particularly to clarify the fundamental human alternatives, by delving as deeply as possible into the roots of things. Liberal education is thus essentially a recovery or rediscovery of root issues and origins.[4]

The liberal arts must give explicit attention to these root issues and origins to an extent not often found in contemporary liberal arts programs.

## CONTENT

### Elementary Education

Historically, the liberal arts have contributed least to the content of elementary education. This is easy to understand when one considers that elementary education tends not to be departmentalized. In today's schools a single elementary teacher is responsible for all aspects of the curriculum in the classroom. Furthermore, unlike secondary schools, the "subject matter" of elementary education is typically not organized in ways comparable to the disciplinary organization imposed by liberal arts and colleges and universities and adopted by secondary schools. The elementary school teacher must deal with reading, beginning writing (even penmanship), basic arithmetic, social studies, health, science, physical education, art, and music—all in addition to human development.

In what follows, I assume that the elementary classroom will continue to be organized much as it is today, with the individual teacher responsible for a broad range of areas. This assumption could, however, be questioned and the difficulties surrounding teacher preparation in elementary education might be significantly alleviated were we to introduce changes in the structures of elementary classrooms. Just as one example, teams of elementary teachers could be formed with some team members expert in mathematics and science and others expert in reading and language arts. Such a change might alter the necessity for a single teacher to know everything—a necessity not easily honored as will become apparent.

In general, elementary schools are primarily concerned with imparting the prerequisite tools and skills for learning, rather than with the actual learning of organized bodies of knowledge. The liberal arts, on the other hand, concentrate almost exclusively on those bodies of knowledge and find it difficult to conceive of the tools and skills as "college level" material. Consequently, the preparation of elementary teachers is usually found in schools and colleges of education, rather than in liberal arts colleges. Elementary teachers sometimes take up 50 percent of their courses in education and most often receive their degrees in education. In contrast, the proportion of courses in education that a secondary teacher takes is usually about 20 to 25 percent of the total in a bachelor's program, and the degree is usually taken in a regular academic major.

The issue of the appropriate contribution of the liberal arts to the content preparation of elementary school teachers is extremely troublesome. On the one hand, some argue that the lack of disciplinary structure in elementary schools is simply a historical accident of the normal school approach to teacher training. Advocates of disciplinary structure point to the slighting by elementary teachers of content areas in which their own preparation was meager. In other words, elementary teachers who had little or no mathematics in their education do not teach elementary mathematics very much or very well. The remedy, from this perspective, would be to insist on rigorous and appropriate disciplinary training for elementary school teachers that would, in turn, make at least possible the imposition of disciplinary structures on elementary classrooms. Or, perhaps, interdisciplinary majors composed of appropriate parts of the disciplines for which elementary teachers are responsible could be developed.

On the other hand, some argue that the development of young children is incompatible with the imposition of a disciplinary structure on elementary education. Advocates of this view suggest that, until about the middle grades, children are largely unable to grasp material cast in the logical structure of a discipline. Philosophically and historically, it is argued that conceiving of the liberal arts as consisting primarily of discipline study is, in any case, overly narrow. It reflects the Germanic tradition of the research university and ignores the earlier liberal tradition that valued the development of compassionate, caring, concerned, and connected human beings—persons with character and an inquiring mind. Indeed, the most trenchant contemporary criticisms of the disciplines, even at the collegiate level, have to do with this tendency to fragment learning. The remedy, so this line of thinking runs, is to extend the integration found in elementary classrooms upwards.

Nor is it easy, in practical terms, to reach a compromise between these two approaches. Let us assume the current structure of elementary schools and insist that elementary teachers acquire at least a minimum of disciplinary knowledge in each of the areas for which they are responsible. If one insists, in addition, that elementary teachers acquire specialized knowledge of how young children learn *and* of how to help them become compassionate, caring, concerned, and connected people, we are potentially asking more of elementary teachers than secondary teachers or even college professors—an unrealistic, albeit interesting, idea.

It is quite essential to appreciate the fact that two entirely different conceptions of liberal education as a whole are represented in the debate over the contribution of the liberal arts to elementary education—the disciplinary vs. the personal development approach to liberal education. I cannot settle this controversy within the confines of this paper. However, either approach will increase the contribution of the liberal arts to the content of elementary teacher preparation requiring either more traditional content or a greater focus on human growth and development.

Yet another area exists in which the liberal arts might contribute to the content preparation of elementary teachers. Elementary teachers must deal with an extremely broad range of subject matter. Thus, whether an academic major is required of the elementary teacher, attention must be given to the wide *range* of content area to be covered in the elementary grades.

Given the introductory nature of most elementary school subjects, the advanced esoteric course work required for a standard collegiate major may not be necessary. More appropriate would be carefully designed basic courses that acquaint elementary teachers with the specific content they must teach. Too often liberal arts departments scoff at the apparent implication that they should teach subjects such as spelling, arithmetic, or reading. So the responsibility falls to education departments, and they are scorned because they "teach college students elementary content." It is absolutely essential to break free of such a simple-minded understanding of the "content" of elementary education. Of course, teachers must know how to spell and do arithmetic, but that cannot be the content of college courses. Rather, that content must be placed in the context of a college level course by paying attention to the logical and disciplinary structures underlying the various elementary content areas and the ways in which those structures might inform the selection of methods for teaching the content to young children.

Lee Shulman[5] has coined the phrase *pedagogical content knowledge* to refer to this approach. These would not be standard courses in "mathematical methods," for example, but would rather concentrate on such things as the most central and powerful concepts, metaphors, and methods of discovery and validation in mathematics itself. Such knowledge would also add to the understanding of the major learning problems students of a variety of ages tend to have in grasping those concepts, metaphors, and methods. Even the most elitist professor of a discipline should be able to appreciate that this kind of study of "elementary" content is worthy of college credit. Moreover, this kind of knowledge of content would be far more valuable to elementary teachers than advanced esoteric courses in the field.

*Secondary Education*

The relevance of disciplinary content areas secondary teachers is obvious and, as far as I am concerned, noncontroversial. Every secondary school teacher should major in the discipline he or she is going to teach, receiving a bachelor's degree in that field, along with an appropriate minor. This is the norm now and at a minimum it should be continued. To note that most secondary teachers do major in the disciplines they teach is not, however, to suggest that all is well with secondary education. As should be apparent by now, a great deal of the liberal arts is relevant to teacher preparation over and beyond the oft-cited requirement that, for example, a biology teacher must know biology. Yet, as noted earlier, all too often an emphasis on the disciplines comes at the expense of ignoring the more humane goals of liberal education. Secondary teachers need to care as much about the kinds of total human beings their students are becoming as they care about their disciplines.

A *good* general education for secondary teachers will address this concern in part, but more needs to be done. Even more than other students majoring in a discipline, future teachers need to be made aware of the fundamental structure of their discipline. They also need to know what the various disciplines contribute to human understanding, how they fit together, their interrelatedness and application. Thus, as noted with elementary teachers, the notion of the *structure of a discipline* is the key to understanding one of the most exciting new contributions the liberal arts can make to teacher education. Furthermore, that structure must be understood as encompassing not only the logical, conceptual framework, but also the complex of human needs and activities that give rise to the discipline in the first place.

## STRUCTURES OF KNOWLEDGE

Neither elementary nor secondary teachers need to know all of the technical details of a discipline required of practitioners of that discipline. Teachers would, however, profit enormously from understanding the various ways of knowing which have developed historically and which are reflected in the basic *structures of the disciplines*. For example, scientific method and process of discovery, inference, and justification are crucial for understanding science; likewise, the ideas of counting, correspondence, and operation are central to mathematics. However, it is not obvious that the structure of a discipline can be learned simply by increasing the exposure to the content of the field. The challenge is to design courses in the various disciplines that can help teachers understand the concepts, methodologies, and criteria of validity in each field and discipline and to develop ways of teaching which draw from that understanding. Thus, not only should teachers generally become competent in subject matter, they should also learn the structure or philosophy of what they teach. Understanding the structure of their fields would enable secondary school teachers to plan their lessons taking into account both the logic of the discipline as well as the needs and capacities of their students. They would be better able to diagnose student difficulties and propose appropriate activities if they had an overall cognitive "map" of their disciplines.

Thus, the liberal arts need to provide prospective teachers with a knowledge of the structure of the disciplines. The teacher, elementary or secondary, must be aware of the fundamental concepts, methods of discovery and validation, major findings and theories, and the way they all fit together. Only with such knowledge can teachers make intelligent choices of how to provide young people access to these fields. Courses in the structure of a discipline are too seldom found and yet they are a critical part of an ideal teacher preparation program. Several such courses should be required for all prospective teachers.

## METHODS OF TEACHING

Ideally, "methods" courses should be the most intellectually challnging and exciting part of the teacher education curriculum. Too often, they are nothing but "bags of tricks" or anecdotal reflections. The question is not *whether*/students will learn how to teach but rather *how* they will learn the way to teach, for even if we eliminated methods courses, students would revert to the way they were taught, pick up hints in the teachers' lounge, or perhaps just read the textbook out loud. The challenge is to make of methods courses what they could and should be. The ideal methods course should combine a survey of the substance and structure of the content area, with the principles of child development and learning theory; the social context of education, along with compassion, caring, and concern must be *connected* with instructional and management strategies that fit the everchanging circumstances of the classroom. The teacher must draw upon the higher order skills of problem-solving, critical thinking, and human concern to decide when and how certain aspects of the discipline should be presented, taking into account the students' different needs, motivations, and backgrounds. Teachers must be brought to reflect on and critically evaluate their teaching performance. What really happened in class today? Why did that example work? Would another strategy have been better suited to get at that concept? Imagine a methods course in which a content area professor, and education professor in the area, an experienced teacher, and a group of student teachers sit down and critically analyze, evaluate, and improve *real* teaching practice.

The "logical" structure of a content area is not necessarily the best "pedagogical" structure as the problems with "new math" taught us. Methods courses must deal with the interaction of the *logical* structure derived from the disciplinary experts in the liberal arts and the *pedagogical* structure derived from the experts in education in the context of human relationships. I conclude that the liberal arts can contribute not only to improving general cognitive skills and content, but also to improving the methods of teaching.

## EXTENDED PREPARATION

As one reviews the wide-ranging potential of the liberal arts to teacher preparation, it quickly becomes apparent that more is required than is typically the case in the 1980s.[6] The general education component of liberal education must be revitalized and reconceptualized for all students to make it a more integrative experience. That will most likely require more, not less, time. If one pays special attention to the higher-order skills and competencies rather then assuming they will emerge on their own, more time will be required. If one goes beyond the disciplines to earlier conceptions of liberal education as preparation for an intelligent life, more time will be needed. Traditional "content" education must be given its due, and as our knowledge grows, so will the pressure to increase the time devoted to regular academic majors. If we take seriously pedagogical content knowledge, the structure of the disciplines, and the liberal arts contributions to methods of teaching, we will need to find room in our curricula for such work.

In short, the liberal arts must contribute more to teacher education, but not simply through increasing the hours required in traditional majors. Indeed, with the exception of a few teachers who teach college level courses in high school, there seems to be no demonstrable connection between advanced content knowledge on the part of teachers and better student performance. On the other hand, many teachers have been justly criticized for lack of basic and higher-order cognitive skills and for the inability to handle the essentials of subject matter in ways appropriate to the capacities of their particular elementary and secondary students.

Some might suggest that we could find room by eliminating the professional component from teacher preparation and allowing liberal arts graduates to learn how to teach on the job. It is not my purpose here to defend the professional component in teacher preparation. Suffice it to say that several recent analyses make strong cases for retaining a professional component. The Holmes Group report, *Tomorrow's Teachers*[7] contains a particularly compelling case for not resting content with the "bright person" (liberal arts only) model of teaching given the reality of the kinds of "high risk" students who will more and more come to populate our schools. The Carnegie Commission report, *A Nation Prepared: Teachers for the 21st Century,*[8] likewise calls for a professional component, albeit at the graduate level. Furthermore, the knowledge base underlying general pedagogical knowledge has increased dramatically in recent years, strengthening the case that we can and must teach people how to teach. If we maintain the professional component, teacher preparation will take longer than four years. We will require extended preparation programs for teacher education of at least five years.

Some advocates of a five-year teacher program argue for a baccalaureate followed by a fifth professional year of educational studies. Such a proposal fits far more easily into the existing models of liberal and professional education than does an integrated program. On the other hand, an integrated five-year program might be more consistent with the contributions of the liberal arts noted above. Of course, myriad problems are associated with actually implementing an integrated five-year teacher training program of a fifth-year program. My point is simply that if the liberal arts are to play their proper role in teacher preparation, and we do not slight professional preparation, it will take at least five years. Perhaps it is time we got on with the job.

This paper is based on "Teacher Education and the Liberal Arts," a report of the Task Force of the Association of Colleges and Schools of Education in State Universities and Land Grant Colleges and Affiliated Private Universities. The Task Force members were Hugh G. Petrie (SUNY-Buffalo), Chair; Richard D. Hawthorne (Kent State University); Richard E. Ishler (Texas Tech University); Cecil G. Miskel (University of Utah); Patricia D. Murphy (North Dakota State); Frank B. Murray (University of Delaware); and Jay D. Scribner (Temple University). The full Task Force Report is available as an Occasional Paper of the Association from Hugh G. Petrie.

## NOTES

1. B. Othanel Smith, *A Design for a School of Pedagogy* (Washington, D.C.: U.S. Government Printing Office, 1980); David Berliner, "Making the Right Changes in Preservice Teacher Education," *Phi Delta Kappan* 66 (October 1984): 94–96; Hendrik Gideonse, "State Education Policy in Transition: Teacher Education," *Phi Delta Kappan* 66 (November 1984): 205–208; Judith Lanier, *Research on Teacher Education* (East Lansing, Mich: Institute for Research on Teaching, Michigan State University, 1984); Lee S. Shulman, "Those Who Understand: Knowledge Growth in Teaching," *Educational Researcher* 15, no. 2 (February 1986): 4–14.

2. Study Group on the Conditions of Excellence in American Higher Education, *Investment in Learning: Realizing the Potential of American Higher Education* (Washington, D.C.: National Institute of Education, 1984).

3. Association of American Colleges, *Integrity in the College Curriculum: A Report to the College Community* (Washington, D.C.: Association of American Colleges, 1985).

4. Jan H. Blits, "The Search for Ends: Liberal Education and the Modern University," in *The American University: Problems, Prospects and Trends,* Jan H. Blits, ed. (Buffalo, N.Y.: Prometheus Books, 1985): pp. 81–100.

5. Shulman.

6. Of course, extended preparation programs are not new. In particular, the Ford Foundation funded a number of Master of Arts in Teaching (MAT) programs in the 1950s and 1960s [see, for example, J.C. Stone, *Breakthrough in Teacher Education* (San Francisco: Jossey-Bass, 1963).] However, most of those programs were abandoned when the external funding dried up. A few did not, and others were started. Bank Street College and the University of New Hampshire are two examples of current extended programs that have been in existence for some time. However, the point remains that, currently, very few extended preparation programs for initial certification exist.

7. The Holmes Group, *Tomorrow's Teachers: A Report of the Holmes Group* (East Lansing Mich.: The Holmes Group, 1986).

8. Carnegie Commission, *A Nation Prepared: Teachers for the 21st Century* (New York: Carnegie Forum on Education and the Economy, 1986).

Chapter Five

# The Holmes Group Proposals: Critical Reactions and Prospects

*Tomorrow's Teachers*[1] is the impossible-to-ignore manifesto of the Holmes Group, an organization of three dozen or so respected deans from the major research-producing schools and colleges of education in the United States. As some of us anticipated, the report has generated an outpouring of reaction. Careful examination of the responses suggests important lessons for those who believe, as do I, that the Holmes Group's conclusions and recommendations are basically correct even if, as members of the group themselves would be quick to admit, no one should believe it is the last word,

Most readers of this chapter are, no doubt, already fully familiar with *Tomorrow's Teachers*. For those who may come to this article less knowledgeable, the Holmes Group argument, in its essence, is for a *profession* of teaching. To that end, group members seek to

> make the education of teachers intellectually more solid; differentiate the teaching staff according to knowledge, commitment, education, certification, and work; create professionally relevant and intellectually defensible standards for entry into the profession; connect the education of teachers to the schools as places of professional practice; and make schools better places for teachers to learn and work.[2]

A handful of premises underlie these recommendations. It is assumed that several kinds of knowledge properly form the basis for teachers' performances, and furthermore, that substantial amounts of that knowledge are in hand. The Holmes Group thus concludes that preparing teachers for entry into the profession within the confines of the baccalaureate program is no longer adequate to the task. Group members assume that preservice professional education must be conducted in settings specially designed for that function. They argue that what we know about other professions, about the emergent profession of teaching, and about learning and teaching demonstrates the need for a different structure for the organization of teaching and, by implication, schools. Finally, they understand that improving the preparation for the teaching profession is not just about intellect; it is also about politics and leadership. This is the reason for the boldness of their message,the insistent way it has been laid before the profession and the nation, and the impetus to organize for constructive action. One cannot but admire what the Holmes Group has done and the energy and commitment they have displayed in doing it.

Which takes us to the reactions to the proposals. Between March and October 1986, both praise and criticism have been received. This analysis proposes to focus, deliberately, on the criticism. Praise has been forthcoming to be sure, but this article does not attend to it. Comments have also been made about what the Holmes Group did *not* cover. I have chosen to omit all those comments that seem to acknowledge that the report could not hope to cover everything. Omissions identified as mistakes have been included.

Focus on the criticism is not just an exercise in masochism. The substance and tone of objections can tell much about what must be overcome, or at least addressed, either within the conceptual frame of the Holmes Group's recommendations or practically, in order to implement them. It may also tell something about the present context within which the recommendations have been advanced. Thus, I ask the reader's indulgence for the following long list of quoted criticism. However, this is the surest way to impart the full flavor of the published negative response to the recommendations of the Holmes Group. Consider, then, the following:

> ... this *mea culpa* approach to reform .... [3]
> This is not just elitism ... but self-aggrandizement for the worst of motives as well. [4]
> ... current research does not justify such a change. [5]
> It's almost arrogant. [6]
> ... the deans represented only one of several different groups of [teacher education] institutions .... [7]
> [To accept the premise that only a research university] was capable—by virtue of its research activities—of turning out 'good teachers' ... would be 'crazy.' ... ' [8]

[The Holmes Group] proposals for graduate education would translate into enrollment losses for some of the participating institutions.[9]
... has conceptual problems ....[10]
... it will create problems in elementary schools.[11]
There are moral, ethical, and economic considerations surrounding a proposal which would create a large and permanent underclass of apprentices ...[12]
If our education deans fail to take on the issue of academic quality in departments other than education, practitioners are likely to conclude that 'quality' is merely an academic synonym for 'generating credit hours'...[13]
It is run-on, redundant, and uninspiring ... points get lost in its verbiage ....[14]
... there needs to be recognition of the fact that at many universities a-cross the nation, the basic tenets of the report are being carried out at this time ...[15]
But another education dean, who asked not to be identified, said he was 'underwhelmed' by the report's 'relatively shallow intellectual content' and the prevalence of 'sweeping statements without any foundation in research.'[16]
We're talking about billions and billions of dollars to implement these proposals. Whether that money will be available on other than a pilot basis seems to me to be unlikely.[17]
... the group's solutions are 'troublesome' ... because so many of the things education deans believe are wrong in teaching and teacher education' are out of their control.'[18]
[The report is] more intuitive than it is objective ... they have violated some of the very principles of academic inquiry which they say in other places are essential to rigorous preparation.[19]
Politically what it does is highlight the status differences among in-stitutions of higher education ...[20]
I am disappointed that the leaders of this group claim unto themselves that responsibility for improving teacher education].[21]
... pseudo-pedantic rationale for eliminating that which barely exists or which they are miserably failing at.[22]
Mob rule and monopolies, both illegal in the United States, operate on the same principle. If you can't compete, eliminate the competition.[23]
... the proposals ... only confirm that the 'ivory tower' syndrome is alive and well ...[24]

Its members seem to be ignoring the advice of the very people who can contribute the most to relevant reform—the practitioners. When will the reformers learn?[25]
[One of the] most controversial recommendations [is to] remove pro-fessional studies from the undergraduate curriculum and place them totally at the graduate level ....[26]
... aggressive recruitment of minority students and greater cooperation

with departments in colleges of arts and sciences are two goals likely to be negatively affected by eliminating teacher education at the undergraduate level.[27]

Many of those now preparing to be elementary teachers would avoid science and mathematics courses altogether if they were not obliged to take them by school education requirements.[28]

The predictable result will be a slump in teacher education enrollments at Holmes Group institutions as prospective teachers enroll in those universities that will license them after earning baccalaureate degrees.[29]

Once alternate routes to licensure [of Instructors in the Holmes Group's three layers of differentiated staff] have been accepted and school officials learn that they can employ bright people at the lowest beginning salaries, who will oppose alternate routes to certification—except possibly deans of schools of education?[30]

... members of the Holmes consortium had little interest in building on the successful innovations of the previous decade ... [31]

We are left to assume that consortium members 'from the major research universities in each of the fifty states' need not cite appropriate references.[32]

... vague prescriptions for change in the liberal arts .... The naivete of the Holmes Group is striking.[33]

... suddenly, we are expected to jettison this important component [developmental clinical experiences which begin in a prospective teacher's freshman year and continue through a full year of internship] ... [and] replace current models of field experience with an entity they call a 'professional development school ... '[34]

... we are given rhetoric that is often trite ... an over abundance of platitudes ... erroneous and undocumented comments.... Unfortunately, they tried to do too much, too soon. And they left us with too many incomplete recommendations.[35]

... sophisticated analysis followed by simplistic solutions.[36]

The essential flaw of contending that we must have more time for teacher education is that the key issue thereby becomes the quantity of preparation, not its quality.[37]

... the role of specialized knowledge mastered in an autonomous graduate school setting is less critical to the professionalization of teaching than is the case for many other professions ....[38]

Why roads paved with good intentions may not take you where you want to go.[39]

... the self-criticism is not very pointed.[40]

... understandably vague ....[41]

The issue, however, is whether it deserves the status of the one best way that the Holmes Group accords it.[42]

Like almost all teacher education reform proposals of the last hundred years, the Holmes plan wants us to increase the amount of time teachers spend in college prior to teaching....[43]

...the Holmes Group finesses the practical problems....[44] The Holmes Group's proposals would significantly increase the costs to individuals of becoming a teacher...will decrease the quantity of those entering teachers.... And the quality of the pool will also decline....[45]

The most troublesome part of the Holmes Group's proposals...has to do with the status schism it will create within the profession.[46]

...why promote...differentiated staffing...? One answer. The Holmes Group institutions expect to be the training ground for Career Professionals [the highest of the three-tier differentiated staff].[47]

The Holmes Group began as a self-improvement effort.... There is little doubt that the Holmes Group's ambitions transcend internal change.[48]

...high implementation costs and reasonable possibilities that the Holmes design for teacher education will not yield gains for school children suggest that it is desirable to encourage variation, demonstration, and evaluation. That the leaders of research universities do not subscribe to this view is ironic.[49]

A heavy dose of criticism, perhaps, yet drawn only from what has accumulated in one policy-oriented teacher educator's file over the past six months. No doubt an active search would reveal even more.

## WHAT HAVE WE GOT HERE?

Some of these statements imply have to be dismissed as revealing the irascibility of their authors. Little time need be spent on them. Other statements are either deliberate misrepresentation, sloppy scholarship, or both. Examples of this are charges that the Holmes recommendations call for the ending of developmentally sequenced clinical and field experiences, or for fitting all professional preparation into the fifth year, or for "one best way" of teacher education. *Tomorrow's Teachers* does none of the three.

Some criticisms lead me to want to coin a term—*ad institutionum.* Such criticism, in effect, says "consider the source" and allows the critic, at least, to dismiss attention without further ado. Yet the fact remains that those critics felt the need to speak. In doing so they implicitly acknowledged that the Holmes deans are, indeed, forces with which to be reckoned.

Part of the *ad institutionum* comment in effect faults the authors for being who they are and not someone else. In fact, however, many of the

Holmes deans were once practitioners, and most are still actively engaged in teaching, albeit in universities. Denying those deans the right to speak on matters of professional preparation (as do some critics) displays an elitist (or perhaps populist?) tendency—a tendency others claim to see in the Holmes deans themselves.

The fact that the Holmes deans are addressing the issues from the particular perspective of their roles as deans is seen as an arrogation of authority. Objecting to leadership initiatives is a curious posture, to say the least; one of the things explicitly expected of deans is the exercise of leadership.

The charges of bad motivation, blatant self-interest, and self-aggrandizement could be classed along with irascible or the *ad institutionum,* but the not-so-latent hospitality merits separate attention. Members of the Holmes Group do not need testimonials, but those who know them see an assemblage deeply committed to improving the profession through the instruments under their control. In making these recommendations, the deans showed a willingness to risk their nests, not feather them, Curiously, still other critics point out the extent to which the Holmes proposals would represent real risks to institutions adopting them. One might ask how both claims can be true simultaneously.

Another line of criticism accuses the Holmes deans of failing to demonstrate the intellectual rigor expected of members of research universities advocating such rigor in teacher education. For example, claims are made that the deans fail to support their arguments with research evidence, that there *isn't* any such evidence, worse, that they commit bad scholarship, and finally, that they fail to endorse experimentation. But are these valid complaints? To argue that research evidence is not presented is to miss entirely the fundamental grounding of the recommendations on the teaching and teacher education research of the last three decades. In point of fact, however, *Tomorrow's Teachers* makes no pretense at being a scholarly effort; it is a manifesto designed to challenge, persuade, and, yes, recruit.

The blunt claim that no research evidence exists to justify the Holmes recommendations appears damaging until one thinks about the logic of the claim: how can research evidence exist for any proposed innovation? If this argument had been applied to the Apollo project, the United States would never have begun it. If this argument had been applied to the reformation of medical education, Daniel Coit Gilman at Johns Hopkins University and Charles W. Eliot at Harvard University would never have launched the curricular and structural innovations which allowed Flexner, thirty-five years later, to do his landmark study which forever transformed the education of physicians. Empirical evidence is not the only basis for action; good theory and the logic of intention and design can be equally compelling bases for movement.

Lastly, the accusation that the Holmes proposals discourage experimentation is actually something of a misrepresentation, given the encouragement to member institutions to develop approaches suited to their own circumstances.

There are criticisms which, in effect, say the proposals are old hat or already being implemented. But to say that people have recommended for one hundred years increases in the amount of preservice teacher preparation ignores the advancing base on which each of those recommendations was made. Further, while examples can be found here and there across the land of already-existing instances of actions on Holmes premises, these are highly isolated exceptions that take nothing away from the basic idea being promulgated—namely that the institutions heavily committed to research in education have a great obligation to mount teacher preparation programs that fully reflect the intellectual and scholarly capacity such institutions possess.

Critics point to negative consequences. Problems are seen for elementary schools. Assertions are made of the incredible costs of mounting the programs nationwide. A slump in teacher education enrollment is predicted. The differentiated staff proposal is seen as creating a permanent underclass of instructors and providing an incentive for school districts to hire untrained people subject to continuous turnover. Finally, fears are expressed that the program would reduce recruitment of minority students, diminish cooperative efforts with arts and sciences departments, and reduce the intellectual content of the baccalaureate experience of the elementary teachers.

The last three concerns may be easily dismissed. A teacher education program at whatever level, baccalaureate or combined baccalaureate and postbaccalaureate, can maintain control of the curriculum simply by specifying necessary pre- or corequisities for entry. Institutions can determine how to recruit minority students, a task that is neither greater nor lesser at the baccalaureate level or beyond. Cooperation with arts and sciences departments would be no more or less difficult whether the programs remain at the undergraduate level or shift to a full five years, combining bachelor's and master's degrees.

The projected huge costs of implementation are based almost entirely on the concept of the foregone income to the teacher candidate, a concept that economists love to discuss and that makes for impressive

numbers. However, such calculations loom large only in the economists' minds; far more important is the commitment of individuals to
undergo whatever preparation is required to equip them properly for
their chosen career.

Finally, entirely well taken are comments respecting the need for
still more thinking about the organization of schools under differentiated staffing; the different curricular requirements of elementary and
special education teacher education programs; and, indeed, all the
specifics of the curricular map for accomplishing the liberal arts, subject matter mastery, and professional preparation goals of teacher
education within a five-year (plus internship) program.

## MEANING?

How should this outpouring of criticism be read?

Both the emotional intensity and the volume of critical comment
invite several observations. The various elements of the huge existing
educational establishment are well-entrenched. The Holmes proposals
represent nothing short of a fundamental reconceptualization of the
whole enterprise. No one should be surprised, therefore, that all the ox-
owners are busy protecting the flanks of their charges. Whether it helps
or hinders the effort to point out this apparent defensiveness is nowhere
near as important as recognizing that the Holmes proposals imply
changes for every part of the professional education enterprise.

It is also true, however, that the potential blocks to action in
teacher education reform are numerous. Teacher education, as David
Imig reminds us, is not the same thing as the education of teachers.[50]
The former is in the hands of teacher educators, the latter in the hands
of the entire college or university. As a result, even within their own institutions, teacher education leadership depends upon the active cooperation of the larger institutional leadership. In the absence of such
cooperation, not much is likely to happen.

The structure of schools is largely determined by state regulation,
as is the certification of teachers. State regulation is an intensely political process. Even with the tremendous energy and initiative being
shown by many of the nation's governors, the outcome of the political
debate over school structure and teacher certification is far more likely
to favor the *status quo* than innovation. Yet when policy proposals of
the sweep of the Holmes recommendations are advanced, considering
the extent to which critical reaction is in response to the existing frame
of reference as compared to the projected one would seem prudent.

The economics of compensation is also vital. Even if the foregone income argument is a weak one in estimating cost of implementation, it remains true that the willingness of teacher candidates to submit to longer and more rigorous training will depend on their perceptions of the intrinsic and extrinsic rewards at the end of the path. But a new salary structure is not likely to be created before the vehicle on which it would be based.

When everything looks equally problematic, what's the best thing to do? Answer: What you believe *ought* to be done within the parameters over which you have control. And that is precisely what the Holmes Group has proposed. It is what they must be encouraged to continue to a successful conclusion.

## NEXT STEPS

The core premises of the Holmes Group proposals are the imperatives derived from the kinds of knowledge with which teachers ought to be equipped and which need to be applied in the practice of schooling. Teachers require a good liberal education, mastery of the subject matters of instruction, and a theoretical and practical grasp of professional knowledge, skills, attitudes, and values. At its simplest, teacher candidates need sufficient time to acquire that knowledge.

While much of the criticism levelled at the Holmes Group has focused on the need to expand the time available for preservice preparation, the Holmes institutions should be encouraged to ignore the *ad institutionum* character of much of it. Ironically, the time argument is not a quantitative one; it is based almost exclusively on the qualitative considerations of the essential knowledge teachers must have. Equally important (though overshadowed somewhat by the particular character of the *ad institutionum* criticisms), the argument from the knowledge bases requires more than just extended time for the students; it will also require a professional teacher preparation faculty trained in the full range of necessary specializations. The great majority of teacher education institutions in America are under great pressure arising from the advances in scholarship about teaching. This pressure is of an inexorable nature and stands independent of any proposals the Holmes Group has advanced, but it may help to explain the intensity of the reactions to the Holmes recommendations *per se.* If the Holmes proposals had not been advanced in March 1985, the pressures on the majority of America's teacher education institutions on this count would still be very great.[51]

If the Holmes Group institutions can afford to ignore the *ad institutionum* criticism several other steps exist that the Holmes deans cannot afford to omit. One of these is to cultivate the assistance of their provosts and presidents. Repeating Imig's observation, teacher education and the education of teachers are not an equivalency. The goal cannot be achieved by teacher educators alone.

In this regard, it may be useful to note that the report of the Carnegie-supported Task Force on Teaching as a Profession[52] may be a better stimulus to garner the attention and commitment of university leaders than the Holmes report by itself. No study has been done, of course, but anecdotal evidence strongly suggests that on many campuses the Carnegie Task Force recommendations have elicited greater attention among central administrators than the Holmes report. While those of us in teacher and professional education have been much involved in discussions of the Holmes report, the higher education community generally seems to have been exposed more to and touched more by the Carnegie document. Given the virtually identical nature of the teacher education recommendations in the two reports, teacher educators interested in pursuing the Holmes recommendations and garnering the engagement of central administration and arts and sciences figures may be well-advised to key to the Carnegie Task Force report at least as much as to the Holmes report.

The second and third observations involve other important, and progressively larger, constituencies. The first of these is the rest of the teacher education community.

That anxieties and irritations run deep among us, should be apparent, just as deep as the real challenges and threats that face us all. Achieving the objective of building teacher education programs that will prepare teachers for the emerging teaching profession is a task that none of us knows how to do; if we did, it would already have been done.

To the extent that this is true, every one of us in teacher education faces major changes, Holmes institutions as well as all the others. The Holmes institutions are embarked on a national quest which must be nutured in the context of teacher education policy in the fifty states. The task of reform will be facilitated in the long run by the greatest degree of openness of communication between Holmes Group institutions and their teacher education peers. The Holmes Group ran into something of a problem in that respect midway through the development of their conceptualization,[53] but the publication of their report has helped greatly. Also helpful has been the expressed willingness of the group, after the initial work of implementation in the charter institutions, to be open to initiatives by other qualified institutions interested in pursuing the broad directions outlined.

The third constituency with whom Holmes advocates and implementers must maintain close contact is the various practitioner groups. They are an important source of wisdom and experience. They are also vital loci of professional political power, both nationally and at the state level.

Conceptually, the relationship to current practitioners in the context of proposals that would radically redefine their roles, responsibilities, and relative status is hardly a trifling matter. There are millions of teachers, hundreds of thousands of administrators at state and local levels, and a very decentralized policy structure. The Holmes proposals and the far-reaching implications that derive from them promise to do more than touch only lightly the "turfs" and functions of the present army of practitioners.

At the same time, the histories of other professional transformations remind us that, while stressful perhaps, to many of the participants the changes were more in the nature of gradual replacement at retirement than enforced retooling or replacement at midstream. And so it will be in teaching as we move to full professional capacity and status.

Based on present and future developments in professional knowledge, changes are inevitable in teachers' roles, the structure of the profession, and the schools themselves. It may take twenty or fifty years, but these changes will come about. The extent to which practitioner groups are fully admitted to and apprised of their development will be critical in determining the pace of transformation. This suggests the need, at both the national level and the local level, to link systematically and deliberately with the pertinent practitioner organizations.

Establishing, maintaining, and capitalizing on such connections should be deemed as much a part of the overhead of the enterprise as the travel and phone budgets linking the participants. These connections are vital to, indeed are an expression of, the concept of collegium central to any true profession.[54]

## NOTES

1. The Holmes Group, *Tomorrow's Teachers: A Report of the Holmes Group* (East Lansing, Mich.: The Holmes Group, 1986).

2. Ibid., p. 4.

3. Barry McGhan, "Holmes Group Criticized for 'Mea Culpa' View of Teacher Education, *Education Week* (June 11, 1986), p. 17.

4. Idem.

5. Lynn Olson and Blake Rodman, "Teacher Educators Finding Themselves in the 'Eye of Reform,'" *Education Week* (March 12, 1986), p. 16.

6. Ibid., p. 17.

7. Robert Jacobson, "Key Goal of Holmes Deans: Support on Their Own Campuses," *The Chronicle of Higher Education* (April 16, 1986), p. 28.

8. Idem.

9. Idem.

10. James H. Sutton, "Some Conceptual Problems in Teacher-Training Report," *The Chronicle of Higher Education* (May 21, 1986), p. 40.

11. Idem.

12. Idem.

13. Ibid., p. 41.

14. Robert Sherman, "Letters," *The Chronicle of Higher Education* (May 21, 1986), p. 41.

15. Carolyn Warner, ibid., p. 41.

16. Lynn Olson, "Reaction to Holmes Report: Plaudits, Skepticism, and Muted 'Sour Grapes,'" *Education Week* (April 23, 1986), p. 1.

17. Ibid., p. 12.

18. Idem.

19. Idem.

20. Idem.

21. Idem.

22. Peter J. Quinn, "Eliminating Competition Suspected as Holmes Goal," *Education Week* (April 30, 1986), p. 19.

23. Idem.

24. Chuck Aswell, "Holmes Plan Said Flawed by 'Mistake of Ignoring Advice of Practitioners,'" *Education Week* (May 7, 1986), p. 13.

25. Idem.

26. Howard D. Mehlinger, "A Risky Venture," *Phi Delta Kappan* 68 (September 1986): 34.

27. Idem.

28. Ibid., p. 35.

29. Idem.

30. Ibid., p. 36.

31. Edward J. Nussel, "What the Holmes Group Doesn't Say," *Phi Delta Kappan* 68 (September 1986): 36.

32. Idem.

33. Ibid., p. 37.

34. Idem.

35. Ibid., p. 38.

36. Alan R. Tom, "The Holmes Report: Sophisticated Analysis, Simplistic Solutions," *Journal of Teacher Education* 37 (July–August 1986): 44.

37. Idem.

38. Ibid., p. 46.

39. Willis D. Hawley, "A Critical Analysis of the Holmes Group's Proposals for Reforming Teacher Education," *Journal of Teacher Education* 37 (July–August 1986): p. 47.

40. Idem.

41. Ibid., p. 48.

42. Idem.

43. Idem.

44. Ibid., p. 49.

45. Idem.

46. Ibid., p. 50.

47. Idem.

48. Idem.

49. Ibid., p. 51.

50. David G. Imig, "The Greater Challenge," *Phi Delta Kappan* 68 (September 1986): 33.

51. The logic of the staffing requirements derived from the advancing knowledge base will prove increasingly and deeply provocative for nearly two-thirds of America's teacher education establishments. As I have argued else-

where, the great majority of the 1,300 or more institutions now approved by their respective states to offer more than 7,200 different certification programs simply do not have sufficient faculty with advanced preparation in professional areas to cover the specializations now nearly universally recognized by teacher education leadership nationally to be required for the preparation function. Hendrik D. Gideonse, "The Coming Reduction in the Number of Institutions Preparing Teachers: Rationale and Routes," in *Improving Teacher Education,* E. Galambos, ed. (San Francisco: Jossey-Bass, 1986).

52. The Task Force on Teaching as a Profession, *A Nation Prepared: Teachers for the 21st Century* (Washington, D.C.: Carnegie Forum on Education and the Economy, 1986).

53. Symptomatic of the problems more than a year ago was my letter to the Chief Institutional Representatives of the American Association of Colleges for Teacher Education which was widely reported in education press (see Cindy Currance, "Teacher Training Standards: Change and Debate," *Education Week* (October 30, 1985), p. 1.

54. Charles W. Case, Judith E. Lanier, and Cecil G. Miskel, "The Holmes Group Report: Impetus for Gaining Professional Status for Teachers," *Journal of Teacher Education* 37 (July–August 1986): 38.

# Part II

# *Teaching Reform*

Chapter Six

# Reform and the Teaching Profession

In a recent essay in the *Phi Delta Kappan,* Larry Cuban, professor of education at Stanford University, argues that there are really two education reform movements in America today and that the changes they are trying to make in our schools often work at cross purposes.[1] One movement pursues an agenda aimed at strengthening the traditional school structures; it focuses on standardized test results, highly structured curricula with a great deal of rote learning, greater bureaucratic control, and a general tightening of existing standards.

The second reform movement is based on the premise that we have to set learning goals higher than ever before, and that our schools need to develop the higher order of intellectual skills in our students— reasoning, weighing evidence, and effectively developing and expressing an argument. This would demand a radical restructuring of our schools to give teachers what other professionals already have—greater control of their working conditions, the opportunity to try a variety of teaching strategies, the time for close work with individual students or with small groups to discuss compositions or student projects, a chance to share ideas with colleagues and develop and evaluate curriculum materials.

Both approaches have much to recommend them. Obviously, we need to set tougher standards for our students and to undo the damage of the looseness of the late 1960s and early 1970s. We need standardized tests as one way of pinpointing weaknesses and highlighting areas requiring more resources and greater effort. But we clearly must do more because we still have not discovered large-scale, effective ways of engaging most students in their own learning and ways of freeing the best abilities of our teachers.

Each of the reform movements may achieve sporadic success but, at bottom, as Professor Cuban argues, one approach will probably preclude the other, and the vision that prevails will be crucial in determining the effectiveness of our schools and the quality of our teaching staff well into the twenty-first century.

## HOW SCHOOLS PROFITED IN THE PAST

Not so long ago, our schools were the beneficiaries of social and economic problems. During the Great Depression of the 1930s, widespread unemployment forced many highly qualified candidates into our classrooms who would normally have gone into other, more lucrative professions. Schools offered a job and security and had the rare luxury of being able to choose from among a surplus of top-flight applicants, many of whom waited years for an appointment to a teaching post. Ironically, a national disaster was a boon to academic quality.

Sex discrimination also helped our schools. Until quite recently, the doors to most professions were closed to women. Teaching, nursing, and librarianship were among the few jobs to which bright women could aspire. But a quick look at the composition of enrollments in law schools, medical schools, and in MBA programs demonstrates how radically the picture has changed. Women have a vastly expanded number of career options. The end of official discrimination in the workplace, although a wonderful advance for women (and minorities), has cut deeply into what used to be our school's richest source of teaching talent.

Selective Service gave another boost to our schools. For a time, particularly during the Vietnam War, many able young men who normally would have chosen other careers elected the option of performing national service in difficult-to-staff, inner-city schools rather than in the military. With the end of the draft, however, these men no longer enter classroom teaching.

Of course, as in the past, large numbers of people continue to be drawn to teaching by their love of children and their eagerness to make a contribution to society. However, our schools are not likely to get the extra boost in recruitment efforts that they once did from economic and/or political adversity. Increasingly, they will have to compete head-on for personnel with the private sector.

## THE ROAD AHEAD

To say the least, the task is formidable. One estimate suggests that, simply to maintain current staff levels, we would have to recruit and retain 24 percent of all college graduates for each of the next ten years. But a recent survey reported that only 7 percent of college freshmen expressed an interest in teaching in elementary or secondary schools. Even so, this low figure represents a significant increase over the 4.7 percent figure for 1982, probably fueled by the publicity given to reform initiatives. The true dimensions of decline can be seen when these numbers are compared with the statistics for the late 1960s—when more than 20 percent of freshman (including one-third of the women) said they were interested in teaching careers.

Furthermore, it is neither feasible nor desirable for nearly one-fourth of our college graduates to become teachers. Our society still needs accountants, doctors, chemists, engineers, and other trained professionals.

What our schools face is a tough scramble for their share of available talent, made even more difficult by the figures that show, at least for the short term, that we have a declining number of college graduates while the number of school children in the lower grades is rising.

## STRATEGIES FOR CHANGE

One answer to the crisis would entail raising salaries and improving working conditions. In recent years, schools had fallen so far behind in competition with the private sector that a great deal had to be done to avoid complete collapse in recruitment. But a strategy that might ensure short-term success in crisis control in scattered districts does not necessarily hold up when projected over the next few years for the whole country.

Last year, the average teacher's salary in the United States was slightly in excess of $25,000. An across-the-board increase of only $1,000 would cost more than $2 billion, not including any fringe benefits or Social Security payements. A pay raise is always welcome, but a salary of $26,000 after several years in the classroom would hardly tempt large numbers of undergraduate students to prepare themselves for social studies or biology teaching, instead of majoring in computer technology, accounting, prelaw or premed programs. What our school systems need to make their teachers' salaries competitive with the private sector is probably something close to a 50 percent across-the-board pay hike—for more than two million people! However, especially in the shadow of Gramm-Rudman legislation, it is utterly un-realistic to expect that anything close to the multibillion dollar package needed nationally would be made available just for teachers' salaries. Incremental improvements have been and will probably continue to be made in many districts. But, given traditional approaches, they would not result in our schools being able to offer teachers the kind of money they could earn in the private sector.

In shortage areas like math and the sciences, our schools are un-likely to be even in the running. In some subjects, college graduates simply are not available or are so few in number that it is inconceivable that corporate giants like IBM or General Electric will allow local school districts to outbid them for the relative handful of physics, chemistry, and math majors that our colleges produce each year. We already see ample evidence of recruitment problems in the widespread use of out-of-license teachers. Our salary improvements, although welcome and long overdue, are not likely to make much of a differ-ence.

After salary increases, the other main recruitment strategy is to im-prove working conditions. Of course, a great deal can be done in this area, which brings us back to money. Many school plants need repairs and cleaning. Supplies need to arrive on time in quantity and quality so that teachers can function effectively. Too often school authorities have not been able to provide staffs with needed support, and too many teachers have come to accept it as a given of professional life that they must dig into their own pockets to compensate for the system's failure to supply basic materials for their students.

## OBSTACLES IN THE ROAD

A deeper, more intractable problem concerns the question of the intrinsic satisfaction that a teacher derives from his or her job. Good teachers know they should not be preparing children to take multiple choice or short answer tests. They want to stimulate their students' minds and liberate their imaginations. They want to encourage students to weigh alternative ideas, sift evidence, learn to marshal facts to support their opinions—in short, learn to think and express them-selves effectively. But a great deal of close work with small groups of students is required to permit teachers to read compositions carefully, make suggestions for revisions, and coach students in clarifying their thinking.

The reality of school life, so tellingly described by Theodore Sizer in *Horace's Compromise,* forces even the most conscientious teachers to trim their principles.[2] In secondary schools, class sizes of thirty and more make it impossible for teachers to do the kind of job they know they should be doing. With a total enrollment of 150 students in five classes, if it takes a teacher ten minutes to read and discuss a paper with each student, one writing assignment would take at least twenty-five hours for grading and conferences. This would be added to the normal burden of lesson preparation and clerical duties. Clearly, many teachers soon get the message that theirs is an impossible job and, if they remain, that they will live with the knowledge they are doing less than they should. A terrible compromise is built into the job.

An obvious reform, then, would include the improvement of teachers' working conditions by reducing class sizes. If we cut each class by 20 percent, a high school English teacher, for example, would have to grade 120 papers for each assignment instead of 150 and spend twenty hours instead of twenty-five. Admittedly, this would be a welcome relief—but it really would not make the whole task any less impossible. The job would remain a crushing burden.

Even this relatively modest reform in working conditions is unlikely to occur given the numbers. A 20 percent cut in class size also means a 20 percent increase in the number of teachers needed and an equal increase in the school budget. If our schools are not sufficiently competitive (and funded) to maintain their current staff levels and replace the people leaving in the next five to seven years, it is unreasonable to expect that there will be enough qualified candidates available, and the money to pay for them, to make even the slightest improvement in class size.

Another weakness of the traditional reform proposals is that they fail to take into account the changing perception of work in our society. My parents and most of their contemporaries had a simple, straightforward idea of what a job was all about: it was a means of putting bread on their table and a roof over their heads. Being employed meant exchanging sweat for dollars.

But workers today have a different idea of what they are doing. As a vice president of the AFL-CIO, I served as a member of the Commission on the Future of Work. One of our missions was to discover what effect workers' attitudes had on the labor movement. We looked at the results of a number of surveys and commissioned several of our own. The findings showed a marked contrast with the attitudes of my parents' generation. Instead of seeing their jobs merely as a means of providing the necessities of life, today's workers are more concerned about the personal satisfaction they derive from what they do—from having the opportunity to use their special talents, from having the discretion to make meaningful decisions about how their work should be done, from being rewarded for high levels of performance. The emphasis now is on fulfillment, control, professionalism.

But in many states and local school districts, what supposedly passes as reform is actually moving in the opposite authority. It may often be part of a political trade-off for, when political leaders are out front in upgrading teachers' salaries or improving school working conditions even in modest ways, it is understood that they must demonstrate to their consitituents that they are getting value for their tax money. It is not good politics to offer voters the same product for increased expenditure. The impulse, then, is to demand something from the teachers and the schools, some sign that things will improve, even if it is little more than a cosmetic change. Therefore, many states have instituted tests for teachers, although in almost all cases they have not been serious professional tests but rather minimum skills tests in reading, writing, and arithmetic.

Along with this has come a wave of increased regulation, which includes a welcome tightening of academic requirements, but also an increased regimentation of curriculum and teaching strategies—and an increased emphasis on standardized test results. Tomes of new regulations have been issued by state legislatures. For example, in his book *Tales Out of School,* Patrick Welsh, an English teacher in Alexandria, Virginia, who favors a few of the new rules, describes some of the reforms pouring down from above:

> Virginia's Legislature was passing new laws and the Department of Education was cranking out regulations affecting what we taught and how we taught it....The reservations of teachers had to do with the seemingly rigid plan for executing the standards, and with the potentially nightmarish bookkeeping requirement. They listed literally hundreds of things that teachers had to do at specific points in students' education.[3]

It seems ironic that the centralized, paternalistic management strategies being abandoned in industry as counter-productive are now promoted in our schools in the name of reform. Therefore, while salaries have risen and gestures have been made toward improving working conditions, teachers are still told that they are not expected to be very bright or creative. They are given sixth-grade arithmetic and reading tests and are increasingly being told what to do, when to do it, and how to do it. This is hardly the image of a profession that is likely to capture the imagination of a bright college graduate who is eager to accept the challenge to make the most use of his or her talent. This reform approach is bound to maintain teaching as an "easy-in/easy out" profession. Although I do not meet any ex-doctors, ex-lawyers, ex-engineers, or ex-actuaries in my travels around the country, legions of former teachers greet me and describe how they spent a few years in the classroom and went on to something else.

As long as teaching is so lightly regarded, better college graduates will continue to turn to other occupations, not only for increased financial rewards and better working conditions, but for greater personal satisfaction and the kind of professional challenge that our highly bureaucratized schools simply cannot offer. The evidence already exists that despite reform efforts (and in some cases because of them) we will be lowering instead of raising the standards of the teaching profession. Not long ago, Baltimore, Maryland tested teaching candidates for basic skills. When the bell rang for the first day of classes, the board of education, because of a shortage of teachers, was forced to hire some who had failed. For several months, full-time teachers went to night school to learn essentially what they would be teaching their own students during the day. Unfortunately, we can expect more of the same, given the poor competitive position of our schools. As a result, taxpayers and politicians will soon question the expenditure of money for the sort of reform that produces such results, and the fate of public education will be placed in jeopardy.

For the sake of argument, however, even if these reforms "succeeded," exactly what kind of schools would result? Teachers' salaries would be improved—a little. Class sizes would be reduced—a little. Academic standards would be tightened. Teachers would not be hired unless they passed tests. If it all sounds familiar, it is because that is what we had a generation ago. What we are really talking about is "the good old days." But we are also talking about the "wonderful" conditions that existed in high schools that had drop-out rates of up to 70 percent! In reality, then, some of our reformers are busy trying to recreate institutions that once failed for a majority of their students.

## A VISION FOR THE FUTURE

There is another reform vision, with different idea of what schools can be and what teachers can do. In an already much-quoted passage, last year's Carnegie report, *A Nation Prepared,* says,

> If our standard of living is to be maintained, if the growth of a permanent underclass is to be averted, if democracy is to function effectively into the next century, our schools must graduate the vast majority of

their students with achievement levels long thought possible for only the privileged few. The American mass education system, designed in the early part of the century for a mass-production economy, will not succeed unless it not only raises but redefines the essential standards of excellence and strives to make quality and equality of opportunity compatible with each other.[4]

What is clear is that replicas of the schools of the 1950s, even at their best, will never educate enough students to levels that will make our nation competitive in the next generation's hi-tech world. Nor will the perpetuation of an industrial model school system, where rote learning dominates, provide the best environment to sustain liberal traditions of rational discourse and promote the humane, democratic values that are the foundation of our society. The only reforms that will succeed in accomplishing this are those that will revolutionize both the structure of our schools and the roles and structure of our teaching staff. Our challenge is to reshape the teaching profession, to attract and retain a fair share of the best and the brightest by offering the rewards and challenges of other professions.

In short, we need to do for teachers what has already been done for almost every other profession—doctors, lawyers, engineers, actuaries. We must assure prospective candidates that they will not be treated like factory hands, strictly supervised at every point in the working day and robbed of every opportunity of exercising their own judgment.

## REALIZING THE VISION

To begin with, we must rethink basic assumptions and work toward a new structure for our schools that would more fully engage both teachers and students and make more effective use of professional personnel.

If we were to build our education system from scratch, it is hard to imagine that we would opt for the highly structured, control-oriented schools that traditional reformers seem determined to resurrect, where students for the most part are expected to sit attentively from nine to three and listen to teachers who have little choice but to lecture, given the large class registers and the tight succession of forty- or fifty-minute periods. Such a proposal would give rise to all sorts of objections— about the possibility of children being able to learn much sitting still for so long a time and about the willingness of a sensible, talented adult to endure that kind of confinement for a whole career.

In *A Place Called School,* John Goodlad describes the deadening effect of such a school structure:

"We observed that, on the average, about 75 percent of class time was spent in instruction and that nearly 70 percent of this was 'talk'— usually teacher to students. Teachers out-talked the entire class of students by a ratio about three-to-one. If teachers in the talking mode and students in the listening mode is what we want, rest assured that we have it . . . .

Clearly, the bulk of this teacher talk was instructing in the sense of telling. Barely 5 percent of this instructional time was designed to create students' anticipation of needing to respond. Not even 1 percent required some kind of open response involving reasoning or perhaps an opinion from students. Usually, when a student was called on to respond, it was to give an informational answer to the teacher's question . . . .

We do not see in our descriptions, then, much opportunity for students to become engaged with knowledge so as to employ their full range of intellectual abilities. And one wonders about the meaningfulness of whatever is acquired by students who sit listening or performing relatively repetitive exercises, year after year . . . .It appears to me that students spending twelve years in the schools we studied would be unlikely to experience much novelty. Does part of the brain just sleep, then?[5]

Admittedly, it is often difficult for anyone to break with old modes of thinking. Most of us have only known the same sort of schools with highly structured programs for both teachers and students, where the bell rang every forty-five or fifty minutes, where there was little or no time or place for reflection or informal discussions, where we packed our books on signal and left English for biology and then packed our books again and went off to French, often leaving questions hanging and puzzlement unresolved, where curriculums had to be "covered" posthaste—not digested or savored.

Although some schools intermittently attempted to depart from this formula, there are still too few models to guide us. We have little choice but to hold our vision steadfast and embark on a period of trial and error.

My own experience suggests that we try, for example, the sort of approach that the Boy Scouts and Girl Scouts have been practicing for years. Both organizations have a series of examinations and tasks that scouts have to pass and master. However, the scout masters never deliver a formal lecture to their groups on the ten knots that have to be learned. Instead, each scout knows what he or she has to do to progress to the next rank and works at his or her own pace. And each time a scout masters one task, the leader signs the individual's record to acknowledge the achievement.

The job of the scout leader is to connect each scout with the appropriate activity that will help the scout complete a specified task. For example, if Johnny had to learn to make a particular knot, the scout master might give him a piece of rope and a book with step-by-step instructions and encourage him to try to figure it out by himself. If that failed, the scout master might try some individual instruction or he might send Johnny to another scout who was a whiz at knot-making for some peer tutoring.

In the same spirit, we must work toward a system that liberates the teacher and student from the batch processing system we now have, that will grant the teacher the flexibility and resources to match the student with an appropriate learning experience. In a period of space travel, most of our schools still use the tools of the horse and buggy age. We have scarcely begun to explore the teaching possibilities of technological advances, not only as more effective learning tools but as ways of giving teachers the opportunity to do the close work with students—the coaching, the small group discussions—necessary to develop the higher levels of intellectual skills for which we must aim.

Teachers still lecture to their classes about the wildlife of Tierra del Fuego or the economics of the Mississippi Delta, subjects that could be more effectively presented by films or video cassettes. And we are still stumbling in our efforts to fit the computer into our curriculums. In a restructured school, teachers would be able to try to match the student with the appropriate materials. In any given "period," some students would work at computer terminals, others would be viewing video tapes, and others still might be consulting reference material. At the same time, teachers would be free to grade papers, prepare and evaluate curriculum materials, conduct individual conferences or seminars, or confer with colleagues and supervise paraprofessionals and other staff members.

## WHAT REMAINS TO BE DONE

All this may be visionary, but it is not illusory. A great many educators recognize what must be done, and some schools are trying to break the old mold. A recent article in the *London Times Educational Supplement* reported on a secondary school's attempts to "break away from the tyranny of the traditional forty-minute period." There are no bells, teachers' desks, or blackboards. Although some required formal classes are taught, in most cases students pursue individual projects at length, with their teachers' guidance, without having to drop everything and rush off to the next period. Scrapping the usual organization allows teachers to have frequent one-on-one conferences with students to review work and periodic discussions with parents and supervisors. One youngster summarized his experience by saying, "I did not like primary school because *the teacher was always gabbing at us.* Here, you're expected to behave like adults."[6] (Emphasis added.) One experimental school does not herald the millenium, and it may fail in the long run, but it still represents the kind of effort we should be making to strike out in new directions.

Along with structural changes, we have to devise new forms of school goverance. Implict in professional status is the ability to have significant control over one's workplace. As things are now, we consistently waste one of the greatest assets that out schools have—the collective wisdom and experience of the teaching staff. Teachers are almost never consulted about suggestions for improving the system. Decisions regarding curriculum content and learning materials are invariably made without input from those who have to live with them in the classroom.

## PARTNERS IN PROGRESS

Schools could be run like a partnership, something similar to the way law firms operate. The logistics of the operation—the supplies, the custodial staff, and general maintenance problems—could be in the hands of a hired manager so that educators could fully devote themselves to the mission of the school. Faculty members could decide for themselves how they wanted to organize the academic decisionmaking process. Regardless of the structure, shared collegial autonomy is a vital distinction between the professional and the hired hand and a necessary step in making teaching an attractive career to top-flight college graduates.

The "partners" in the school I envision will be highly qualified and highly paid professionals earning professional-level salaries. They will have received their credentials not only through earned academic degrees but through an extensive, supervised internship program and a rigorous, national (although not government) examination akin to the medical and law boards, devised and monitored by members of the profession.

Where staff shortages persist, as they most likely will in math and science, a variety of recruitment methods could be tried that would not compromise instructional quality. For example, in addition to the permanent corps of professional career teachers, we could develop a cadre of able people who would teach for four or five years as a form of national service that would be recognized for salary, seniority, and pension credit by large corporations. It would be in the self-interest of companies such as IBM or General Electric to lend members of their staffs to our schools to ensure that the next generation of mathematicians, chemists, and physicists were being adequately prepared in our nation's classrooms.

To walk through our nation's schools today is to go back in time. Most teachers labor, isolated from their colleagues, in self-contained classrooms, forced by unmanageable class sizes to lecture most of the time or put notes on the board to be copied by their students who, for the most part, are expected to absorb chunks of state-mandated curriculums that must be covered in $x$ number of days. For the most part, youngsters are expected to be passive and, on the designated day, disgorge what they were fed. Bells ring with regularity and all parties rush off to more of the same. Reflection, doubt, questioning, sharing—all these are reserved for another time and another place. If the halls and classroom nationwide are orderly and the results of standardized tests are respectable and all teachers are modestly qualified, many of today's reformers will feel that their work is done.

Such an achievement is not to be scorned. But to accept it as the ultimate goal of our schools is to set our sights far too low. The world now unfolding will punish our nation severely unless we achieve new levels of excellence in our classrooms. We need to recognize that this cannot be done with old formulas and traditional structures. We have to create new schools for a new generation of teachers and students.

## NOTES

1. Larry Cuban, "Persistent Instruction: Another Look at Constancy in the Classroom" *Phi Delta Kappan* 68 (September 1986): 7–11.

2. Theodore R. Sizer, *Horace's Compromise: The Dilemma of the American High School Today* (Boston: Houghton Mifflin, 1984).

3. Patrick Welsh, *Tales Out of School* (New York: Viking, 1986).

4. Carnegie Forum on Education and the Economy, *A Nation Prepared: Teachers for the 21st Century,* The Report of the Task Force on Teaching as a Profession, (New York: Carnegie Corporation, 1986) p. 3.

5. John Goodlad, *A Place Called School* (New York: McGraw-Hill, 1984) pp. 229–30.

6. "Wiping the Slate Clean" *London Times Educational Supplement* (October 31, 1986), p. 11.

STEPHEN L. JACOBSON

Chapter Seven

# Merit Pay Incentives in Teaching

In *A Nation At Risk,* the National Commission on Excellence in Education's 1983 report on the state of American education, and in at least eight other major reports issued in 1983,[1] teacher compensation is identified as a central concern of educational reform. There appears to be a consensus among these reports that, if the teaching profession is to attract and retain high caliber individuals, teachers' salaries must become more competitive with those offered by other professions. As Boyer argued, "Our society pays for what it values. Unless teacher salaries become more commensurate with those of other professions, teacher status cannot be raised; able students cannot be recruited."[2]

While most educational policymakers agree that teacher salaries need to be raised, particularly at the entry-level, considerable disagreement exists over whether salary increases can also be used to improve teacher performance. Of the various compensation reforms proposed, merit pay proposals have stirred the most heated debate.

These pay incentive proposals explicitly link teacher salary differentials to evaluations of performance, even though research on teacher compensation provides only limited support for the premise that the availability of increased monetary rewards can effectively motivate teachers to improve the quality of their work. While some argue that classroom teachers are no different than workers in other occupations where money is effectively used as an incentive,[3] others contend that teachers are motivated more by the content and process of their work than by the opportunity for extra compensation.[4]

Contemporary advocates of merit pay incentives, such as Presi-

111

dent Reagan, are of the opinion that our schools will improve only if teachers are "paid and promoted on the basis of their merit and competence."[5] Yet, in practice, pay incentive plans for teachers have a well-documented history of failure.[6] As Murnane and Cohen observed, "The history of merit pay suggests that while interest in paying teachers according to merit endures, attempts to use merit pay do not."[7]

This chapter examines some of the major issues and problems surrounding the proposed use of merit pay incentive plans in public education, beginning with a discussion of merit pay in theory, a discussion developed through a variety of theoretical perspectives drawn from industrial psychology and labor economics. Next follows a brief history of merit pay's use in public education and a working definition of merit pay in its contemporary context. Central to this examination of pay incentives in practice is a typology of the performance criteria used in existent merit pay plans and recent proposals to identify meritorious teaching. As we shall see, the term *merit pay* has become a catchall designation for a variety of compensation plans that use very different criteria to define meritorious performance.

## MERIT PAY PLANS IN THEORY

Of all the recommendations to come out of *A Nation at Risk,* merit pay was perhaps the most likely to generate national interest because it reinforces the public's perception of how the free enterprise system ought to work. Johnson nicely summarized the rather simple rationale behind merit pay, stating that "[i]f teachers are paid competively on the basis of performance, they will work harder. The system will reward effective teachers and encourage them to remain in classrooms while nudging ineffective, unrewarded teachers to leave."[8]

This apparent simplicity belies a rather complex relationship that must exist between the availability of rewards and subsequent teacher behavior. These conceptual underpinnings are perhaps best explained by Vroom's expectancy theory.[9]

### *Expectancy Theory*

Vroom's model of employee motivation describes the process that links the availability of rewards to worker behavior and suggests that teacher performance can be influenced by monetary incentives only if the following conditions exist:

1. teachers have a high expectancy that meritorious performance can be achieved through increased effort;

2. teachers believe that high instrumentality exists between meritorious performance and the likelihood of reward; and
3. teachers find monetary rewards attractive.

Merit pay advocates implicitly assume the first and third conditions listed above, i.e., meritorious teaching performance *can* be achieved through increased effort, and teachers find monetary rewards *highly* attractive. Once high instrumentality between superior performance and increased monetary rewards is achieved, merit pay proponents predict that teachers will increase their effort and therefore improve their performance. Implicit in this position, however, is the belief that unless monetary rewards are contingent upon performance, teachers withhold their effort. Assuming that teachers *do* withhold effort, the expectancy approach can be used to provide alternative explanations for this behavior; explanations that challenge the assumptions of merit pay supporters.

Vroom's theory suggests that on-the-job experience provides individuals the opportunity to reevaluate expectancies, i.e., their subjective estimates of the relationship between effort and performance. If, for example, experienced teachers come to believe that conditions of their employment, such as overcrowded classes and outdated materials, prevent increased effort from improving performance, then their motivation to perform in the future will be diminished. Therefore, even if instrumentality between performance and reward is high, low expectancy could cause teachers to withold their effort.

Another explanation has to do with the relative attractiveness of monetary rewards. As noted previously, merit pay advocates assume that monetary rewards are *highly* attractive to teachers. If this is not the case, i.e., money is not a primary motivator of teacher behavior, then the expectancy approach would predict little change in teacher effort, even if instrumentality and expectancy are high. In other words, people are not motivated to work harder for rewards they do not find especially attractive. This issue is examined in greater detail in the section on the two-factor theory.

### Equity Theory

Merit pay advocates suggest that their proposals derive theoretical support from equity theory.[10] Equity theory advances the notion that compensation equity exists when employees believe that "what is" is what "should be." Stated another way, workers are satisfied with their compensation when: (1) equals are rewarded equally, and (2) unequals are rewarded unequally. Merit pay advocates contend that our best teachers are dissatisfied with the uniform salary schedule because teachers identical in experience and education are paid the same salary regardless of differences in performance, i.e., unequal effort yields equal reward, and teachers whose performances are identical will be compensated differentially if they differ in experience and education, i.e., equal effort yields unequal reward. The most troublesome case of inequity exists for high-quality junior teachers who are paid less, often substantially less, than senior colleagues who may not be performing well.

Pay inequities inherit in uniform schedules, coupled with the fact that these schedules primarily reward longevity, lead supporters of merit to argue that our present system for compensating teachers encourages poor teachers to remain on the job, drives good teachers from the profession and discourages high-quality individuals from entering. By making monetary rewards performance-based, merit advocates argue that incompetent teachers are provided a strong incentive to seek employment opportunities outside of the profession because teaching will no longer be financially rewarding. Yet the strength of this argument depends, once again, upon how central monetary rewards are to teacher labor market behaviors, i.e., are teachers primarily motivated by money?

## *The Two-Factor Theory*

Perhaps the best-known theory of employee motivation is Herzberg's two-factor approach, which suggests that employee behavior is influenced by two categories of rewards: (1) motivators and (2) hygiene factors. Herzberg defines *motivators* as rewards intrinsic to the content of one's work; rewards that can effectively stimulate psychological growth, a necessary precondition for job satisfaction and enhanced performance. These intrinsic rewards include: achievement, recognition, responsibility, advancement, and work itself. In contrast, Herzberg contends that rewards extrinsic to the content of one's work or *hygiene factors,* " . . . act in a manner analogous to the principles of medical hygiene. Hygiene operates to remove health hazards from the environment of man. It is not a curative; it is, rather, a preventative."[11]

Herzberg contends that while hygiene factors, such as salary, help to reduce job dissatisfaction by making the conditions of work less unpleasant, they have little affect on positive work attitudes and improved performance because they do not promote psychological growth. In other words, salary incentives can be used to prevent teacher dissatisfaction . but cannot be used to cure poor teacher performance. Instead, Herzberg's work suggests that school policymakers wishing to improve teacher performance must be more attentive to making intrinsic rewards available. Indeed, when teachers have been asked to self-report their reward preferences, they typically focus on teaching's intrinsic benefits. For example, Lortie found that the most frequently reported attractors to teaching are: (1) the opportunity to work with children, and (2) the belief that teachers provide an important service to society.[12] Although Lortie acknowledges that normative expectations of teachers being "dedicated" professionals may inhibit them from acknowledging the extent to which material benefits influence their behavior, intrinsic rewards consistently rank higher than monetary gain in teacher opinion surveys.[13]

Studies of the effects of extrinsic rewards on motivation suggest that pay incentive plans could even undermine teacher performance if monetary rewards become more important than the content of the work itself and teachers develop self-serving ways to obtain these rewards with a minimum of effort.[14]

Although the two-factor approach predicts that the provision of pay incentives will not motivate teachers to improve their performance, the theory *does* suggest monetary rewards *can* play an important role in improving teacher retention by reducing job dissatisfaction.

Recent reports by the Holmes Group[15] and the Carnegie Forum on Education and Economy[16] have broadened the scope of compensation reform to include the potential motivating effects of intrinsic benefits by recommending that teachers' roles and responsibilities be restructured. In *A Nation Prepared: Teachers for the 21st Century,* the Carnegie Task Force is quite explicit in addressing teachers' intrinsic needs, "[g]iving teachers a greater voice in the decisions that affect the school will make teaching more attractive to good teachers who are already in our schools as well as people considering teaching as a career."[17]

The compensation proposals of the so-called second wave of reform are far more consonant with the underlying tenets of the two-factor approach than were proposals of the "first wave," which focused almost exclusively on monetary incentives. By attending to the intrinsic rewards teachers report they desire most, these recent proposals are more likely to improve teacher performance than merit pay.

A very different perspective on merit pay incentives, one that focuses as much on the organization as on the individual, is provided by a branch of microeconomics that Murnane and Cohen call the "contracts literature."

## The Contracts Literature

The contracts literature suggests that an organization's approach to compensation should depend upon the nature of the work required of its employees. The usefulness of the contracts literature is that it stresses the importance of organizational trade-offs between the benefits of employee performance gains and the costs of performance evaluations. This cost-benefit analysis is based on three assumptions:[18]

1. Worker's preferences are not completely consonant with the employing organization's goals. If there are no adverse consequences for them, workers prefer to work less hard than the organization would like.
2. Monitoring the output of individual workers or the actions of the individual workers is costly.
3. Imperfect monitoring will induce workers to attempt behavior that makes them appear productive relative to other workers, but in fact is contrary to the goals of the organization.

Applied to teacher pay incentive plans, the contracts literature focuses on the criteria used for performance evaluation. Murnane and Cohen suggest that merit pay plans that reward teachers on the basis of student gains on standardized tests are analogous to piece–rate compensation; a payment algorithm that attaches a unit price to each unit of performance output measured. Piece-rate compensation works best in industries where a worker's output can be measured easily and at low cost, e.g., the number of shirts ironed by a laundress.

Murnane and Cohen suggest that the benefit of piece-rate compensation is that it provides workers incentives to find new ways to increase production; the cost of piece-rate compensation is that these new production methods can include opportunistic behaviors, such as neglect of machinery, as employees reallocate their time in an attempt to increase output. Applied to teaching, opportunistic teachers may respond to performance incentives based on mean student achievement gains by choosing to attend only to cognitive aspects of student performance, while ignoring affective needs. Murnane and Cohen contend that teaching does not satisfy the production conditions under which piece-rate compensation works most effectively, and, if merit pay plans that reward on the basis of test scores are implemented, the curriculum will be narrowed to only those subjects that are tested.

The contracts literature further suggests that, due to their inherent vagueness and subjectivity, merit pay plans that reward teachers on the basis of classroom evaluations will fare no better than plans that reward student outcomes. Murnane and Cohen suggest that,

> Merit pay is efficient when the nature of the activity in which workers are engaged is such that supervisors can provide relatively convincing answers to the following two questions posed by workers:
> 1. Why does worker $X$ get merit pay and I don't?
> 2. What can I do to get merit pay?[19]

The imprecise nature of teaching makes these questions difficult for individuals supervising merit plans to answer, and produces a number of unintentional consequences. Among these dysfunctional side effects are:

1. teachers who become angry when supervisors cannot identify specific actions that will result in meritorious performance;
2. teachers who are unwilling to discuss classroom problems for fear that they will hurt their chance for merit;
3. teachers who are dissatisfied with their evaluation, because teachers typically rate their own performance higher than do their supervisors; and
4. disagreement over whether the best teacher or the teacher whose performance is the most improved should be rewarded.

Murnane and Cohen argue that merit plans that reward teacher evaluations lower faculty morale and change the principal's role from "being a coach into being a referee."[20]

Unlike employee motivation theories, in which the success or failure of merit depends upon the perceptions of the individual, the contracts literature indicates that merit pay incentives are inappropriate in public education because they are too costly to the organization. Whatever gains are realized in terms of improved performance are paid back, with interest, in terms of dysfunctional consequences to the morale of teachers in the district. As a result, Murnane and Cohen conclude that merit pay's goal of putting the "power" of money into the evaluation process, in order to improve teachers' performance, is misguided.

## THE HISTORY OF MERIT PAY

Recent interest in merit pay belies the fact that pay incentive plans have been used frequently during the past century.[21] The use of merit pay appears to have peaked during the early 1920s when perhaps as many as 40 to 50 percent of America's school districts had so-called merit plans in effect. But, during the 1930s, merit pay slowly gave way to the uniform salary schedule, due, in part, to the fact that merit was often determined by a teacher's sex and/or level of instruction.

The crisis in American education spawned by the Soviet Union's successful launching of Sputnick in the late 1950s renewed public interest in compensating teachers on the basis of performance. As a result of this interest, 11.3 percent of school districts with student enrollment greater than 6,000 had performance-based pay incentive plans by 1968. But, once again, merit pay plans were abandoned as unworkable, with difficulties in measuring performance and teacher union opposition commonly cited as the principal reasons for these failures.[22] The Educational Research Service found that, in 1978, only 4 percent of school districts still had a merit pay plan in effect.[23] By 1979, only thirty-three of the nation's largest public school districts (districts serving communities with a population greater than 30,000), had a merit system in operation, down 80 percent from 170 districts in 1959.[24] Even in private schools, where union opposition would be less of a factor, pay incentive plans are the exception rather than the rule, with only 7 percent of Catholic high schools using merit pay in 1983.[25]

By 1985, with over more than 99 percent of America's teachers employed in school districts that utilize uniform salary schedules, Murnane and Cohen could identify only seven districts that had used merit pay for at least five years, and had paid awards of at least $1,000 or had a student enrollment of more than 10,000. These surviving programs were found in wealthy districts that could hire teachers selectively, pay them well, and provide excellent working conditions. Two characteristics typical of these surviving programs were that merit awards were given inconspicuously and every teacher received an award of some size. Although inconspicuous awards distributed among all faculty members may reduce competition and make everyone feel special, these are hardly the program characteristics merit pay advocates envision. Indeed, Murnane and Cohen note that merit pay in these districts does not appear to have strong effects on the way teachers teach. Nevertheless, the growing perception that American education is not adequately preparing its citizens for the challenges of the twenty-first century has, once again, renewed interest in the use of performance-based pay incentives for teachers.

## MERIT PAY IN PRACTICE

Under a "pure" merit pay system, salary differentials would be determined exclusively on the basis of differences in performance, but, recognizing that teacher union opposition makes the prospect of dismantling the uniform schedule highly unlikely, recent merit pay proposals have recommended monetary incentives that would supplement, rather than supplant, existing salary schedules. Therefore, the term *merit pay incentive plan* is used in this section to identify a school district compensation system that rewards "meritorious" teaching performance with monetary awards over and above those provided by the uniform schedule.

Although other incentives, such as sabbaticals, tuition assistance, and/or attendance at professional conferences can be offered, merit awards usually take either of two forms: (1) a temporary salary increase, i.e., a once per-annum bonus for which a teacher competes on a yearly basis; or (2) a permanent salary increase, i.e., a monetary award that, once earned, becomes part of a teacher's base salary, regardless of subsequent performance.

Merit pay awards are usually used to recognize individual achievement, although they can also be presented in recognition of meritorious performance by an entire instructional unit. By shifting pay incentives from the individual to the instructional team, *group incentive plans* are intended to promote teacher cooperation, as opposed to teacher competition, a factor often cited as a detrimental side effect of merit pay plans.

Noticeably missing from our definition of merit pay is how meritorious performance is identified and measured. Merit pay advocates implicitly assume that the factors that contribute to meritorious performance can be identified. But, like pornography, "meritorious" performance appears easier to identify than define.

## WHAT COUNTS AS MERIT?

The common thread running through recent merit pay reform proposals is the belief that teachers' salaries should reflect their contributions to the educational enterprise. Yet, considerable disagreement exists among recent merit pay proposals as to what legitimately counts as merit. As Monk and Jacobson note, "[s]ome writers use the term *merit pay* but disagree over how merit should be assessed. Others eschew the use of the term, but nevertheless propose what amounts to a plan of differentiated payment based on an assessment of teachers' contributions."[26]

Although the presage criteria used by uniform schedules may be objectionable to merit pay advocates, years of experience and educational training are easy to measure. On the other hand, as Lipsky and

Bacharach suggest, "The selection of performance criteria for use in merit pay plans is a process fraught with peril."[27]

To address this issue, Monk and Jacobson developed a typology of performance criteria recommended by recent merit pay proposals as contributions worthy of additional renumeration. These criteria include: (1) the quantity of work performed by a teacher; (2) the efficiency of a teacher's work; (3)the level of a teacher's accomplishment; and (4) the importance of a teacher's accomplishment.

## THE QUANTITY OF A TEACHER'S WORK

Although the provision of salary add-ons, based upon a measure of the quantity of an individual's work, does not represent a significant departure from traditional compensation practice, extra pay for extra work rewards are among the most commonly recommended incentives in recent merit pay proposals. For example, Tennessee's "Master" teachers have the opportunity to accept ten-, eleven-, or twelve-month contracts that provide 15, 35, or 60 percent pay supplements.[28]

Murnane and Cohen found that the opportunity to earn extra pay for extra work was a characteristic typical of the few merit pay incentive plans that have endured in public education. These authors suggest that the success of this approach is that it allows teachers with additional financial needs the opportunity to meet those needs. Yet, the potential effectiveness of extra pay for extra work incentives, particularly those offered as contract extensions, may be of limited use because most (79 percent) public school teachers indicate that they would rather teach ten months than twelve months, even if opportunities for other professional activities existed.[29]

A variation on the quantity of work theme is the use of pay incentives to reduce rates of teacher absenteeism. At least two school districts in western New York State currently have incentive programs that provide monetary bonuses for teachers with exemplary attendance records. In one district, perfect attendance pays a $150 bonus, one absence pays $75 and two absences $50. Three or more absences and a teacher is no longer eligible for an attendance bonus. In the second district, a "pari-mutuel" attendance incentive pool was created that will "payoff" for teachers who are absent less than seven days in 1987. Each day less than seven, the mean number of teacher absences in the district in 1986, pays a teacher an additional share from the total pool.

## THE LEVEL OF EFFICIENCY

Called "old style" plans by some authors,[30] the level of efficiency approach to merit ties salary levels to rating scale evaluations of teacher classroom behaviors. Monk and Jacobson contend, "[t]his input-based approach to the measurement of teacher efficiency has gained widespread use in American education. Much of what now passes for teacher evaluation relies heavily on the use of periodic classroom observation."[31]

Merit as teacher efficiency assumes that positive correlations exist between identifiable teacher behaviors and high levels of student achievement. Checklists of teacher input behaviors often include: classroom organization and management, inservice growth, professional attitude, school community service, and even personal fitness and appearance.

The teacher efficiency approach is often criticized for stifling teaching creativity because teachers are under considerable pressure to conform to administrative perceptions of good teaching, e.g., if classroom discipline is a high administrative priority, teachers may feel that they have to be more attentive to keeping students seated and silent than with what their students are learning.

Substantive questions exist as to which teacher behaviors, if any, are significantly related to student achievement (questions beyond the realm of the present discussion) but, even if such questions could be resolved, old style merit plans reward the potential for high achievement rather than the accomplishment itself.

## THE LEVEL OF ACCOMPLISHMENT

Whereas merit as teacher efficiency rewards the process of teaching, merit as accomplishment evaluates teacher performance through measurements of student gains on standardized achievement tests. These output-based evaluations, or "new style" plans, are concerned primarily with the product of a teacher's endeavors. As Murnane and Cohen observe, "[t]he attractiveness of this strategy is that the evaluation problem is solved by actually measuring certain dimensions of each teacher's output, and thereby avoiding the subjectivity of the evaluations under old style merit pay."[32]

Although merit as accomplishment is arguably less subjective than merit as efficiency, the use of student outcomes to measure teacher performance is often criticized because of difficulties in disentangling an individual teacher's contribution from the influences of other factors, e.g., the contextural influences of other students in the classroom. An additional criticism of this approach to merit plans is that it encourages opportunistic behaviors, e.g., teachers teaching exclusively to the test and focusing only on those students they judge most likely to do well on the test.

## THE IMPORTANCE OF THE ACCOMPLISHMENT

This approach to merit differentially rewards teachers on the basis of differences in their duties and responsibilities, and, as Monk and Jacobson note, "[t]he teacher need not work harder, may not be more efficient, and need not accomplish more. The relevant points are that (1) the teacher makes a *different* contribution, and (2) the market value of the various possible contributions can vary."[33]

The teacher career ladder, a commonly proposed variant of merit pay, falls under this dimension. Career ladders are compensation systems that create a staged profession that proceeds from the Apprentice to Master Teacher. As teachers move up a career ladder, their professional responsibilities and compensatory rewards increase. A model teacher career ladder was developed by the Congressional Merit Pay Task Force:

> *Apprentice Teacher:* An individual with a degree from an accredited institution of higher education who has met all state requirements for initial certification, could begin teaching at $15,000.
>
> *Professional Teacher:* A fully certified teacher with five years experience, some in-service training or post graduate course work, and at least four positive annual evaluations, would receive a base fifth year salary of $20,000.
>
> *Senior Teacher:* A certified Professional teacher with a master's degree in his or her area of concentration, and at least eight of ten positive annual evaluations, would receive a base tenth year salary of $30,000.
>
> *Master Teacher:* A certified Senior teacher with additional study beyond the master's degree and more than ten years of consistently positive evaluations, who has demonstrated "best practice" and is willing to accept in-service or summer-training responsibility for other teachers would receive $35,000 and a minimum $10,000 annual bonus for continuing positive evaluations and in-service contribution.

Scarcity bonuses also fall under the heading of incentives that reward the importance of the accomplishment, i.e., differential pay for teachers in subject areas where shortages exist, e.g., mathematics or science, or for teachers willing to work in less desirable schools, e.g., schools that serve large numbers of disadvantaged students.

Rewarding the importance rather than the level of an accomplishment is often criticized for being less of an attempt to make teacher salaries performance-based than market sensitive. As a result, this approach to merit justifies paying a second-rate physics teacher more than an excellent history teacher, simply because it is harder to find a physics teacher than a history teacher—hardly the outcome merit pay proponents had envisioned.

Many recent pay incentive plans have incorporated a number of the criteria types described, for example, Houston's Second-Mile Plan offered the following rewards in 1982:

1. *Outstanding Educational Progress:* $800 per teacher in district schools that exceed predicted academic gains on standardized student achievement tests.
2. *High-Priority Location:* as much as $2,000 per teacher willing to work in district schools that have a high concentration of educationally disadvantaged students.
3. *Critical Shortage:* scarcity bonuses for teachers of subjects where shortages exist, e.g., $800 for mathematics or science, $600 to $900 for special education, and as much as $1,000 for bilingual education.
4. *Professional Growth:* $300 for each additional six credits of college coursework (or seventy-two hours of in-service training) related to a teacher's area of instruction.
5. *Attendance:*$100 per day for unused absences up to five, a teacher with perfect attendance can earn an additional $500.[34]

Clearly, the only category in Houston's plan directly related to student outcomes is Outstanding Educational Progress. The other categories, though serving important district and teacher needs, hardly represent meritorious teaching. Indeed, of the four criteria types Monk and Jacobson describe, only Teacher Efficiency and Level of Accomplishment are related to student performance. And so, it appears that in practice, merit pay has become an all-encompassing term used to describe a variety of compensation packages—compensation packages that appear to have little in common except for the fact that they have monetary rewards that can be selectively distributed among teachers.


## CONCLUSIONS

In this chapter, merit pay incentives plans were examined from a variety of theoretical perspectives focusing on both the individual and the organization. The central premise of merit pay, that monetary rewards can effectively motivate teachers to improve their performance, is based upon the assumption that teachers are primarily motivated by money. Yet, the theoretical underpinnings of teacher motivation suggest that the quality of teacher performance is more a function of intrinsic rewards than salary. For example, increases in recognition and responsibility are more likely to promote enhanced performance than increases in pay. But even if teachers *were* primarily motivated by money, merit pay incentives would still be inappropriate because teaching does not satisfy the production conditions under which this type of piece-rate compensation works most effectively. The products of teaching are not easily tallied in a ledger. Focusing only on those products that can be quantified may result in opportunistic teacher behaviors, the costs of which can easily override potential gains in performance. Due to teaching's imprecise nature, focusing instead on performance evaluations to determine merit can also produce dysfunctional side effects, such as lowered faculty morale and adversarial relationships between teachers and supervisors. Indeed, pay differentials based on inherently subjective performance evaluations could ultimately produce salary inequities as egregious as those found under the uniform schedule.

Examining merit pay in practice revealed that merit pay is more a subject of debate than a practical reality in 1987. Pure merit systems are currently non-existent and the characteristics of the few surviving merit plans hardly exemplify the type of program of which pay advocates are desirous. Difficulties in measuring teacher performance accounted for the demise of past merit pay plans, yet little suggests that any less confusion exists in identifying merit now than in the past. Indeed, the performance criteria of recent merit pay proposals suggests that meritorious teaching means different things to different people.

Although little encourages the belief that merit pay incentive plans can effectively improve teacher performance, advocates of merit pay are probably correct when they argue that the public would be more willing to support higher teacher salaries if salary increases were pegged to performance. This quid pro quo virtually assures a resurgence of merit pay schemes. Yet, merit pay in the 1990s will probably be very different than merit pay in the 1920s and 1960s; that is, it will represent only one part of the overall teacher compensation algorithm. For example, teacher productivity is but one of four factors that the Carnegie Task Force recommends for differentiating teacher salaries; the other factors being level of certification, job function, and seniority. Under the Carnegie plan, teachers would progress through a sequence of licenses, certifications, and advanced certifications granted by a National Board of Professional Teaching Standards. At each new level of certification, teachers would assume new job functions and responsibilities, with salaries increased accordingly and additional increments accrued through seniority. Teacher productivity would be measured by schoolwide student performance, thereby providing group, rather than individual, salary increments.

The fact that the Carnegie report has been favorably received by a broad spectrum of educational leaders, including individuals who are often at odds (e.g., district superintendents and teacher union leaders), suggests that it may be the prototype of future merit pay plans. Rather than speculating over the appropriateness of performance-based incentives in public education, scholars of teacher compensation should grasp this opportunity to evaluate and compare the effectiveness of the myriad compensation reforms that have been and will be implemented. As Kirst notes,

> There is a widespread belief that teacher quality is crucial to increasing the academic attainment of students, but states are unsure what mix of reforms will work best to improve the teaching force. Few states can afford to fully fund the entire range of possible reforms. Consequently, the states are trying all kinds of interventions—including career ladders, higher base salaries, improved working conditions, and forgivable loans—without a clear notion of which approaches will yield the best results.
>
> Fortunately, there is such diversity in the approaches to reform taken by the states and local districts that we have what amounts to a nationwide experiment to determine which approaches work best.[35]

The continued willingness of American taxpayers to finance improvements in teacher compensation will depend, to a great extent, upon the public's perception that compensation reforms can produce improvements in educational outcomes. Maintaining the momentum of educational reform, therefore, requires both a careful monitoring and evaluation of programs as they are implemented, as well as a commitment to a research agenda that will examine cause-and-effect relationships between compensation reforms, including teacher pay incentives, and educational outcomes.

## NOTES

1. These reports included: Ernest Boyer, *High School: A Report on Secondary Education in America* (New York: Harper and Row, 1983); Education Commission of the States' Task Force on Education for Economic Growth, *Action for Excellence* (Denver, Col.: Education Commission of the States, 1983); C. Emily Feistritzer, *The Condition of Teaching: A State by State Analysis* (New York: Carnegie Foundation, 1983); John Goodlad, *A Place Called School: Prospects for the Future* (New York: McGraw-Hill, 1983); National Science Board Commission on Precollege Education in Mathematics, *Educating Americans for the 21st Century* (Washington, D.C.: National Science Foundation, 1983); Theodore R. Sizer, *Horace's Compromise: The Dilemma of the American High School Today* (New York: McGraw-Hill, 1983); Twentieth Century Fund Task Force on Federal Elementary and Secondary Education Policy, *Making the Grade* (New York: Twentieth Century Fund, 1983) and United States House of Represen-

tatives, Committee on Education and Labor, Merit Pay Task Force (Washington, D.C.: U.S. Government Printing Office, 1983).

2. Boyer, p. 168.

3. William F. Casey, "Would Bear Bryant Teach in the Public Schools?" *Phi Delta Kappan* 60 (March 1979): 500.

4. Susan M. Johnson, "Merit Pay for Teachers: A Poor Prescription for Reform," *Harvard Educational Review* 54 (May 1984): 175–185.

5. Speech at Seton Hall University, South Orange, N.J., May 1983, reported in Johnson.

6. See, David K. Cohen and Richard J. Murnane, "The Merits of Merit Pay," Project Report No. 85-A12, Stanford Education Policy Institute, School of Education, Stanford University, November 1985; David B. Lipsky and Samuel B. Bacharach, "The Single Salary Schedule Vs. Merit Pay: An Examination of the Debate," *NEA Research Memo* (Washington, D.C.: National Education Association, 1983); or Wayne J. Urban, "Old Wine, New Bottles? Merit Pay and Organized Teachers," in *Merit, Money and Teachers' Careers,* Henry C. Johnson Jr., ed. (Lanham, Md.: University Press of America, 1985).

7. Richard J. Murnane and David K. Cohen, "Merit Pay and the Evaluation Problem: Understanding Why Most Merit Plans Fail and a Few Survive," Project Report No. 85-A14, Stanford Education Policy Institute, School of Education, Stanford University, November 1985, p. 3.

8. Johnson, p. 176.

9. For a more complete elaboration of Expectancy Theory, see Victor H. Vroom, *Work and Motivation* (New York: John Wiley and Sons, 1964).

10. For a more complete elaboration of Equity Theory, see J. Stacey Adams, "Injustice in Social Exchange," in *Advances in Experimental Social Psychology,* vol.2., L. Berkowitz, ed. (New York: Academic Press, 1965): pp. 267–299, or Karl E. Weick, "Equity and the Perception of Pay," *Administrative Science Quarterly* 11 (1966): 415–18.

11. For a more complete elaboration of the two-factor theory, see Frederick Herzberg, *Work and the Nature of Man* (New York: Crowell Publications, 1966).

12. Dan C. Lortie, *Schoolteacher: A Sociological Study* (Chicago: University of Chicago Press, 1975).

13. See, for example, Feistritzer, *Profile of Teachers in the U.S.* (n.p.,1986).

14. Edward L. Deci, "The Hidden Costs of Rewards," *Organizational Dynamics* 4 (Winter 1976): 61–72.

15. The Holmes Group, *Tomorrow's Teachers: A Report of The Holmes Group* (East Lansing, Mich.: The Holmes Group, 1986).

16. The Carnegie Forum on Education and the Economy, *A Nation Prepared: Teachers for the 21st Century,* The Report of the Task Force on Teaching as a Profession (New York: Carnegie Corporation, 1986).

17. Ibid., p. 24.

18. Murnane and Cohen, pp. 3–4.

19. Ibid., pp. 11–12.

20. Ibid., p. 16.

21. Urban.

22. See Samuel B. Bacharach, David B. Lipsky and Joseph B. Shedd, *Paying for Better Teachers: Merit Pay and its Alternatives.* (Ithaca, N.Y.: Organizational Analysis and Practice, Inc., 1984); or Murnane and Cohen.

23. Paul J. Porwoll, *Merit Pay For Teachers.* (Arlington, Va.: Educational Research Service, Inc., 1979)

24. Ibid.

25. *The Catholic High School: A National Portrait.* (Washington, D.C.: National Catholic Education Association, 1985).

26. David H. Monk and Stephen L. Jacobson, "Reforming Teacher Compensation." *Education and Urban Society* 17 (February 1985): 223.

27. Lipsky and Bacharach, p. 7.

28. Carlton H. Stedman, "Tennessee's Master Plans for Teachers, Supervisors, and Principals," *Journal of Teacher Education* 34 (March-April 1983): 55–58.

29. C. Emily Feistritzer, *Profile of Teachers in the U.S.* (Washington, D.C.: National Center for Education Information, 1986) p.39.

30. Robert D. Bhaerman, "Merit Pay? No!" *National Elementary Principal* 52 (5) 1973: pp. 63–69; Lipsky and Bacharach; Murnane and Cohen.

31. Monk and Jacobson, p. 226.

32. Murnane and Cohen, p. 5.

33. Monk and Jacobson, p. 227.

34. Leslie Miller and Elaine Say, "This Bold Incentive Pay Plan Pits Capitalism Against Teacher Shortages," *The American School Board Journal* (September 1982): 24–25.

35. Michael W. Kirst, "Sustaining the Momentum of State Education Reform: The Link Between Assessment and Financial Support," *Phi Delta Kappan* 67 (January 1986): 341–45.

R. JERRALD SHIVE AND CHARLES W. CASE

Chapter Eight

# Differentiated Staffing as an Educational Reform Response

The National Center for Education Statistics (NCES) has projected that 1.65 million additional public and private elementary and secondary school teachers will have to be hired between fall 1985 and fall 1993 in order to meet demand. That staggering number includes attrition for reasons such as retirement as well as an increase in demand from about 2.4 million teachers in 1985 to about 2.7 million in 1993. Further, NCES estimates that supply as a percent of demand will fall to 63 percent by 1993. Clearly, the existing conditions generate a number of alternative responses by the affected school districts. Some possibilities include the following:

1. Lowering standards where permitted by state law and regulations, thus allowing teachers to enter the profession with less than adequate preparation. The data indicate that this alternative is probably now being adopted on a fairly broad scale.[1]
2. Raising salaries in order to attract more and better candidates into teacher education. Although some modest gains have been made on this front, any increases which will attract new and significantly larger numbers of bright graduates into the teaching profession are simply not forthcoming.
3. Finding more cost-effective ways to utilize existing staff in order to maintain or improve quality while at least restricting the growth in demand.

This last alternative suggests that a system which will modify present school organizations, reallocate staff to fill new roles, and provide
pay that is commensturate with the new staff positions, may result in
filling the demand for new teachers while maintaining standards and
improving the delivery of instruction. Differentiated staffing (D/S) is
such a system. D/S recognizes differences in the preparation and teaching skills among the adults who serve students in schools. D/S does
away with the single classification of "teacher" by differentiating
among teachers based upon teaching functions in order to optimally
use their expertise. Teachers, in such a system, are not interchangeable
and tasks are assigned according to whether they are curriculum tasks,
instructional tasks, leadership tasks, or other responsibilities that effectively make use of teachers' skills or training. Any and all staff positions
could be open to differentiation. D/S also provides incentives for
teachers to remain in the classroom by creating new roles and responsibilities. This is a break with the existing tradition that the primary
avenues of advancement for successful teachers have led out of the
classroom.[2]

The coming shortage of teachers is a reality: the nation will once
again need many teachers within a short timeframe; this is an issue
policymakers generally understand. However, many persons and
organizations in education have depicted other equally important considerations for changing school organizations to some form of D/S:
providing opportunities for alternative responsibilites and career advancement for teachers without leaving teaching; recognizing differences in motivation and attainment; creating work structures that allow
professionals to make professional decisions; making the work life of
teachers more collegial; and, establishing teams of adults to serve
groups of students in an individual and a collective manner, with
adults who have different levels of preparation, experience, and commitment.[3]

Differences between D/S and career ladders have sometimes not
been clear (Center for Public Sector Relations, 1985). Career ladders
usually provide for progression through three to five career steps in a
hierarchy based upon professional evaluations of the candidate's
teaching effectiveness. The professional evaluations replace seniority
and training as the primary criteria by which someone proceeds along
a salary schedule. In fact, under career ladder plans, a district has multiple salary schedules in effect, one for each of the career ladder steps.
By comparison, D/S plans differentiate among teachers at the same
level according to tasks performed or roles and responsibilities fulfilled. Teachers are differentiated not by career ladder steps but accord-

ing to their expertise, which may result in a number of differentiations on the same career ladder step. For example, an intern or a career teacher will not carry out duties identical to those of all other interns or career teachers who are on the same career ladder steps.

D/S is not the same as differentiated pay, however. Different salary schedules might be proposed in order to attract teachers to academic areas of short supply or to attract teachers to work settings that are generally perceived as being less than desirable.[4] D/S systems, on the other hand, base pay on professional tasks performed rather than criteria related to the market place. D/S adds additional salary schedules or hourly rate structures for teacher aides, media specialists, proctors, teacher assistants, resource persons, interns, and other adults who serve students. D/S is not merit pay, wherein some teachers are judged as being more competent than other teachers with the same responsibilities.

D/S in effect adds a horizontal structure comprising several self-contained subunits to the career ladder concept. That is, a master teacher, for example, might work with apprentice teachers or develop curriculum or work on research projects while also teaching as a part of a larger subunit or team. Aides, resource persons, interns, novice teachers, and others, might assist in teaching or other planning or professional development activities. Thus, D/S encourages the formation of teams made up of teachers who are on different steps of a career ladder as well as other adults who have differing roles and responsibilities based on their training and expertise. The teacher becomes a professional who has technical assistants to help him or her with the instructional process. D/S results in the creation of a whole new organization based on new roles and responsibilities with pay consistent with the differentiation in assignments. As with master teacher plans, it is important that teachers be involved with faculty evaluations and see themselves as key to the success of the D/S organization. Senior staff members in the D/S model function as team leaders, each with specific responsibilities. D/S is a vehicle for teacher specialization which enables a district to recognize achievement and leadership by teachers within their D/S responsibility.

The D/S model also encourages continuous interaction among members of the instructional teams on matters related to instruction, research, curriculum, or instructional design. This professional interaction helps alleviate the problem of isolation from adults so frequently felt by classroom teachers.[5] It also permits teams to be structured by faculty members. If a particular faculty member has training and experience in curriculum development of staff evaluation he or she can work on a D/S team that needs those skills. This structure thus expands the diversity of individuals used in schools. Also although D/S permits specialization along subject matter lines, the teams may be interdisciplinary such as an English/language arts/social studies team or a math/science team. The team structure provides a system and personnel that can match expertise with the instructional needs of individual students for variable times. The team structures also influence overall school organization and allow flexibility in curriculum and instruction.

D/S teams also establish a possible vehicle for group decisionmaking on matters affecting overall school policy. Goals, objectives, instructional evaluation, curriculum and materials development, professional development, and staff evaluation are matters which can be dealt with by the D/S teams. Broader issues related to school policy such as discipline, grading, curriculum requirements, and/or student counseling can also be dealt with through the D/S mechanism. It is conceivable that team leaders in a school could be members of an administrative council that worked on such planning and policy matters with the principal. D/S then becomes an organizational mechanism to deliver improved instruction for individuals or groups of students while also meeting a whole set of much broader institutional goals by granting D/S teams group decisionmaking authority. This is also consistent with recent recommendations from teaching groups that teachers be central to the decision process in schools.

D/S emphasizes what is done rather than how good someone judges the teacher to be.[6] Because teachers must demonstrate competency in their assigned roles, and because they are also involved in the evaluation process, D/S can make significant contribution toward overcoming the notion that only administrators can judge the competency of teachers.[7] Further, Maxine Greene and others have noted that different role requirements can be more readily defined, observed, and judged than competency defined as "better than."

A number of school districts implemented D/S plans in the 1960s and 1970s. These include Toledo, Ohio; Sarasota County, Florida; Denver, Colorado; Montgomery County, Maryland; and Temple City, California.[8] However, teacher strikes, the complexities of implementation, and the confusion of D/S systems with merit pay slowed the movement in the late 1970s and very early 1980s. Like many other changes in schools, minimal amounts of time, effort, and money were expended in providing staff members with the necessary preparation and training for the adoption of new behaviors and understandings essential in D/S.

In 1983, career ladders and, to some degree, D/S plans received new impetus with the release of the report on the National Commission on Excellence in Education.[9] The report called for school boards, administrators, and teachers to "cooperate to develop career ladders for teachers that distinguish among the beginning instructor, the experienced teacher, and the master teacher." It also states that "[m]aster teachers should be involved in designing teacher preparation programs and in supervising teachers during their probationary years." Since the publication of the Commission report, other groups and experts have suggested career and/or D/S plans. John Goodlad, for example, suggests a complete system of career ladders and D/S.[10] T.H. Bell has proposed a career ladder system of three steps: beginning instructor, professional teacher, and master teacher.[11]

Meanwhile, twenty-five states have adopted, or are in the process of considering, developing or preparing career ladder and/or D/S plans.[12] These include the Tennessee Master Plan, the Florida Education Association/United Report, the Virginia Career Ladders Plan, and other state plans in North Carolina, Delaware, Texas, Colorado, Utah, Idaho, and California.[13] Some states have also adopted guidelines which permit local variations in the implementation of career ladders and D/S. In the Charlotte-Mecklenberg, North Carolina master teacher plan, three levels of teachers exist with job differentiation by level.[14] By comparison, a voluntary system of D/S assignment creates flexibility and efficiency but also more organizational difficulties in identifying and utilizing talent.

Very recently the Holmes Group, in their report calling for the reform of the teaching profession, called for a career ladder of four steps and a six-year preparation program that would encourage differentiation from teachers who were prepared in other kinds of programs. Holmes Group teachers would complete programs that include half-time paid internships in the sixth year of preparation and that emphasize the integration of research with classroom practice. The career ladder program would enable teachers to move from teacher candidate, to intern, to career teacher (after appropriate experience and evaluation), to professional career teacher (upon completion of an advanced degree).[15] The Holmes Group report emphasizes the requirement that roles and functions of teachers be related to expertise, preparation, and performance. Many current career ladder plans simply define levels of positions with little or no attention to roles, responsibilities, and team organization. The Holmes Group report sets forth a career development plan so that teachers with successful experience and advanced preparation can remain teachers but may also take on additional leadership responsibilities in the areas of curriculum, instruction, and staff development. As a case in point, the Tennessee Plan, for example, proposes eleven- and twelve-month contracts for master teachers so that they can, for example, teach gifted classes, assist with curriculum development and help other teachers. Thus, some D/S is combined with career ladders.

To envision the functioning of a differentiated staffing model, assume twelve teachers in self-contained classrooms each teaching twenty-five students per period during five period days. This results in 1,500 students being served for one-hour periods each day. At a cost of 25,000 per teacher, the total cost for personnel in this traditional organization would be $300,000. For illustration purposes, the following salary schedules might apply to interns, novice teachers, career teachers, and professional career teachers in a differentiated school:

| | |
|---|---|
| Intern | $7,500 (half-time seeking certification) |
| Novice | $18,000–$22,000 (beginning teachers with supervision) |
| Career | $20,000–$35,000 (autonomous and fully certified) |
| Professional Career | $33,000–$50,000 (fully certified with an advanced degree) |

The salary schedules for novices, career teachers, and professional teachers overlap in order to permit salary growth at each level and also to provide incentive and opportunity for moving to the next higher level.

Given the same $300,000 budget, a school might employ personnel in a D/S school team in the following manner:

| | |
|---|---|
| 2 Professional Career Teachers | $70,000 |
| 3 Career Teachers | $75,000 |
| 5 Novice Teachers | $100,000 |
| 4 Interns | $30,000 |
| 2.5 Resource Persons | $25,000 |

The professional career and career teachers would be eleven- or twelve-month contracts. Their status would be the result of systematic evaluations in addition to experience and preparation. Each of their roles and responsibilities would be different, and each would make specific contributions to the overall functioning of the instructional team. One career teacher might supervise interns, another might help novices evaluate and improve their teaching. The third career teacher might work with the resource people to ensure that they make the greatest possible contribution to the instructional process. A professional career teacher might coordinate curriculum planning and development for the team while the second professional career teacher might help the team to design and carry out research projects aimed at determining how instruction and learning might be improved and evaluating particular programs. Most teachers would maintain some direct teaching responsibility. The resource persons would serve as aides, technical assistants (media and/or computer), community consultants, paraprofessionals, or library/materials specialists. The clear result of such a model is a whole new structure and way to approach planning for delivery of instruction to these 1,500 students. Also twelve teachers have now been replaced by fourteen professionals and two and one-half resource persons, improving the adult-to-student ratio in the classrooms and encouraging greater individualization of instruction. There has been no total increase in the cost of personnel.

Some differentiated staffing plans have actually led to reductions in the overall operation costs of a school district.[16] Although the funds required for the operation of a D/S system may be no greater than the funding required for a traditional organizational model, new funds will be needed for implementation and planning. There will be new costs in professional development and in organizational change.[17]

In a D/S system, the entire team has responsibility for curriculum development and planning, the professional development of interns and novices, research and the coordination of instructional resources. However, one teacher at each of the two higher career ladder steps has overall responsibility for the success of the team in one of these tasks. Because the team works together to achieve these goals the usual feeling of isolation in self-contained classrooms in negated. Career teachers have responsibility for the professional growth of novices. D/S becomes a structural vehicle for collaberation and staff development.[18] The team works together to achieve instructional, curricular, and planning goals, and teachers are not treated as though they are equally effective or interchangeable parts. Such a D/S system might also include study grants, sabbaticals, and travel funds for teams that demonstrate success in carrying out their goals and objectives. Primary among these objectives would be improved teaching.

The D/S model does make certain assumptions:

1. Roles and responsibilities can be defined, and they can be defined in ways that are flexible and can change over time. Teachers might alternate responsibilities every three to five years. This requires constant evaluation of faculty and programs as well as the willingness to change. For the same reasons, faculty may prefer a D/S system because teachers

are not "locked in" to carrying out the same tasks and fullfilling the same roles for their entire teaching career as they are in a more traditional structure.

2. Teachers will see career ladders and D/S as an opportunity for professional growth as well as salary improvement. It should be noted, however, that some researchers have disputed the claim that career ladders and D/S plans are effective as teacher incentive programs.

3. Differentiated staffing can provide incentives for teachers to remain in the profession as teachers while providing differentiation in roles and responsibilities. They are not forced to seek new careers in administration, for example, in order to impact curriculum and school policy. Faculty members know that they can continue to teach while seeking professional improvement.

4. D/S is not simply an increase in workload for teachers. Rather, D/S is intended to promote professional growth and teacher autonomy.

5. Organizational changes necessary to carry out D/S can be implemented. To be sure, these organizational changes require a supportive school philosophy, as well as goals and objectives which reflect school district resources. Organizational support is a key to the success of career ladder or D/S plans.[19] Such organizational changes must not be just an increase in bureaucracy but must give teachers real decision-making authority. Also, when systems change, the authority and decision making roles of principals and teachers are changed. A change in one element of the system necessarily changes many other elements. Prestige, status, staffing patterns, use of time, scheduling, curriculum, and school climate will be altered.[20] The planning and organizational development process will need to be extensive, but many models from a variety of types of organizations exist to guide the process.

6. New concepts of staff training and professional development will be necessary in order to maximize the talent and expertise of teachers in their roles as well as to facilitate the operation of the new organization. Experienced teachers can also have considerable influence over the successful growth of new teachers in a D/S system. In at least one study, teacher leaders have reported the greatest immediate professional growth in a teacher mentoring system.[21] The differentiation of teaching roles may also enable teachers to better understand various levels and types of professional expertise and provide a focus for professional development programs.[22] For example, support personnel—counselors, social workers, special education teachers—could work with D/S teams to enhance team members' abilities to work with different student needs.

Professional teaching organizations have generally opposed merit pay plans and career ladder plans if they are simply variations of merit pay.[23] Likewise, teacher organizations have tended to oppose systems requiring more work for the same amount of pay. Therefore, it is important that D/S systems do not just add to the work of regular classroom teachers. Richard W. Moore notes that teacher organizations are also cautious about endorsing master teacher plans that may take teachers out of the classroom.[24] If they are the brightest and most talented, they are exactly the teachers who are most needed in a strong teacher organization.

It is important that a district consider the policy motivation for adopting a D/S system.[25] Is the motivation to force out incompetent teachers, attract candidates to teaching, retain better teachers, keep teachers in the classroom and/or to improve educational effectiveness? The policy motivation for D/S affects both the structure and operation of the schools. For example, should D/S role and responsibility assignments be voluntary, team assigned, or centrally assigned? Much of the current research suggests that decisionmaking should be decentralized at least to the team level.[26] In any case, the reasons for adopting a D/S system will determine the roles, responsibilities, structure, and evaluation of the D/S system.

Differentiated staffing can make important contributions toward reforming how a school conducts business, the roles of teachers, and the career growth and development of teachers. The numbers of adults serving students can be increased without new operation costs. However, a school district must be prepared to plan carefully and invest time and resources in bringing about the organizational change. The various calls for reform in schools and personnel preparation, as well as the impending shortage of qualified educational personnel, now present favorable conditions for changes in educational policy and practice.

## NOTES

1. Emily Feistritzer, *The Condition of Teaching: A State by State Analysis* (Princeton, N.J.: The Carnegie Foundation for the Advancement of Teaching, 1985); and Virginia Robinson, *Making Do in the Classroom: A Report on the Misassignment of Teachers* (Washington, D.C.: Council for Basic Education, 1985).

2. Bob Palaich, *Restructuring Careers in Teaching* (Denver, Col.: Education Commission of the States, 1983).

3. Carnegie Forum on Education and the Economy, *A Nation Prepared: Teachers for the 21st Century* (New York: Carnegie Forum on Education and the Economy, 1986); and the Holmes Group, *Tomorrow's Teachers* (East Lansing, Mich.: The Holmes Group, 1986).

4. Robert O'Reilly, "Selected Legal Considerations Bearing upon Alternative Salary Plans for Teachers" (Paper delivered at the annual meeting of the Midwest Conference on Alternative Salary Plans for Teachers, Lincoln, Neb., November 3, 1983), p. 10.

5. Maxine Green et al., *The Master Teacher Concept: Five Perspectives* (Austin, Tex.: Research and Development Center for Teacher Education, 1984).

6. Kenneth H. Hansen, *Policy Options for Education Reform* (Portland, Ore.: Northwest Regional Educational Laboratory, 1984).

7. Greene et al., *The Master Teacher Concept.*

8. Fenwick English, "AFT/NEA Reaction to Staff Differentiation," *Educational Forum* 36 (January 1972): 193–198; Dal Lawrence, "Controversy and Apprehension among Principals Nearly Killed the Toledo Plan," *The American School Board Journal* 172 (July 1985): 22–23; Robert J. Starr, "Reconstructing Differentiated Staffing to Improve Teaching-Learning," *Peabody Journal of Education* 53 (July 1976): 315–17; and Carl W. Swanson, "The Costs of Differentiated Staffing," *Phi Delta Kappan* 54 (January 1973): 344–348.

9. National Commission on Excellence in Education, *A Nation At Risk: The Imperative for Educational Reform* (Washington, D.C.: U.S. Government Printing Office, 1983).

10. John I. Goodlad, *A Place Called School: Prospects for the Future* (New York: McGraw-Hill, 1984), pp. 302–3.

11. T. H. Bell, "The Master Teacher," *School Business Affairs* 50 (July 1984): 41–3.

12. Center for Public Sector Labor Relations, *Teacher Compensation and Evaluation in Public Education* (Bloomington, Ind.: Indiana University, 1985).

13. Southern Regional Education Board, State Actions: Career Ladders and Other Incentive Plans for School Teachers and Administrators (Atlanta, Ga.: Southern Regional Education Board, 1984).

14. Palaich, "Reconstructing Careers in Teaching," pp. 2–4.

15. Holmes Group, *Tomorrow's Teachers,* pp. 10–14.

16. "Save—For a Change: Ideas to Cut Costs," *Nation's Schools* 90 (August 1972): 25–40; and Swanson, "The Costs of Differentiated Staffing."

17. P. Berman and M. W. McLaughlin, *Federal Programs Supporting Educational Change: Implementing and Sustaining Innovations* (Santa Monica, Calif.: The Rand Corporation, 1978).

18. Susan J. Rosenholtz, *Political Myths about Educational Reform: Lessons from Research on Teaching* (Denver, Col.: Education Commission of the States, 1984).

19. Ibid.

20. Association of Teacher Educators, *Developing Career Ladders in Teaching* (Reston, Va.: Association of Teacher Educators, 1985); and Carol Camp Yeaky and Gladys Styles Johnston, "Overview of Differentiated Staffing," *Planning and Changing* 9 (Fall 1978): 131–48.

21. Ann Weaver Hart, "Formal Teacher Suspension by Teachers in a Career Ladder" (Paper delivered at the annual meeting of the American Educational Research Association, Chicago, April 1985): 20–22.

22. Association of Teacher Educators, *Developing Career Ladders in Teaching,* p. 4.

23. O'Reilly, "Selected Legal Considerations Bearing upon Alternative Salary Plans for Teachers."

24. Richard W. Moore, *Master Teachers* (Bloomington, Ind.: Phi Delta Kappa Educational Foundation, 1984), p. 26.

25. Hansen, *Policy Options for Education Reform.*

26. Hart, "Formal Teacher Supervision by Teachers in a Career Ladder," pp. 10–14; and Yeaky and Johnston, "Overview of Differentiated Staffing," p. 139.

SUSAN MOORE JOHNSON AND
NIALL C. W. NELSON

Chapter Nine

# *Conflict and Compatibility in Visions of Reform*

In 1983, when the publication of *A Nation at Risk*[1] riveted public attention on the failings of U. S. education, commentators and educators generally agreed that the problems of teaching and schooling demanded rapid and responsible action. A succession of reports by educational experts left few doubters.[2] This compelling concern moved politicians and practitioners to initiate state-level hearings and local studies in an effort to diagnose the problems of schooling and to propose remedies. But politicians and the public did not expect a measured and disinterested inquiry; they demanded quick answers. Soon a consensus began to emerge: teachers were the primary source of schooling's difficulties.[3] In some states, governors and legislators competed to be the first to reform the teaching profession, and plans for merit pay, mentor teachers, career ladders, salary raises, competency tests, and revisions of tenure and certification laws moved rapidly through school boards and legislatures.[4] Together, these new policies promised major changes in the composition of the teaching force and the structure of teaching.

Despite the initial flurry of excitement and expectation, the prospects for reform of the teaching profession looked dim by early 1986. There had been but modest changes in state and local practices, and teachers were increasingly expressing cynicism, while legislators were voicing disenchantment.[5] The Tennessee Education Association reported that almost 90 percent of teachers surveyed said that the state's career ladder had affected morale negatively, while almost 93 percent said that the money should have been spent to reduce class size.[6] Statewide initiatives in Tennessee and Florida faced challenges from teachers, their unions, the courts, and legislators. One Tennessee lawmaker voiced his dissatisfaction with his state's career ladder program:"It is not working. Tennessee teachers seem to be as demoralized as I've ever seen them about public education . . . ."[7] In the "Metropolitan Life Survey of the American Teacher," Louis Harris found that 64 percent of their nationwide sample of teachers believed that the reforms enacted in their states reflected the views of administrators rather than teachers.[8]

Faced with evidence of failing reforms, politicians did not, as many expected, abandon educational concerns for more timely or tractable problems. Instead they seemed intent on refining their plans, redirecting their dollars, and recapturing teacher enthusiasm.[9] Governor Graham of Florida proposed an overhaul of the master teacher program in his state.[10] Governor Kean of New Jersey promised that the "second wave of teacher reform" would have some "different themes" from the first, including greater empowerment of teachers and "really significant pay increases tied to performance." "Teachers are the ones in the classroom," he said. "They should have more to say in what goes on."[11]

There was little evidence, however, that the second sweep of reform initiatives would differ significantly from the first, for the diagnosis of the problem and the vision guiding the reformers remained much the same. Despite Governor Kean's promise to attend to teachers' concerns, Governor Ashcroft of Missouri said, "We've come to the conclusion that the key is assessment," while Governor Alexander of Tennessee reported that among the central issues identified by the Governors' Task Force were "seven [issues] that education groups are not as interested in as we are."[12]

It is notable that the prominent educational reformers of the past four years have been legislators, governors, and chief state school officers, whose primary advisors—businessmen and academics—have contended that schooling would be improved with better teachers and more accountable teaching. In their view, standards for teacher selection were flimsy, competitive incentives were virtually nonexistent, and productivity was inexcusably low. They envisioned school districts that were efficient, competitive, and accountable, that would attract a different kind of teacher—an academically able individual who simultaneously seeks public service, modest monetary incentives, and staged career opportunities.

Although many of those outside the schools shared this view of the problem and confidence in the solution, most teachers did not. Recent research on effective schools had confirmed their hunches that the faculties of such schools were effective because they worked collegially in schools structured to support good instruction. Cooperation, not competition, was at the center of such an enterprise.[13] Teachers in such schools could rely on strong leadership by the principal, a clear statement of organizational purposes, and enforcement of policies on student attendance and discipline. Such a workplace would enable them to do their best work.

Having acknowledged the presence of some weak colleagues, teachers generally reported that the difficulties of schooling were centered not in them, but in the conditions of their work—low pay, large classes, bureaucratic demands, inept administrators, low professional status, diminished parental support, and an increasingly demanding and unresponsive student population.[14] Their eyes were not set on some far-off image of efficient excellence, but on the practical complications and daily hazards of teaching. How could they see ahead to a school that would guarantee high test scores and successful graduates when there were not enough books for students? How could they demonstrate greater professional expertise when the district supervisor imposed a recipe for success that they thought could not possibly succeed?

Studies of successful corporations have demonstrated the limitations of the rational, top-down model of change.[15] Those who best understand how to improve the structure of work are usually those who do that work, not those who direct and assess it from above or outside. Kanter's research has illustrated the importance of empowering workers to put their ideas to work in the interests of the organization,[16] and Callahan has documented the failures of scientific managers in their crusade to fix public education.[17] However, the legislated school reform of the past three years was quintessentially top-down. Because policymakers saw the teachers as the problem, they sought to impose their notions of how education could be improved.

In retrospect, one of the most interesting features of this period was that although the reformers and the teachers may have both recognized the need to improve the schools, they proceeded with different and often contradictory visions of what those schools should be like. Not only did the reformers seldom seek to reconcile these differences in drafting legislation or school board proposals, but most seemed not to have even recognized them. Nevertheless, they acted with confidence as if they knew what was best for teachers, and eventually they responded with dismay and annoyance when those teachers did not share their views. For although politicians could legislate change, they could not implement it; they needed teachers' compliance and commitment. Having recognized that the new programs would not significantly improve the conditions of their work, many teachers eventually dismissed the reforms as mirages, the would-be reformers as shortsighted. The reform movement was not guided by a common vision.

In an effort to better understand the fate of such staffing reforms, we conducted research in a diverse sample of local school districts between May 1984 and January 1985. Through interviews with 151 teachers, administrators, and union officials in four districts, we sought to understand the types of reforms that were being introduced, the source and substance of those initiatives, and the responses of teachers and their unions to them. (The methodology is described in the Appendix.) In two of these school districts, administrators had initiated local reforms. In the other two, teachers were responding to comprehensive legislation passed by the state and intended to restructure teaching. Here we examine the various perspectives that policymakers and teachers brought to the issue of staffing reform in these four sites. We conclude that in some cases, competing, and often conflicting, visions impeded successful adoption and implementation of the changes. In others, there were opportunities for the participants to recognize and to reconcile different views about what was wrong and what corrections were desirable. In such cases, the reforms appeared to have better prospects of success.

## LOCAL INITIATIVES IN MIDLAND HEIGHTS AND EAST PORT

In Midland Heights, a wealthy suburban district, and East Port, a large urban system, local administrators set out to reform staffing practices. Teachers in the two districts responded quite differently to their initiatives. In neither case did teachers and administrators begin with a uniform view of what was best for their schools. However, in East Port, teachers and administrators did acknowledge similar problems and use the collective bargaining process to reconcile their views and devise workable solutions to those problems. By contrast, a top-down reform intended to increase accountability among teachers in Midland Heights never gained professional acceptance.

The superintendent in Midland Heights conceived of the reform there—Staffing for Excellence—as a response to parental pressure to "move against poor teachers," who were widely agreed to be very few in this school district of highly qualified staff. He had discussed his concern with principals and finally told them: "What I'm going to recommend to the board [is to] give you assistance in working with teachers that you've identified as being problem teachers." He envisioned a highly accountable district where administrators exhaustively evaluated staff, dismissed the weakest teachers, and satisfied an outspoken and demanding public. Such a school district would be compatible with the values of its business-oriented community. The superintendent said: "I've worked in a number of school districts and I think this is the best group of teachers I've ever worked with. If I had to change teams, I don't know of anybody I'd change with. But if I could swap some players, there's a lot that I would swap." The personnel director shared this vision of a refined staff, explaining that following a layoff due to declining enrollment,"the poor teachers got more visible." Staffing for Excellence, he said, was designed to "take a serious look at our staff and to counsel some people out, or to actually improve others, make some changes."

The head of the teachers' association regarded Staffing for Excellence as a program of harassment rather than one of refinement:

[It's] not a program, but simply an administrator hired to kick the principals around to get them to be tougher in the evaluation process . . . . Don't get me wrong, I'm not saying they shouldn't be dealing with those teachers who aren't performing properly, but this is much more far-reaching. This is harassment. They're not dealing with the problems they have, and the recommendations they make are unrelated to the problems or deficiencies they've cited.

Most teachers whom we interviewed shared this view. Midland Heights teachers, who were required to hold a master's degree in each subject area in which they taught, considered themselves an unusually qualified professional corps. Negotiated layoff provisions guaranteed that no teacher, however junior, would be let go unless a fully qualified senior member was available to take his or her place.

Teachers reported that the anxiety and distrust generated among good teachers by Staffing for Excellence was unwise and unwarranted. They saw no need for a districtwide program focusing money and effort on a few inadequate teachers. However, they did envision a different kind of school system, one in which school officials actively supported a superior staff by encouraging their professional growth and autonomy. Teachers and principals commonly agreed that staff morale was very low. Staff reported that they were misunderstood and undervalued by the central office administrators. They would have endorsed a change that emphasized their many accomplishments and provided the opportunity for new inquiry and programs rather than one that highlighted the shortcomings of a few. They envisioned schooling as a supportive, reinforcing, and empowering endeavor rather than one that sorted and discarded its weakest members.

In a second response to public concerns about school, the Midland Heights superintendent instituted a Commission for Excellence that established a committee structure for teachers, administrators, and community members to assess their schools. It elicited some suspicion, but more support from teachers, for although it was spawned in the central office, this study commission enlisted teachers as agents rather than objects of scrutiny. The superintendent saw in the national movement toward excellence "something ....for us," and hoped to understand "are we evaluating [staff] performance effectively?" Teachers could accept the logic behind these motives, but they viewed it with some cynicism. One said, "If things go as normal, they'll pull out what can be used to their benefit financially." Another said, "I'm afraid we'll be ignored or [that it will] become a tool used against us." In fact, the final report of the committee reflected the prevailing teachers' view that school officials should be more involved with and responsive to teachers: "The problem of staff morale and poor communication with central office administrators are the overriding concern of this committee. This poor working relationship has far-reaching negative effects on our educational community. We feel it is imperative to address these problems as soon as possible."

In East Port, there was more consensus among school officials and teachers about the prevalence of staffing problems in their schools. It was generally agreed that restrictive provisions in the teachers' contract regulating assignment and transfer had compromised the quality of education and were disrupting the teachers' professional lives. Stories abounded about mismatches in teacher qualifications and assignments—the Italian teacher who didn't speak Italian, the kindergarten teacher who was assigned to teach physics. Principals complained that they had lost all control over staffing in their schools, recounting incidents of unexpected and often ill-prepared teachers arriving at their doors in September. Teachers told of their frustration with sequential bumping procedures that moved them from school to school and department to department, year after year. Most of these problems resulted from a teachers' contract that prescribed seniority-based staffing decisions often augmented by inept administration. Initially, the union had expected that seniority guarantees would serve teacher interests, but teachers increasingly viewed them as problematic.

Initially a group of principals participating in a school site management project drafted proposals for revising the East Port contract. These principals wanted to stabilize staffing in their schools and restore administrators' discretion over teacher assignments to the school site administrators. In reporting their work to the superintendent, the deputy superintendent expressed these principals' collective vision of a collegial relationship between teachers and administrators:

> We should be striving towards a constructive relationship with our teachers and their representatives. A contract which will ensure that is one which provides for a productive workforce which meets the goals of the system while at the same time ensuring equitable and reasonable working conditions. Our current contract does neither. It is a codification of years of paternalistic past practices which were, by and large, accommodations to resolution of short-term conditions.

The report further criticized the teachers' contract for being seniority-bound, providing insufficient instructional time, and not including adequate standards for teacher performance.

A central office administrator explained the difficulties that principals had encountered:

> They used to go bananas because they'd get people whom they hadn't planned on—a problem or a misfit from another place. They'd set up their courses around the teachers that they knew they were going to get, or thought that they were going to get, and then they would find out that they were getting a teacher from another place on transfer because it was [the teacher's] absolute right to transfer—[a teacher] who couldn't possibly handle photography or geography or whatever it was at that particular school. That's just absolutely no way to say you have an academic program.

Although teachers and their union leaders were wary of East Port management's motives in seeking to negotiate more discretion for principals, constraints on seniority rights, and a wider array of evaluation ratings, they did acknowledge the wisdom behind such initiatives. After school officials had won many of these revisions through contentious negotiations, teachers generally acknowledged that the changes were warranted. One said: "I don't think it was an unreasonable compromise. That may sound strange coming from a teacher, a building representative, but it's after having seen teachers who took advantage of the principals and who always had the [union] and their lawyers behind them. The principals need some support." Another, who called herself "a staunch believer in seniority," concurred: "Without [seniority] we don't have much. I do feel though, as an educator, this new system is fair . . . .A lot of people passed through here for many years who were unprepared. It's not fair to ask the principal to run the schools with a group of poor teachers. You have to give them some choice." The president of the union also regarded the agreement as fair and consistent with teacher interests: "Ninety percent of the members are more happy than unhappy." Writing in the union's newspaper, he observed: "To improve the quality of education, to restore public confidence in the school system, and to secure adequate funding for public education, such cooperation is not only desirable, it is vital."

This consensus was achieved in part because teachers and administrators initially identified similar problems in their staffing policies. However, collective bargaining also provided the forum for devising alternative means of achieving the more appropriate assignments that both parties thought were necessary.

Although they were both logically initiated, there were notable differences between these reform efforts in Midland Heights and East Port. Staffing for Excellence, a top-down measure derived from a vision of business-like accountability, was inconsistent with teachers' views of what they and their schools needed. They resisted the initiative and school officials viewed that resistance with contempt. Meanwhile, through their work on a study commission, the teachers expressed their vision of a collegial, responsive administration. Ultimately, that vision prevailed as Staffing for Excellence was abandoned, the superintendent resigned, and the school board searched for a replacement who would be more responsive to staff. By contrast, in East Port there was greater consonance among teachers, administrators, and community members about what schools needed—more discretion for principals, more stability for staff, mor accountability for teachers, and more certainty that teaching assignments would match curricular needs.

## STATE INITIATIVES IN MARLIN
## COUNTY AND CANYON UNIFIED

In two other districts of this study, reforms originated outside the district. Administrators and teachers in Marlin County, a large southern district, and Canyon Unified, a western rural secondary system, were expected to implement laws passed by the states. While Marlin County participants sought to subvert the intent of the legislation and to minimize its negative effects, Canyon Unified teachers and administrators worked to adapt state-level reforms to the circumstances of their district. Again, there were important differences between the visions that guided the reforms in these districts.

Business leaders had set the course of reform for Marlin County when the statewide business community moved to promote educational excellence that was measurable and competitive. Marlin County's superintendent characterized that vision in two short sentences: "Show us some progress. Reward your best teachers." He explained that the governor had appointed a council to study performance-based incentives:

> They were charged with coming up with the whole concept of merit pay in the state. They took all these people from business and industry and education and put them together to try and develop a plan that was workable. In the meantime, the governor came up with his own plan and said, "I have to have this thing in by the deadline." And he imposed it and just said, "Here is the master plan."

Two prominent features of the legislation that eventually emerged were a Master Teacher program and a Merit Schools program. Meritorious teachers were to be selected on the basis of classroom observations. Meritorious schools were to be identified as the top one-fourth of a district's schools, measured by standardized student test scores.

The governor, whom teachers had initially regarded as their advocate, had shifted to embrace the vision of the business community which promoted competition among schools with prizes for the winners. A leader of the teachers' association explained:

> [At first,] he didn't want anything exotic. He just wanted teachers to make more money without having to go into administration ... He fell in love with merit pay. He said so and we can't shake him. Now what he's started with has turned into a monster, with more plans, locally bargained merit schools; there's no end to this stuff.

Both teachers and administrators in Marlin County anticipated that the Merit Schools program, which distributed substantial financial rewards to outstanding schools, would demoralize staff and undermine public confidence in schools that were not selected, confidence they had sought to equalize across the district since desegregation. Most of the faculty reported that selecting a few schools as "meritorious" ran counter to their vision of egalitarian education. One said, "Forget it. I'm vehemently opposed to it. This is not industry. We're not producing Cokes or selling insurance. We're working with kids." Another spoke of the absence of educational insight in the plan: "This meritorious schools plan is the same old political rhetoric. It comes from ignorant politicians. People who are ignorant about education, the classroom, and teaching."

Marlin County teachers voiced similar concerns about the Master Teacher program: "You have to make the basic salaries competitive rather than worrying about merit pay for some. It makes for divisiveness and unhappiness. Let's get rid of the poor teachers. This is a Band-Aid operation." Another said, "It pits teacher against teacher and ruins sharing, the team approach, and collegiality."

The visions of education held by state reformers and teachers in Marlin County were not simply different, they were contradictory. Advocates of merit pay and merit schools sought to promote competition and ranking. Opponents believed that such competition and ranking obscured the prospect of schools that might be supportive, collegial organizations.

Initially, Marlin County teachers and administrators lobbied against the governor's proposals, but when those efforts proved unsuccessful, they sought to turn state programs to their own advantage. Together, union leaders and school officials sought to subvert the intent of the Merit Schools plan while reaping its financial benefits. The state required that the most successful one-fourth of the district's schools, as evidenced by standardized test scores, be recognized as meritorious and rewarded with substantial cash bonuses. In response these local readers devised an alternative proposal, eventually accepted by the state, that would minimize the competitive components of the plan and equalize the financial awards among the schools. Some might argue that by their actions, Marlin County endorsed the reform effort, but the local school officials and teachers never did share the vision of schooling that inspired these reforms. Instead, they planned to wait out public enthusiasm, to secure the financial benefits of the legislation, and to protect the schools as best they could. As one union official explained, "What we have here is a whole lot of damage control."

The legislative reforms that Canyon Union teachers were to implement resembled those of Marlin County. But these programs, which included a Mentor Teacher program and requirements for more thorough teacher evaluation, originated not from the business roundtable or the governor's office, but from the chief state school officer, whose electoral platform stressed the importance of committing teachers, administrators, and school board members to goals of excellence, and who envisioned a state in which local districts were "raising academic and behavioral expectations for all students...."[18] Although his rhetoric seemed to echo that of politicians and business leaders, Canyon Unified teachers saw him as an educator, a former elementary teacher, whose platform derived from instructional priorities, enjoyed wide public support, and therefore deserved their attention. The reform included a Mentor Teacher program and requirements for more intensive teacher evaluation. Many teachers were wary that the Mentor Teacher program was merit pay in disguise. But generous across-the-board pay increases that would compensate teachers for longer school days and years and instructional improvement grants to promote curriculum development were also included. Although the proposals were not fully consistent with teachers' visions of what their schools needed (smaller classes, more teaching materials), they were not at odds with them. They introduced the controversial mentor teacher positions, but they also provided for more professional initiative and teaching time.

Central office administrators in Canyon Unified viewed the reform legislation pragmatically. The assistant superintendent believed that it created the conditions for better education by providing new state money for local districts. The teachers' union opposed those components of the legislation that dissatisfied them, such as the Master Teacher plan. As one administrator said, "They don't like the competition at the school level about who's the best teacher and who's the worst." Yet when it became clear that school officials were intent on implementing the law, the union cooperated and negotiated its details. Mentor teachers in Canyon Unified would assist probationary teachers, thus minimizing the status differentiation among current staff. Although this program lacked broad support from faculty, some found it compatible with their own goals. One said that she had been "dreaming of a project for five years" that would allow her to become involved in teacher training, "sharing ideas and discussing materials," and "being able to communicate effectively in more than one curriculum area." It was this collegial side of the mentor teacher program rather than its competitive edge that was consistent with teachers' visions of their work.

Similarly, the legislation called for the regular evaluation of staff. Teachers initially feared that local administrative enthusiasm for a Teacher Power instructional model might compromise their instructional freedom. However, as it became clear that the program would not be imposed on veteran teachers, they acknowledged that changes in the weak existing evaluation program were necessary, and support for the program gradually grew. Here, as in East Port, reform proposals were not simply incorporated wholesale into the schools. Rather, local teachers bargained each piece separately, adjusting the policies to fit the needs of their local districts and their views of teaching and schooling.

Teachers in Marlin County and Canyon Unified responded differently to legislated reforms. In neither district were they persuaded that the state had accurately diagnosed the ills of schooling and prescribed appropriate remedies, but in Canyon Unified teachers believed that a substantial part of the legislation was consistent with their view of what was needed, while in Marlin County most teachers saw the new reforms as misdirected. Although this consistency or inconsistency of vision was not the only factor that influenced their responses, it was the primary one.[19]

## CONCLUSION

The experiences of these four districts provide some insights for those who would reform the schools. The message is not that teachers have the only perspective on school improvement that counts, but rather that the difficulty reformers have faced in implementing reforms has not resulted primarily from ignorance or teacher resistance. The teachers and the reformers saw things differently from the start. Efforts to fix the teaching profession began before they had faced and reconciled those differences. External reformers focused primarily on the failings of teaching and foresaw a teaching force that would attend to the public's new priorities and be moved by financial incentives. Teachers considered the routine realities of their work, the limitations of school resources, and the organizational complexity of their schools. They contemplated school reform and envisioned well-equipped schools, well-paid staff, attentive students, and responsive administrators. By 1986, many reformers concluded that teachers' vision was re stricted by blinders, while many of those same teachers suspected that they had been hoodwinked.

If better, or even comparable, teachers are to be attracted to the profession during the coming staff shortage, we cannot disregard the teachers' views.[20] It is not enough to merely include teachers in the discussions of reforms as many politicians have recently proposed. Their expectations must be actively solicited, understood, and accomplished. As Governor Kean acknowledged after three years of reform efforts: "We believe that teachers are the ones who can make the schools better, and we don't feel people have been listening enough to teachers....Any further reform will fail without them."[21] For prospective teachers will not assume jobs that are unsatisfying or undoable, even if their pay becomes competitive with that of electricians or engineers.

Recent reform proposals from the Carnegie Commission[22] and the California Commission on the Teaching Profession[23] would have teachers redesign and regulate their own work. These recommendations comprise a very different blueprint for teaching and schooling than those that would prescribe curriculum, promote competition, and prod professionals into greater productivity. It is not yet clear whether such plans can gain credence with the policymakers who must fund them. In attending to the failings of public education, school officials may well need to specify goals more clearly, review school effectiveness regularly, and hold teachers accountable for responsible professional action. But they must also ensure that teaching is professionally rewarding, that it approaches the vision that beginning teachers had of its opportunities and rewards. Much of the reform movement has followed from a conventional management-controlled view of organizations. If that view is not wrong, it is certainly incomplete.

The research reported here was funded by a grant from the National Institute of Education. The authors wish to acknowledge the considerable contribution of Jacqueline Potter, research assistant on the study.

## NOTES

1. The National Commission on Excellence in Education, *A Nation at Risk: The Imperative for Educational Reform* (Washington, D.C.: U.S. Government Printing Office, 1983).

2. Ernest Boyer, *High School: A Report on Secondary School Education in America* (New York: Harper and Row, 1983); John I. Goodlad, *A Place Called School* (New York: McGraw-Hill, 1983); Theodore R. Sizer, *Horace's Compromise: The Dilemma of the American High School Today* (New York: McGraw-Hill, 1983); The Twentieth Century Fund, *Making the Grade* (New York: The Twentieth Century Fund, 1983).

3. Willis Hawley, "False Premises, False Promises: The Mythical Character of Public Discourse About Education," *Phi Delta Kappan* 67 (November 1985): 183–87.

4. U.S. Department of Education, *The Nation Responds: Recent Efforts to Improve Education* (Washington, D.C.: U.S. Government Printing Office, 1984).

5. Lynn Olson, "Pioneering State Teacher-Incentive Plans in Florida, Tennessee Still Under Attack," *Education Week* (January 15, 1986), 1, 24, 25.

6. Ibid., p. 24.

7. Ibid.

8. Louis Harris and Associates, *Metropolitan Life Survey of the American Teacher* 1985 (New York: Metropolitan Life Insurance Company, 1985).

9. J.R. Sirkin, "Governors Appear Set To Propose School Reforms," *Education Week* (March 5, 1986), pp. 1, 16.

10. Lynn Olson, "Master-Teacher Conversion Proposed," *Education Week* (February 12, 1986), p. 4.

11. J.R. Sirkin, "Governors Appear Set," p. 16.

12. Ibid.

13. See, for example, Stewart S. Purkey and Marshall S. Smith, "Effective Schools—A Review," *Elementary School Journal*, vol. 83, pp. 427–52; Michael Rutter et al., *Fifteen Thousand Hours: Secondary Schools and Their Effects on Children* (Cambridge, Mass.: Harvard University Press, 1979); Susan J. Rosenholtz, "Effective Schools: Interpreting the Evidence," *American Journal of Education* 93 (May 1985): 352–88.

14. *Metropolitan Life Survey of the American Teacher* 1985.

15. Thomas J. Peters and Robert H. Waterman, Jr., *In Search of Excellence: Lessons from America's Best-Run Companies* (New York: Warner Books, 1982), pp. 29–54.

16. Rosabeth Moss Kanter, *The Changemasters* (New York: Simon and Schuster, 1983).

17. Raymond E. Callahan, *Education and the Cult of Efficiency* (Chicago: University of Chicago Press, 1962).

18. Bill Honig, "The Educational Excellence Movement: Now Comes the Hard Part," *Phi Delta Kappan* 75 (June 1985): 675–81, 678.

19. See Susan M. Johnson, Niall C.W. Nelson, and Jacqueline Potter, *Teachers Unions, School Staffing, and Reform* (Cambridge, MA: Harvard University Press, 1985), pp. 93–107.

20. Linda Darling-Hammond, *Beyond the Commission Reports* (Washington, D.C.: The Rand Corporation, 1985.

21. J.R. Sirkin, "Governors' Education Task Forces Begin Hearings: State Policy Agenda is Goal," *Education Week* (January 8, 1986), pp. 1, 16.

22. The Carnegie Task Force on Teaching as a Profession, *A Nation Prepared: Teachers for the 21st Century* (New York: The Carnegie Corporation, 1986).

23. The California Commission on the Teaching Profession, *Who Will Teach Our Children?: A Strategy for Improving California's Schools* (Sacramento, Calif.: The California Commission on the Teaching Profession, 1985).

## APPENDIX
## RESEARCH METHODOLOGY

The field sites for this study were chosen after an analysis of teacher contracts from a stratified, random sample of 155 districts in eleven states. They were selected to provide diversity across a range of site variables: staffing reform initiatives, location, size, socioeconomic status, urban/suburban/county character, enrollment trends, NEA/AFT affiliation, and length and history of bargaining.

Our investigative fieldwork model drew upon document analysis, intensive interviewing, and transient observation. We examined teacher contracts, school board policies, administrative memoranda, seniority lists, assignment rosters, arbitration decisions, state laws, and newspaper reports. These documents provided information about the origin, development, and implementation of staffing policies.

Through intensive interviewing, we explored the course of reform initiatives at the four sites. Subjects were selected purposefully rather than randomly to achieve a balanced sample and include those with particularly relevant perspectives or experience. Semistructured interviews were conducted between May 1984 and February 1985 at the district, school site, and classroom levels. We began with central office administrators and union leaders. Based on their recommendations, we then selected between four and nine schools, representing all grade levels, in each district. Every effort was made to choose schools that provided a balanced and representative sample from each system. At the school site, we interviewed principals and union building representatives, who then recommended a selection of teachers for further interviews.

In total, we conducted 151 interviews, each lasting between thirty and ninety minutes. Subjects were assured of confidentiality and informed that neither they nor their districts would be identified in reporting the findings.

Transient observation of individuals, interactions, and physical surroundings was used to test and corroborate findings gathered through document analysis and interviews. Cross-checking and triangulation helped to confirm the validity of the data and to counteract potential sources of bias and error.

# Part III

## *Critical Perspectives on Current Reform*

LINDA M. MCNEIL

## Chapter 10

# *Exit, Voice, and Community: Magnet Teachers' Responses to Standardization*

Now that a number of articulate intellectuals have pointed out the deficiencies of American public schools, it seems to have fallen to the technicians rather than the scholars to "fix" what is wrong with our schools. While university deans and professors discuss the "second wave" reforms that call for professionalizing teaching and restructuring school management, state agencies and school boards are busy implementing the "first wave" reforms. Most of these reforms are sweeping, aimed at stemming the "crisis" of American education by setting uniform minimum standards for school practices. And because most of these reforms originate with management, they frequently define the "crisis in American education" as a "crisis in teaching."

These standardizations include adding minutes to the school day and days to the school year, controlling the number of minutes or hours teachers may take students away from the classroom, setting specific behaviors against which to measure instructional performance, and assessing teaching by testing students with exams not written by their teachers. The very pessimistic view of teaching implied by many of these "reforms" may be justified by that small percentage of teachers that are not fully literate or competent in their subject field. The negative assumptions about teacher effort are perhaps justified by those teachers who have burned out or never learned to communicate their subject knowledge to students.

The irony of the reforms built upon these negative assumptions, is, however, that *they help bring about* mechanistic, disengaged, depressed teaching or, at best, boring teaching. They are also helping bring about the exit of some of our best teachers, who see their professional, creative teaching threatened, even negatively rewarded, by standardized reforms which disregard teacher initiative. Standardized reforms by definition attempt to neutralize individual differences; teacher-neutral reforms then have a levelling effect which brings down the best while elelevating (perhaps) the weakest.

To date, we have had little empirical evidence of the effects of standardized reforms. While some districts and states are reporting out student test scores, there has been little evidence of the effects specific reforms have had on classroom practice, on students' analytic understanding of content—tested only in fragments—or on the role of teachers. The effect on teachers is especially important because many of these reforms have deliberately been designed to shift the locus of control over content and over instructional and evaluation methods away from classroom teachers. Whether shifting authority for instructional style and testing improves teaching is critical because, as the reforms demonstrate, they are aimed at solving the "problem" of bad teaching by tightening management over what teachers do.

Research in progress at the time such reforms were implemented in a large urban district offers new documentation of the effects of top-down management reforms on teachers in magnet high schools.[1] Rather than conform to the spirit of letter of the reforms unreflectively, these teachers very actively weighed the reforms against their instructional goals and their program's philosophy. These teachers were among the "best" in their district; many owed their teaching assignment in a magnet to their reputation of expertise that preceded them and caused them to be recruited. While none of them was a perfect teacher, all were competent and conscientious prior to the enactment of state- and district-level standardized reforms. Theoretically, none of these teachers fits the negative stereotype of teacher that the standardized reforms were designed to "improve." Yet, reforms aimed at lifting the minimum standards had significant impact on the professional discretion and performance of these teachers. And the procedures for evaluating minimum performance had even greater impact on teaching style and on the ways these teachers could assess the work of their students. The effect, or potential effect, in each case was that the standardized reform decreased rather than increased instructional quality in these teachers' classes or caused them to resort to overt accommodations while thinking of leaving teaching.

The teachers were not without resources. At each of these magnet schools, the faculty coalesced into a body with common perspectives and common practices supporting the distinctiveness of the school. This development of a faculty culture helped teachers resist the imposition of standardized practices such as detailed curricular guidelines or districtwide final examinations (all of which ran counter to the purpose of the distinctive magnets). Magnet school faculties were specifically recruited for their competence in curriculum development and interest in the specialized purposes of their respective schools. Thus, as a group these teachers tended to focus their attention on special curricular emphases and the resources available to support them. Their magnet specialties included career emphases such as fine arts, engineering, and medical professions and a specialized pedagogy for the gifted and talented.

Even more important than their affiliation with the magnet specialties, the teachers in the various magnet programs developed a strong collective identity based upon their allegiance to a generalized vision of high-quality teaching. They collectively supported and demonstrated ideas of engaging, divergent, intellectually substansive teaching as the best kind of teaching for all schools. Many of them perceived magnet schools as a group to be the only schools where such teaching was possible in the context of extreme, and growing, standardization in the school district. Magnet schools were a haven where such "professional" teaching was supported.

Over time, as pressures to standardize threatened to undermine their professional judgments on content and method, a culture of community became for many an inadequate response to the conflict between being hired to specialize (and thus fulfill magnet specialties) and being evaluated according to standardized criteria. As long as that standardization remained merely a general policy, the strength of faculty culture sustained teachers in their efforts to engage students, to bring their personal and professional stores of knowledge into the classroom, to affirm their professional skills in developing curriculum, planning classroom activities, and evaluating their students. When the standardized reforms became more rigidly enforced and tied directly to grading and teacher pay, faculty culture became insufficient as a buffer between professional goals and institutional regulations. Up to a point, the magnet teachers were able to turn their resistance to administrative controls into a strong faculty culture identified with excellence and teacher professionalism. They resisted participating in their own deskilling. When an imposed deskilling threatened to change their teaching, many found that a faculty culture was not adequate to protect them. Rather than be so deskilled, some of these teachers are now planning to leave the profession.

The strength of this model of faculty culture is in notable contrast to the situation found in a study of Midwestern high schools. There, teachers, under pressure from school administrators' emphasis on control goals at the expense of educative purposes, tended to take their resistance out on their students.[2] These teachers tightened their own control over students and course content, teaching defensively and reducing rich course content to "school knowledge," easily conveyed and tested but scarcely credible to the students as worth their efforts to learn for themselves rather than merely for passing tests. These teachers began inadvertently to participate in their own deskilling, in the separation of their professional knowledge from their treatment of school subjects.

The following analysis describes the way the magnet school teachers built a sense of community and a shared culture in defense of their ideas of what it meant to be "really teaching." In addition, examples from magnet teachers' experience will be compared to an organizational model of employee response to institutional dislocations in an attempt to show how management practices may have unintended consequences, even to the point of becoming a part of the problem they are aimed at solving. It is at this point of internal contradiction that examination of magnet faculty culture helps inform the debate on appropriate school reforms.

## MAGNET FACULTY CULTURE

The sense of faculty culture among magnet teachers arose from both positive and negative forces, from factors within the school and from outside. As, in Metz's words, "a meaning system which provides teachers with a way to feel competent in their work in the circumstances in which they find themselves,"[3] the magnet faculty culture included a sense of identity with the special purpose of the particular magnet and, in addition, a sense of being identified with educational quality. The faculty culture that was visible, both to the teachers and to an observer, was a sense of cohesiveness as a group combined with a sense of professionalism as an individual within that group. That sense of professionalism, in the subject fields and in teaching methods, is especially crucial to the continued motivaion of these excellent teachers because their district tends to reward minimum efforts, especially those efforts conforming to standard procedures and standard measures of evaluation.

*Internal Factors Shaping Faculty Culture*

For teachers at school-within-a-school magnets, the faculty culture develops first around the unique subject specialty. Magnets such as those devoted to the engineering professions and the program for gifted and talented are located as subprograms within large high schools. Such programs are placed in existing schools not only to integrate the student body and faculties of those schools, but to increase the student populations to levels high enough to keep the existing schools from closing. Such schools tend to be in very poor, often minority, areas, many of which can hardly be called "neighborhoods" because of encroaching warehousing, manufacturing, highway construction or other nonresidential, nonretailing land uses. Very often the poverty of the area, combined with declining enrollments, meant that the "neighborhood" school had been declining (or at least not improving) in quality over time prior to the establishment of the magnet. Pressures from residents for the central administration to keep the school open helped determine the location of the magnet program when desegregation plans were put in effect. Locating attractive magnet programs in inner city schools would attract anglo children to those schools, thus integrating them, and would keep the low-enrollment, usually single-race neighborhood from closing.

The magnet teachers, all of whom choose to work in integrated schools, feel less distance from the minority population of the larger school than from the mediocre academic quality districtwide which that larger school represents. The magnet teachers then identify first of all with the magnet speciality of which they are a part and second with the expectations that the magnet offers high-quality education to students of all races. It is interesting that teachers within a magnet whose courses fall outside the magnet specialty still develop this strong identification with the program. History teachers at the high school for health professions care intensely about that program, usually because they become involved with the students' enthusiasm for it, even though their own courses rarely touch on medical issues. Similarly, non-science and engineering teachers at the high school for engineering professions have developed a strong subculture or identity, as a subgroup, committed to the magnet school's reputation for *quality* rather than *specialty*. Several have even commented (as have some other students and parents) that in many instances their courses are of higher academic quality than some of the specialized magnet courses for which students transfer to this school.

These positive feelings of being a part of a cohesive faculty are not merely an observer's interpretations. While the spirit is perceptible to a long-term visitor to a given program, it is often also expressed by the teachers themselves. Several have said, despite the school's scarce resources and many problems with the central administration, that "if you can't teach here, you can't teach." The feeling of "ownership" of the program has led a number of the teachers to recruit other good teachers to the school. One science teacher was explaining in an interview that he had enjoyed teaching in an inner city school but that a woman who had taught with him before transferring to the magnet called him several times to invite him to apply for openings. He finally relented, drawn by the students and the goals of the program, by the culture of the school (although he did not use that term), even though the move meant coming to a school with inferior labs. He named five magnet teachers hired away from his old school. Coming to work with specific colleagues with whom they felt compatible personally and professionally was a strong incentive for teachers joining this faculty.

Others came to the magnets because of the students; they wanted to be a part of the "high expectations" of the school. Both engineering and medical high school teachers said that the key to the faculty life at their school was the "high expectations" for the students, both on the part of the teachers and the students themselves. Because students volunteered to attend these magnets, and in fact had to compete for admission, teachers knew that students and their parents were committed to the program (at least to giving it a chance for that student). In view of the fact that most of the magnet students had to ride the bus for long distances each way, the teachers sensed that students and parents had a serious investment in the educational and desegregation goals of the magnet schools. The faculty culture of high expectations, then, corresponded to student expectations. Teachers and students knew that even if students changed their academic or occupational interests and did not become engineers or doctors after high school, they had nevertheless had an opportunity for a first-rate education. For many of the minority students, the magnets are tickets to higher education; several expressed in interviews that they would have had higher grades and more extracurricular activities if they had stayed at their home school. But like their friends who did stay, they would have been lacking in direction, in quality courses (especially in math), in exposure to the possibilities of going on to college. Each spring the teachers saw magnet minority students admitted to fine colleges and saw many of them awarded sponsored scholarships needed to act on those admissions. These and other manifestations that the high expectations could be realized brought teachers together in a common purpose and helped solidify their sense of community as a faculty.

Other magnet teachers felt a part of a faculty culture of professionals trusted to develop curriculum and innovative educational programs. In some cases the magnets are variations on existing vocational schools. However, those in the arts, engineering, medicine, and foreign languages are examples of programs which had to be developed from scratch. It was hoped that students would be attracted to them and that their relation to the city's economy would both attract industry support and produce graduates who saw a future in professional specialties after studying in those areas in the magnet schools. The programs vary in their degree of conceptualization and resource availability before staffs were hired; many of the observed teachers had helped originate or shape the magnet programs and thus had a very keen sense of professional participation. Others had helped recruit good teachers they had known at other schools, informally building the program in directions to which they felt a commitment.

Those teachers whose specialties had no analogue at traditional high schools in the area had the opportunity to design the courses which would create the magnet focus; this added a further professional component to their work. They became involved in developing curricula (often in conjunction with advisory boards, central office personnel, or other teachers in the program) and in working out prerequisites for the courses and standards for assessing the courses and students' performance in them.

Teachers whose courses did not relate directly to the magnet specialty (English courses, for example) still felt a part of something unique. At one magnet school with a career-related specialty, the nonspecialty teachers felt they too received the benefit of the students' sense of purpose. As mentioned earlier, the nonspecialty teachers sometimes felt their courses to be the stronger, academically richer, and more ably taught part of the program. More than one of these teachers expressed in interviews that students may have come to the school because of the magnet specialty, but they left with a good, overall college-preparatory education. At this school, the nonmagnet teachers formed almost a subculture; this was especially noted among those who had several years' experience at the school.

One of the magnets studied was not centered around a career-oriented or topical specialty but around a pedagogy and type of student.

The high school for the gifted and talented was not the only magnet to admit students by entrance exams and strong academic records; it certainly was not the only magnet to attract extremely bright, scholarly, creative students. But its particular focus centered upon these students—those defined as intelligent, gifted, and creative. The pedagogy of the school was one which was committed to high levels of student involvement in learning. This faculty had the strongest cohesiveness because in addition to a commitment to quality instruction, its members shared a definition of what quality instruction meant in the teaching of gifted children. Their high school, a school-within-a-school, is the only high school magnet to be in a sequence of related magnets at the elementary and middle school level. It drew students from other middle schools besides the middle schools for gifted and talented, but shared with their own feeder schools, especially at the elementary level, a philosophy of teaching and learning. This philosophy required student involvement in open-ended learning activities, student research and discussion, student planning of some instructional activities, and an assumption that serious teaching and learning will result in unexpected outcomes. The processes of learning are central to this program. One teacher at the school described the students as "wanting to investigate things, wanting to become more their own person, wanting to develop their strengths." For students to develop their own abilities, they need the support of gifted and creative teachers, teachers who can be resourceful, flexible, and very knowledgeable.

> I think what's different about being a [gifted and talented magnet teacher] is the way we can teach, because [of] . . . the way we feel about the kids . . . There is no place in this district, except for maybe some of the smaller schools with good teachers, where kids can get quality and love and care and personalized attention that they get here . . . .The kids are interesting and the teachers are interesting.

The faculty culture at this school was reinforced by a shared commitment to a way of teaching; that attention to methods of teaching cut across and overcame what could have been barriers to collegiality based on subject matter divisions. In some ways, the school appears traditional, students are divided by grade; subjects are taught according to traditional academic department designations. There are no courses unique to the magnet as there are at career-oriented magnets such as fine arts or medicine. The only truly different subject comes in the annual student project, in which students have to research a topic of interest, work with a mentor if possible, and produce a paper and other presentation of the information in a way that demonstrates new thought or original treatment of the topic. These projects are under the guidance of a teacher who has been selected (or who chose to work with the project after the students had submitted their proposals). This semester-long project results in collections of student poetry, musical compositions, scientific experiments and discoveries, work on citywide Model United Nations team competitions, involvement in a student-developed business, and a variety of other creative ventures. With all of the nearly 400 magnet students working on a project, the teachers' commitment to this pedagogy is stretched; they do not have time released from classes to work with students on projects. The projects are visible symbols of the positive factors of teacher professionalism and commitment to teaching which characterize this magnet faculty.

One other positive factor operates to undergird the magnet faculty cultures, and that is the autonomy to develop curricula. In a state where textbooks are state-adopted and many other issues have been mandated from a state-adopted and many other curicular issues have been mandated from a central level (state or district), creative, intelligent teachers guard dearly the privilege of developing lessons of content and learning activities for their students. Several of the magnet teachers have expressed this component as their chief reason for teaching at a magnet school. One teacher said that he had taught in an honors program at another school before joining the magnet faculty. Now that that honors program had been phased out, he was pleased to be a part of another faculty where a teacher "could do [your] own thing." Another described his principal as a successful magnet principal because "he hired professional teachers who feel comfortable here and he leaves them alone" to develop their courses. The coordinator at the gifted and talented high school magnet said that their program has a real hold on teachers, who feel an "ownership" of the program.

The positive aspects of the faculty culture of these magnet teachers center on their feelings of specialness for the magnet focus of their school, for the participation in quality education inplied by being at one of the academic magnet schools, for the chance to work with teachers who share their definitions of pedagogy, for the privilege of teaching students who also share a commitment to the program, and for the sense that the uniqueness of the magnet school specialty allows them the chance to work as professionals in curriculum development and teaching strategy.

*External Factors*

While these internal forces shape the magnet faculty culture by af-firming the best in the program other external factors reinforce the feeling of being part of a special culture by representing negative pressures against which the magnet teachers join in reacting. These include tendencies within the district to devalue teachers as professionals, to exclude them from policy decisions, and, more recently, to impose incentives that reward teachers who confirm to standard and top-down directives on curriculum and student testing. Added to these are methods of evaluating teacher performance which deemphasize unique qualities and concentrate on standardized teacher actions and student test responses. These teachers who have been hired to specialize, in teaching style and in content, are now experiencing "reforms" that remove the trust that they will develop meaningful courses and replace it with directives to stay in the specialized magnet but standardize classroom content and pedagogy.

One teacher expressed his frustration with new evaluation policies this way: "I'm not a teacher any more. I'm just a worker now." He was reacting to several trends which have been developing in an effort by administrators to reform what have been traditionally very poor quality schools statewide. Rather than target poor-quality schools with added resources or attempt to reeducate very weak teachers, or give them specified times within which to improve, reformers are imposing generalized remedies to which all have to conform. Some of these appear harmless but are devastating to good teachers.

The most distressing to the magnet teachers of regular academic subjects is that "proficiencies," or basic elements to be covered in each course, are now developed at the central office and sent to teachers at the beginning of the semester. These proficiencies usually just skim the surface of the subjects and so should not interfere with magnet teachers' curricula. Because their students will have to take the same tests as other students in the city, however, the magnet teachers feel the need to make sure their students do well on the tests in order not to reflect badly on the magnet program. They have to take time out to explain which parts of the lesson will be important to learn for learning's sake (and for teacher-made tests) and which will be part of the district's proficiency exams. For complex scientific issues, the proficiencies represent a very low level of "factual" treatment of content; the students in a magnet science class may, for example, go beyond the simple formula for photosynthesis to learn about the enzyme processes at work. Such is the case in biology at the gifted and talented magnet. The teacher must remember to have students write into their notes the formula as it will appear on the citywide proficiency test, a multiple-choice, Scantron-graded test that counts as 20 percent of the students' course grade and that is tied directly to the teachers' salary. The magnet teachers are frustrated not only that the content is trivialized in the proficiency lists and proficiency tests, being reduced to facts even if the subject itself is inherently more complicated than that rendering implies. They are also frustrated that so much of the evaluation of their students is now out of their hands; the central district computers score and weigh in the proficiency test along with other test numbers sent in by the teacher at the end of the semester. The teacher does not know the students' course grades until the students see them. Most of these teachers are so committed to educational quality that they agree that the district needs a policy for upgrading instruction, for creating disincentives for very lazy or uneducated teachers. But the only magnet teachers who as a group seem to favor the proficiencies are selected English teachers, whose proficiency tests resemble the reading comprehension tests of SRA and some aptitude tests; they test for main ideas and interpretative skills rather than for mastery of specific content. They are reading skills tests rather than subject–matter tests. Most of the other teachers who do not feel undercut by the proficiency tests are those in specialized courses, especially specialized magnet courses like Engineering II, for which no proficiencies are available or for which the teacher has to create the relevant proficiencies, thus making them compatible with their own course goals. Teachers in these circumstances feel their professionalism to be enhanced rather than undermined.

The centralized testing of students is merely one component in those negative factors causing teachers to develop a strong faculty culture. Teacher testing is also an issue. The statewide tests for teachers wanting to keep their previously earned "lifetime" teaching certification, and thus their jobs, have made national headlines. The test questions printed in newspapers appear so simple that the governor and state education agency seem to be justified in thinking that only the the dumbest, laziest, least educated teachers should be afraid of failing; and their elimination can only improve education in the state. The problems go beyond the simple content of the test. First, several people have found errors in sample questions, leading teachers to wonder whether to answer with their best guess or their guess of what a C-student test-maker would think the right answer to be. More important, after many years of teaching, teachers in the state feel insulted that their jobs could be taken away by a brief test when no one has seriously evaluated their teaching. The magnet teachers are little threatened by the statewide test, and in fact many took a substitute local test developed the year before the state test took effect; they are more offended that the reforms, aimed at the lowest level, affect all equally.

Even less popular with magnet teachers is the evaluation form within the district which assesses teachers according to a checklist of attributes to be observed by a principal or assistant principal. That check-list, derived along principles of classroom management, lists overt behaviors which are supposed to be the stock in trade of "good" teachers. The uniformity is especially ironic given the mandate that magnet teachers have to specialize.

Two examples will demonstrate the philosophy behind these checklists, a philosophy directly counter to magnet teachers' views to teacher professionalism. One item on the list is that teachers "vary ver-bal responses" to students. One especially well-informed, diligent biol-ogy teacher is a shy young man of Scandinavian heritage from the Mid-west. He is soft-spoken and serious. When he tells students, "that's good," they know they have done a very good job; they take his opinion very seriously because of his command of his subject and the richness of his presentations to them. This excellent teacher was graded down on his evaluation because he was more likely to say something brief and undemonstrative like "that's good" rather than produce a the-saurus-like set of verbal responses to his students. He later discovered that several science teachers in the regular program, who know much less biology but who are more effusive, received higher evaluations. For what he considered to be "real biology teaching," there were no items to be checked off.

An English teacher at another magnet had a similar experience with an administrator's checklist. Another item on the list is that teachers must respond to student comment with praise. This teacher was beginning a lesson on *Julius Caesar* when the evaluator walked in. Knowing that the checklist included an item about having a catchy opening to attract students' attention to the lesson, this teacher turned to the quote she had written on the board and read it in a very dull, almost sleeplike voice: "Friends, Romans, countrymen, lend me your ears." The class did not respond, so she asked, "So, do you think one of you could have read that passage better than I did?" One eager boy volunteered. He stood and read the passage with great dramatic emo-tion. He turned to the teacher, quite pleased with his performance; tongue-in-cheek, she asked, "Do you really think you did a better job than I did? Well, let's just let the class decide." The class voted; there were no votes for the teacher and loud cheers and clapping for the stu-dent, who accepted his applause with bows and smiles. The teacher, playing to the evaluation game, had her catchy opener. The class was eager to get on with the rest of the speech. Later she discovered that the evaluator had graded her down for her failure to praise the boy's speech. The evaluator had taken literally the question, "You don't really think you did a better job than I did, do you?" and had missed the fact that the teacher set the boy up for cheers and applause. He definitely received praise. The distance between the items on the checklist and the ideals these teachers set for their teaching, ideas not easily conducive to standardized evaluations, engender resentment, and frustration. Those negative feelings tend to fine their expression in an even stronger sense of cohesion among the magnet faculties.

## PARTICIPATORY DESKILLING

These teachers' responses are in contrast to those of teachers observed in a study of some Midwestern high schools. The teachers in that study experienced some of the same problems as the magnet school teachers did: a sense of distance from and conflict with administrative policy that stressed controlling students and processing them through credentials, with little regard for the quality of instruction or for teachers' professional contributions to school policy. In that study, the teachers responded to their diminished authority in the school as a whole by increasing their control over course content (reducing student participation) and over students themselves. In schools that valued procedure over quality instruction, the teachers created their own efficiencies. This often included watering down assignments, reducing course content to lists, slogans, and other bits of information requiring scant student involvement; few resources beyond the teacher; and little challenge to teachers' presentations. These teachers were often as intelligent and as educated as the magnet teachers and, indeed, had once had the same idea of what teaching ought to be. But in the absence of a strong faculty culture, of a collective sense that might buffer them from the indifferent or intrusive administrative policies, they often taught defensively, mentioning topics, then apologizing or backing off from a complex presentation of the topic in favor of a version that demanded little of the students.[4]

In attempting to avoid student resistance to school work, these teachers ironically created another kind of resistance: students depreciated school-supplied knowledge as lacking in credibility. In interviews they told of learning information only for the test. The teachers had erected walls between their own personal and professional knowledge in order to meet students in a ritual of exchanging "school knowledge" for course credits. By bracketing their personal knowledge from course content, these teachers were unwittingly participating in their own deskilling, in a splitting of their craft from their classroom practice.

The research on magnet schools was desigend specifically to

analyze student's access to knowledge in schools where there was administrative support for the educational purposes (and not just the control goals) of schools.[5] Examples of engaged students and involved, skilled teachers working under conditions established and supported by elaborate administrative structures and policies seemed to offer the perfect counter to the deskilled teachers previously observed. The magnet teachers seemed uniquely qualified to offer positive examples of what "real teaching" could be. As long as pressures on them to conform to district policy remained fairly abstract, the teachers in the magnet programs could turn their energies into developing community with their colleagues and students based upon the goals of their special programs. However, as controls became more rigidly enforced, many have found that the moral support of faculty culture is inadequate to sustain their goals of "real teaching."

## EXIT, VOICE, AND LOYALTY

No simple model exists to explain the way magnet teachers are coping with standardized policies that directly conflict with their assignments to specialize. As individuals, they are reacting differently, some with humor, some with angry letters, some with a kind of withdrawal into silence. Most, however, continue to teach as they always have, altering lessons only slightly to incorporate proficiency requirements. Where whole units have to be discarded in order to give swift coverage to broad, superficial content mandated by proficiencies, the teachers are less pleased but accommodating in order not to penalize their schools' or students' scores by failing to "cover" the material. Their responses do not seem to otherwise alter their classroom treatment of students or content. Rather, they are altering their long-term calculations about what it means to teach.

Hirschman's metaphor of "exit, voice, and loyalty" may shed some light on these teachers' responses as they attempt to avoid falling into teaching patterns they distrust.[6] In this analysis of how workers can accommodate to organizational dislocations, Hirschman was interested in how organizations maintain equilibrium. Although the magnet teachers are more interested in maintaining the equilibrium of their classroom than of the overall organization, his categories of responses remind us that workers do have choices when they come to disapprove of management policies.

Hirschman sees "voice" as a political response, staying in the organization and attempting to change management policy according to one's position of leverage or one's ability to galvanize collective resistance from within. Choosing voice enables one to postpone exit (and its uncertainties for both the organization and for the person) without acquiescing into real loyalty of a position of loyal opposition.

For the magnet teachers, loyalty has been a better response because it could be directed toward the specific magnet program, their own colleagues and students, rather than to the school district, or even the school, as a whole. Within the culture of their program, loyalty to its history of specialness and uniqueness could be combined with voice, internally, in shaping the program of which one was a part. A collective sense emerged that reinforced the individuals' interpretation of what the program was supposed to be. As new standardized policies came from the district office, upsetting the program's practices, teachers within the school could accommodate to them or express collective concern to the relevant administrator. An example was the spate of rules emerging from the state's attendance laws, part of the infamous "no pass no play" legislation of the summer of 1984 (a sweeping package of legislation known as Texas House Bill 72). These academic-oriented teachers had no problem with the rules requiring athletes to pass their courses before they could play in sports; they *did* object when attendance rules became so rigidified that teachers could no longer take students away from the school building for enrichment.

To compensate for inadequate library materials, computer equipment, and other resources, magnet teachers in these high schools go to great effort to take groups of students to the public and university libraries in the area. They also take advantage of industry and medical facility invitations to visit, arrange mentorships, or to make regular use of equipment off campus. Then, the school district instituted a strict attendance policy that regulated the minutes per semester that students must attend each class. Missing a class without an illness excuse was an unexcused absence; six unexcused absences resulted in failure of the course. The state's version of these rules was aimed at stopping the practice in small towns (and some suburbs) of dismissing school early on Friday to allow students to travel to football or basketball games and of letting athletes (band members or others in ongoing school-sponsored activities) miss class whenever they had scheduled extracurricular events. The rules were aimed at the worst offenders and intended to *raise* educational quality.

For schools such as these magnets where personnel are already conscientiously involved in raising educational quality, the letter of the rules was, when enforced, counter to the spirit. Teachers soon found they had to play word games in order to continue their instructional activities. "Extracurricular" was soon joined by "co-curricular" and "curricular" as designations for trips away from school. Elementary teachers had less trouble in justifying a field trip: a trip to the beach, for example, could include a journal entry about the trip (English), identification of shells (science), a tour of a historic building (social studies), and measurement of tidal patterns (math).

Such juggling of labels and activities meant that students could miss a whole day of school without being "absent" from one subject. For high school teachers, the outside activities posed greater tests of semantics. If the government teacher wanted to take his class to the nearest university library, one hour would be needed just for the round trip; the government class period would be, in effect, used up just with travel. Staying to use the library would intrude into the students' next class, resulting in an absence. Over the course of the year, the magnet teachers learned to juggle paperwork, official category designations, semantics, and their own instructional needs. Gradually, they worked with one another and their magnet coordinators to assure at least some continuation of these very essential school-leaving activities.

As long as the standardizing pressures remained general and not tied to sanctions, the reliance on faculty culture for moral support and imagination needed to deal with them remained effective. "Voice" was exercised within the context of a program to which one was "loyal."

## EXIT

Such generalized policies eroded teacher authority over content and instructional method, but did not entirely threaten teachers' professional discretion. Collective discomforts received collective responses and some collective relief. The responses shifted as standardizations intruded more into classroom knowledge and assessment of students. The district began piloting multiple-choice proficiency exams the semester this research began; some administrators stated they hoped that the proficiency exams could come to replace teacher-made exams. This intention is now denied by personnel interviewed who had a hand in designing this evaluation system. Their expressed intent was to ensure enough uniformity across the district, so that what was called "algebra" at one school would be one of the same quality as "algebra" at a good school. The expectation was that administrators, who felt their hands to be tied in dismissing poor teachers , would have the means of identifying and documenting incompetent teachers.

The first round of tests in the major subject fields were so at odds with teacher-given final exam grades that the tests had to be revised and refined. Teachers were less concerned with the lack of match than with the many errors and eccentricities in the tests. Those teachers opposed to the tests resented the imposition of content and the pacing and treatment of content. For example, teachers who wish to present history according to issues would be forced to follow a chronology instead so that their students would have covered the same time period as other students in the city by the end of the first semester. By selecting facts (sometimes as few as forty or fifty items) amenable to a multiple-choice, Scantron-graded format, testers were reducing content to isolated pieces; teachers could not discern from the number of right answers whether students could actually work math problems or reason out governmental procedures because the test did not include essays or other means of assessing students' integration of knowledge. Teachers whose courses had included in-depth coverage, as models of inquiry, perhaps to the exclusion of covering everything in the text, found that their extra efforts at developing the material would be negatively rewarded if the proficiency test included questions on the materials left out of the lessons.

These magnet teachers, who had avoided participating in their own deskilling in response to increasing administrative controls, now find that they are being deskilled in a way that is imposed policy. Like elementary teachers who have been deskilled by the introduction of so-called teacher-proof packaged curricula, these teachers see their course goals prespecified, their tests supplied by a vendor who made up the questions after getting suggestions from various committees.

This remained a general problem until second phase of the innovation was put into place: the linking of teachers' pay levels to students' performance on these tests. In a complicated formula, a school's test scores are averaged; also, students' scores are documented teacher-by-teacher. Rewards are made on the basis of having a certain percentage of the students pass the tests. This raises serious individual and political problems.

First, if the questions trivialize the course content, then the best might result in low test scores and the most mediocre, checklist teaching might produce higher scores. Second, there is pressure to look at aggregates to such an extent that the school-within-a-school magnets are not broken out for analysis when the numbers are printed in the newspaper. Suburban schools appear to have higher pass rates than two of the highly academic school-within-a-school magnets; even though this may hamper recruiting in those magnets if parents seek programs with higher scores for their children, it protects the neighborhood school where the magnet is housed. Without averaging in the magnet students' scores, those schools would have serious problems in meeting the required pass rates.

Within this context of "losing" curriculum development and student assessment, many of the best teachers in these magnet schools are talking about leaving. A coordinator interviewed for two hours ended her enthusiastic advocacy of the teaching philosophy behind the program and of the content of the magnet specialty by saying 'I'm going to give it one more year." A teacher of an honors science course wants to bring students into the ethics ans aesthetics of scientific inquiry as well as into the facts; to date, no proficiency test exists for his course. He stated on tape, giving permission to be quoted by name, that if and when a proficiency is developed for and imposed on that course, he will quit teaching. Interestingly, he is one of several teachers who are brilliant in math and science and have come to teaching from successful jobs in industry. They love to teach but will return to industry rather than go through the motions of teaching without being able to incorporate their considerable knowledge of the field into their courses. (And students are choosing these magnets *because* of the reputations of these teachers).

Hirschman describes exit as the "economic" response, the response that calls to mind the fact that there is a market of other, competing organizations. He states that the effects of exit are almost all indirect; the changes come because of significant departures, and they may or may not be the changes intended by those leaving.

This particular state has just instituted a competency test to be taken by all current teachers if they wish to retain their certification; state agency officials estimate that failure and fear of failure will cause several thousand teachers to resign or retire. Their leaving will create an even greater teacher shortage, but will presumably be worth that shortage if it means that incompetent teachers will have been driven out of the classroom (such is the strong language used by the governor and other backers of the testing). There will be no way to gauge how many of the teachers leaving were the ones we most wanted to retain. The national reform reports call out for recruiting highly qualified teachers and for giving them more responsibility and better pay. The number of highly professional teachers who are leaving rather than be deskilled by centralized standardizations will be hidden among those who leave because of incompetence.

## FACULTY CULTURE AND COLLECTIVE ACTION

This set of case studies raises complex questions about faculty culture. As we have moved from a view of faculty culture as an organizational component to be "managed" to a view of faculty culture as evidence of participation in shaping the informal and even formal working of organizations, the tendency is to equate faculty culture with benign qualities. Indeeds, the first year of data collection of this study seemed to indicate that the kind of faculty culture that emerges in magnet schools would be sufficient to buffer teachers from deskilling, from pressures to teach to minimum standards, and from cycles of low expectations of teaching and learning. The support of a cohesive identification with program content and quality, and kindred fellow workers, did provide a kind of empowerment for these committed teachers.

However, as policies came down to the individual teacher classroom, faculty culture could not overcome vulnerabilities. There is beyond the individual magnet faculty cultures in this district a broader culture of fear. The extremely strong central administration, dominated by an influential superintendent and his usually supportive board, is built on a view of teachers as workers to be managed rather than as fellow professionals with which to work. As one teacher said of his principal, "he thinks he has a bunch of incompetents working for him." Badly needed reform policies have failed to distinguish between those teachers who are incompetent and those who should be supported, rewarded, and encouraged to stay in teaching.

Within this negative climate teachers feel very vulnerable. Although union membership is rapidly growing since the development of these new policies, collective bargaining is not allowed for public employees in this state, and their union has not been a persuasive voice because of its historical marginality to school policy. Each teacher is on an individual appointment; although administrators speak of the difficulty of getting rid of "bad" teachers, the same former administrator who made that case in an interview responded to my curiosity about teachers' fears by almost shouting. "They *should* feel vulnerable; they *are!*" To exercise voice on major policies might cause one to lose one's assignment at a good school, to be docked pay or evaluated with negative marks on the checklist, or to be fired or hassled into leaving.

Faculty culture alone is not strong enough, at least in these schools, to overcome the vulnerabilities teachers feel. Faculty culture should be seen neither as a tool of management (although management does benefit from favorable public relations generated about the magnet schools because of these teachers' efforts) nor as a panacea for ameliorating teachers' working conditions. Research on faculty culture shows it to be problematic, capable of reinforcing the best among our teachers, but only when the imposition of deprofessionalizing policies does not limit their choices to leaving the profession or giving up on "real teaching."

The actual number of magnet teachers leaving this district or leaving the profession will not be known until the end of the current school year. Those who have said that they are leaving include an exemplary history teacher; a history and English teacher who regularly spends his own money buying paperbacks for his class and taking his students all over town to take advantage of libraries, theaters, and other cultural events; two science teachers recruited from industry; a magnet coordinator; an excellent French teacher; a nationally acclaimed debate coach; and a chemistry teacher (who left at midterm). And there are others. Having selected magnet schools as examples of positive models of teaching and learning, I have stayed in them long enough to watch their fragility under siege. Some other teachers have noted that the superintendent has announced his retirement; they are waiting to see if the new superintendent will have a more favorable view of teacher professionalism. Others note that these reforms, while local in their specific characteristics, are in fact, part of a national trend, especially as other states rush to emulate this one in instituting reforms. They are not sure that a change in prsonnel is all that is needed. They are more likely to wish for a change in the language of assessment, a change in the focus from tests whose scores may make good newspaper copy but whose numbers miss what goes on in schools. If they have to wait too long, we will lose them.

## EXIT, VOICE, AND POLICY

The specific situation of these magnet teachers, with their unique magnet programs and course specialties, serves as a model for examining the broader population of public school teachers. The emergent faculty cultures of which they are a part show the teachers to be active shapers of their professional roles and of their work place and program. The reforms adopted by their district and state see them to be the objects of reform rather than the active shapers; their performance is "evaluated" by checklists of uniform behaviors and instructional vocabulary; their students are "evaluated" by tests designed and scored by personnel distant from their classrooms. Their time with their students is increasingly restricted by regulations disembodied from concern for content or attention to particular students (or groups of them). The reforms are predicated on the assumption that the "problems" of American education are "problem" teachers. The concept of teachers as workers to be managed more efficiently gives educational policymakers one handle on school reform: "improving teaching."

The Hirschman model of employee response to institutional problems allows us to shift the conception of teacher back to subject, to actor, to participant. A teacher may exert voice, may exit, may foster community and a collective response to policy.

In a sense, these are "best case" teachers. Although their school facilities are often far from adequate and their pay modest, these people exemplify that segment of our teachers who have helped build programs, who have been specifically recruited to them, who are competent and committed. They have chosen to be in schools trying, however awkwardly, to affirm equity and excellence at the same time, without having to sacrifice one for the other. The real "crisis in teaching" may not be that they do not always succeed, but that reforms which objectify them, which relegate them to a status of workers to be managed, may make it impossible for them to succeed at all.

Generic management policies that reduce all professional practice to lowest common levels will not produce inspired teaching. In the Midwestern schools described in *Contradictions of Control,* such policies (although milder by far than those in the current case study) made teachers feel the devaluing of their efforts. In response, they split their personal knowledge from their classroom knowledge and succeeded in distancing not only themselves but their students from significant, complex course content. The magnet teachers have been able to coalesce around collective faculty cultures that affirm engaged teaching, preventing the kind of deskilling which results in going through the motions of teaching without putting one's knowledge of the subject and of the students at risk in the classroom. As controls become tighter, originate at greater distances from classrooms, and leave less room for personal and collective discretion, the magnet teachers are likely to choose exit over voice or participatory deskilling. As our "best" teachers, they will not be willing to subordinate their vision of teaching to the efficiencies of standardized assessments. Their faculty cultures have demonstrated their resilience and resourcefulness as active shapers of their teaching environment. To reduce them to objects of universal reform rather than tap this resourcefulness is not a failure of teaching but of management. Those who make and implement educational policy, especially policy reforms, do not need lists of official praise words but serious examination of the ways such policies become a part of the causes behind the crisis in teaching. And those teachers and researchers who view "faculty culture" as an unquestionably benign factor in ameliorating teacher workplace conditions need to examine very seriously the relation of faculty culture to issues of power and policy in that workplace. Generic management can succeed when teachers withdraw into comfortable "cultures" just as when they memorize the praise words just before the principal's assessment visit.

## NOTES

A slightly different version of this paper was presented at the symposium "Faculty Culture in Public Schools: Its Sources and Outside the School" of the Annual Meetings of the American Educational Research Association (San Francisco, April 1986).

1. Case study data cited are drawn from a two-year study of magnet high schools as examples of schools whose educational quality is related to formal, structural support at the district level. An ethnography of classroom processes and an analysis of school organization, this research included extensive classroom observations (a minimum of one semester in each school); interviews with students, teachers, and administrators; and archival and documentary investigation into school histories and policy. The study was conducted in a large urban district whose student population included more than 100 home languages, whose anglo population of students averaged approximately 20 percent during the course of the research, and whose magnets were primarily a response to a court-ordered plan for the hispanic-black-anglo dominant population groups. The magnets are primarily based on career specialties, including fine arts, scientific and engineering fields, medical and law enforcement specialties and petrochemicals. A magnet based on a pedagogy rather than a career topic is the high school for gifted and talented. The research was funded by a grant from the National Institute of Education (NIE); research results and interpretations reflect the ideas of the author and not NIE or Rice University.

2. An ethnography of the administrative contexts of students' access to knowledge in classrooms, as reported in Linda M. McNeil, *Contradictions of Control: School Structure and School Knowledge* (New York and London: Routledge and Kegan Paul, 1986); and Linda M. McNeil, "Defensive Teaching and Classroom Control," in *Ideology and Practice in Schooling,* Michael W. Apple and Lois Weis, eds. (Philadelphia: Temple University Press, 1984), pp. 114–42.

3. Mary Haywood Metz, University of Wisconsin-Madison (personal interview, 1985).

4. Linda M. McNeil, "Defensive Teaching and Classroom Control." See also Linda M. McNeil, "Empowering Students: Beyond Defensive Teaching in Social Studies," a paper presented at AERA (San Francisco, 1986).

5. See McNeil, "Empowering Students: Beyond Defensive Teaching in Social Studies" for a discussion of ways these magnet teachers bring students into active learning.

6. A. O. Hirschman, *Exit, Voice and Loyalty: Responses to Decline in Organizations and States* (Cambridge, Mass.: Harvard University Press, 1970).

ANDREW GITLIN AND ROBERT BULLOUGH JR.

Chapter Eleven

# Teacher Evaluation and Empowerment: Challenging the Taken-For-Granted View of Teaching

## INTRODUCTION

Teacher evaluation is widely understood as a means for improving teaching. Most schemes focus on developing a set of teacher behaviors thought to enhance student test scores. Implicitly, the view of teaching communicated by such schemes imparts the view that teaching is synonymous with instructing—to teach is to dish out content in palatable bits to young people. In this view, teaching is concerned primarily with the technical means by which to disseminate information. The way teachers understand their work, or whether they recognize the ethical political implications of their decisions, matters little. What is important is behavioral change; teachers need to demonstrate proper technique. Within this framework, teacher evaluation is not likely to lead to basic reform of teaching practices; rather, it tends to confirm and reproduce current school roles and relations, those very roles, and relations that may be most in need of change. For those interested in school transformation, this is a troubling realization. Clearly, it is time to rethink teacher evaluation in the light of what we believe to be the proper professional role of teachers within American public schools.

In this paper we will: (1) critique the dominant forms of teacher evaluation in terms of their assumptions about teaching and teacher empowerment; (2) propose an alternative model of evaluation—horizontal evaluation—that attempts to go beyond technical views of teaching by placing teachers in the center of the evaluation process; and (3) present results of a recent study suggesting that given the necessary analytic tools, teachers can effectively evaluate other teachers and will come to see evaluation differently, as an essential part of the role of teacher and one with political and ethical considerations.

## DOMINANT MODES OF TEACHER EVALUATION

### Administrative Supervision

The most common form of teacher evaluation, administrative supervision, is a key component of several of the current school reform efforts, including competency-based teacher education, many teacher effectiveness programs, and career ladder and merit pay programs. The aim of administrative supervision is to change teacher behavior in ways congruent with what experts have determined to be good teaching. Reflecting its historical roots in scientific management, administrative supervision emphasizes efficiency quality control, and inspection (Smyth, 1984). Occasionally, teachers may be given a voice in goal setting, but, for the most part, the challenge is for them to meet pre-established organizational goals that tend to be concerned with issues of immediacy and practicality.

The purpose and structure of administrative evaluation are well illustrated by the Florida Performance Measurement System (FPMS) (Smith, 1984). FPMS encourages teachers to master "121 specific teacher behaviors that have been shown through research to be directly related to increased student achievement and improved classroom conduct"(Smith, 1984, p. 1). Thus, a good teacher is one who demonstrates all 121 behaviors, regardless of teaching context or differences in personality, interest, or ability.

To achieve this purpose, a rating scale has been developed that focuses only on the "presence or absence" of the desired behaviors (Smith, 1984, p. 2–3). Whether a teacher works in an innercity school or a wealthy suburb does not matter. Ostensibly, the observer doing the rating is merely collecting data; the only judgment required "is at the level of whether a particular teacher behavior fits an item on the instrument," (p. ii) such as handling materials in an orderly manner or giving specific academic praise. The more tally marks, the better the teacher.[2]

FPMS may be effective in changing teacher behavior. Nevertheless, it is troubling on several accounts. First, at a time when teachers are being called upon to take a more active role in school reform and to become more professional, the effect of the evaluation process reinforces hierarchical distinictions between the developers of FPMS and teachers. Administrative evaluation keeps teachers dependent on others to determine what they should be doing in the classroom; at the same time, teachers are being held responsible for many of the shortcomings of American schooling. Moreover, evaluation is viewed as something outside the realm of teaching. The emphasis is on value neutrality, on tallying marks, when the important objective is evaluating teachers' inderstanding of what they are doing and why they are doing it. This is essential to improve the quality of educational experiences offered to young people. Furthermore, the focus on technical skills connected, however tenuously, to standardized test scores obscures the ineluctable link between teaching and ethics; knowingly or not, teachers' actions either enhance or impede progress toward a just society. Some teacher actions may be defensible on the grounds of efficiency, even while being morally repugnant.

## Peer Evaluation

As the name suggests, peer evaluation is not inherently hierarchical; generally, teaching is understood to include peer evaluation. Unfortunately, the potential of peer evaluation schemes to empower teachers by involving them in the evaluation process is often not realized. Furthermore, even when teachers are placed at the center, the assumption is still that evaluation should focus only on technical skills. These points are well-illustrated by the peer evaluation system developed by the Kalamazoo Public Schools. The program strived to make teachers accountable. Like FPMS, teachers were evaluated on the basis of a rating scale of good teaching behaviors developed by administrators.[3] Teachers were supposed to use the scale on other teachers. Thus, the only significant difference between FPMS and the Kalamazoo program was that teachers replaced administrators as raters. While teachers are apparently in control of evaluation, in reality, the values placed upon teacher actions are set by others—those who created the scale. Moreover, because the scale emphasizes techniques such as classroom control and organization, the operational definition of good teaching excludes ethnical and political considerations.

Much the same can be said for the peer evaluation system advocated by Van Hoven[4] in which tenured teachers evaluated nontenured teachers. While the stated aim is teacher development, the process is inherently hierarchical. Nontenured teachers are very likely to find themselves in an untenable position: because of the fear of negative tenure and retention judgments, they must conform to the wishes of the tenured teachers regardless of whether they agree with them. Once again, contrary to its stated arms, peer evaluation, in effect underscores teacher compliance with current standards.

## Clinical Supervision

Initially, clinical supervision appears to avoid many of the pitfalls of other peer evaluation schemes. Minimally, it places the teacher at the center of the evaluation process while attempting to "enhance the learner's self-sufficiency and freedom to act . . . [and] increase teachers' incentives and skills for self-supervision and for supervising their professional colleagues." The claim is, therefore, that clinical supervision is a further means for empowering teachers. To achieve this aim, clinical supervision has a five-stage structure: preobservation conference, observation, analysis and strategy, supervision conference, and post conference analysis. The preobservation conference is a time for supervisor and teacher to develop rapport. In the observation stage, "instead of recording general descriptions, the observer should get the stuff down verbatim . . . and as objective an account of nonverbal behavior as he [or she] can manage." During the analysis and strategy stage, the supervisor attempts to make "sense out of the observational data." To do so, the supervisor looks for demonstrable patterns in the data. In the supervision conference, the supervisor tries, among other things, to identify problems and issues that are treatable, to make explicit issues that have been sensed intuitively, to help the teachers develop techniques of self-supervision, and to consider the teachers' vocational satisfaction and technical competency. The final stage, the postconference analysis, assesses whether supervision is productive and considers modifications for supervisory practice.[5]

In many ways the nonhierarchical structure and purpose of clinical supervision seems well-suited to a more professional conception of teaching. However, as McFaul and Cooper report, when peer teachers used the clinical supervision model, discussion centered on the "tricks of the trade."[6] They argue that constrained school conditions such as teacher isolation, a standardized curriculum, and the reactive nature of teacher decisionmaking, caused teachers to focus on technical questions of what they could effect in the classroom. In short, the commonsense view of teaching as instructing went unchallenged. Those who tenaciously hold to a different view, that clinical supervision can make a difference in how teachers understand their work, argue that these constrained work conditions can be changed if the model is used in ways that reflect its original purpose. Smyth for example, asserts that those who claim:

> peer clinical supervision is unworkable because of the less than optimal conditions in schools, become entrapped in the helpful self-fulfilling prophecy that schools will remain the way they are, because of the way they are! I . . . claim that if ownership and control of clinical supervision is genuinely invested in teachers, then they have the self-critical capacities to ultimately transcend the technical aspects of their teaching, and begin to use it to raise larger questions about the "ends" of teaching and the institutional frameworks and structures within which it occurs.[7]

From Smyth's point of view, nothing is fundamentally wrong with the model—only with its use.

Advocates of clinical supervision seem caught in a vicious circle in which school conditions limit the use of the model, which makes it unlikely that debilitating school conditions will be confronted. The model itself, however, may not have enough built-in safeguards to avoid being confined to a narrow technical view of teaching and evaluation. Indeed, clinical supervision encourages a technical focus through its emphasis on objective observation, the need for supervisors to find patterns whose consequences are *demonstrable* in the data, and the stated priority of the supervision conference to leave the teacher with something concrete and treatable. In addition, no explicit method exists for analyzing technical concerns in relation to values and aims. Thus, while the model has some promising elements, it has had limited success in challenging taken-for-granted views of teaching as merely instructing.

In summary, most teacher evaluation schemes help reproduce a view of teaching as a technical enterprise little concerned with the broader aims of education. They reinforce hierarchical structures and give comparatively little power to teachers within the workplace. Moreover, they foster a view of evaluation as distinct from teaching and as being the peculiar realm of experts. Given these weaknesses, such schemes are not likely to lead to transformation of teacher roles or relations.

## THE HORIZONTAL METHOD

Horizontal evaluation was developed, in part, as a corrective to the flaws of other evaluation schemes.[8] It has three unique features: (1) In contrast to other methods where teachers have little if any control over the evaluation process, in horizontal evaluation, the teacher being evaluated helps set the agenda for the postconference analysis. (2) While most evaluation schemes determine teacher quality by referring to process/product research findings that reflect a technical view of good teaching, horizontal evaluation establishes appropriateness by examining the values that underlie a particular action, decision, or speech act. And, (3) while most evaluation models focus exclusively on the techniques of teaching—means—horizontal evaluation focuses on the relationship of means to ends, thereby encompassing the political-ethical aspects of teaching. To further clarify these aspects of horizontal evaluation further, a description of the model, and the methods it uses to structure peer dialogue follows.

*Intention and Practice*

Dialogue structured by the horizontal method often begins by considering the teacher's intentions or purposes. For example, a teacher might state that his or her intention is to get all students to obey the rule, "raise your hand before speaking." An observer might then ask why that rule is important and what its purpose is? The question attempts to bring forth the implicit values the teacher holds—values that will be used as grounds for establishing appropriateness. These values reflect the prejudgements embedded in teachers' purposes and must be made explicit.

Whether intentions are stated in advance or emerge from dialogue, they should not be viewed as reified concepts that, once determined, guide practice forevermore. Rather, means and ends should be viewed fluidly, as everchanging in the light of new data. The goal is to see aims and means reflexively, as part of a reciprocal process.

Intentions ←                    →Practice

The discovery of discrepancies between means and ends often results in the modification of intention or practice or both. Where intentions and practice are congruent, practice and/or intentions are reinforced. But, congruence is not assumed to be beneficial prima facie. Congruence is only deemed desirable if the assumptions underlying both practice and intention, once exposed and critically assessed are found to be appropriate. To make the discussion of assumptions more likely, horizontal evaluation provides specific analytic tools, as illustrated below, including communication analysis, historical perspective, and alternatives for achieving desired aims.

Alternative Methods

Intentions ←                    →Practice

Communication Analysis     Historical Perspective

*Communication Analysis*

Communication analysis refers specifically to a process that aims at uncovering prejudgments reflected in speech acts. One relevant model for guiding analysis of speech acts is Habermas's "Universal Pragmatics."[9] Habermas has identified four validity claims present in all speech acts: comprehensibility, truth, sincerity, and appropriateness. These four claims help us identify and clarify the underlying prejudgments embedded in what we say and do and help direct their critical assessment. All four claims are always present, explicitly or implicitly, in any communication act; however, all four need not be raised for each sentence or utterance being analyzed. It is often sufficient to work with one claim while being aware of the others. In practice, the direction of the discussion will suggest which claims need to be raised.

As applied to the horizontal evaluation model, the first claim—comprehensibility—would simply consider whether the teacher's statement is understandable. Often, language is ambiguous or meaningless; the language of educators is sometimes intentionally obfuscating. While this claim is obviously important, it is something that would normally occur in conversation where the aim is to understand: "Did you say that you thought the students' behavior was determined by the fact that they are in the low group?"

Applying the second, or truth claim, to a statement such as, "The students behaved as they did because they are in the low group," is a bit more involved. The main point is to discover whether the statement is a true description of the situation and of those involved. To clarify this issue, the teacher could, for example, raise a series of questions about the accuracy of describing this group as low. Further questions might focus on the link between being in a low group and behaving in a particular way, and on the extent to which behavior is caused by being a member of the group of because or other factors. One can see the richness and variety that might come from a careful consideration of what can be agreed upon as the "facts" of the situation.

Statements that appear obvious must be discussed to explicate their meaning; this highlights the importance of Habermas's sincerity validity claim. If the observer and the teacher are to understand the statements, establishing the truthfulness of the claim is necessary. Both must ask themselves and be willing to be questioned by the other about whether they are stating actual perceptions and feelings. What is the purpose of the statement? Is it strategic—to secure the desires of the speaker—or a clear comment about perception and feelings? One step in the clarification process is to grasp the way our interests and values color our views of seeming reality. Of concern here are the preunderstandings that we have acquired from living in society and working within schools. For example, categorizing groups of students as "high" or "low" may occur because the signficance of such labels is never considered; they are simply accepted as having obvious meanings. Habermas's formulation emphasizes what we intuitively know—that our prejudices and values influence what we see happening in teaching. Thus, what I truthfully utter indicates both my understanding and that which I accept without reflection. A way of getting at this is by examining the feelings we hold about the categorizations we use in our sincere statements to organize the social world. Our talk may even disclose tensions or discrepancies between our feelings and understandings and the way we communicate them. Through this type of analysis, teachers can lay hold of the systematic distortions built into their utterances.

The final validity claim—appropriateness or labelling justifiable or right?—helps in separating what *is* from what *ought to be.* At this point, teachers must place a value on their actions and offer reasonable justification. This claim can be discussed in at least two ways. First, is the labelling in accordance with the purposes and norms of the institution? And, second, can the institutional norms be supported by reasons that we mutually agree are right? Inherent in these questions is the belief that teaching is a moral activity about which ethical judgments are inevitably made. The concerns of the teacher can no longer be merely technical—Did I reach my objective?—but must also concern the justifications—the reasons why—of both intentions and the means used to reach them.

## Historical Perspective

To broaden and contextualize the critical assessment of teaching, horizontal evaluation encourages participants to use the historical perspective method. This method encourages teachers to make judgments about their teaching in the light of their understanding of the influence of past events on current practice. While communication analysis can explicate and assess the normative values that inform practice, the historical perspective clarifies further the way values have been established.

If, for example, the teacher is working in an open classroom, comparison of past and current forms, as well as the assessment of the social context within which they developed, may help her see her own actions and understandings as influenced by larger societal and professional developments, which themselves must be scrutinized.

Finding the roots of our understandings through historical perspective also takes teachers into a consideration of their biographies. A decision, for instance, to make students stay in for recess may very well be grounded in the teacher's own experience of schooling while a student. The key is to identify the general themes that shape classroom life in order for teachers to assess more accurately the appropriateness of their actions, such as keeping in students for recess.

## Alternative Methods

The concern of many evaluation schemes is to help teachers identify alternative practices, techniques that "work." The suggestion of alternatives—of other ways of understanding a situation and of behaving—is also part of horizontal evaluation. The purpose is to illuminate the educational implications of taking a different approach—not simply to change behavior. For example, if the teacher is conducting a large group discussion, the observer might suggest that the class be broken into small groups. One reason for making this suggestion would be because the observer believes it better-suited to achieving the teacher's aim. The more important reason, however, is to help both participants consider the educational possibilities inherent in a given situation and to help them make decisions based upon a critical understanding of the values reflected in particular choices.

## Challenge Statements

In addition to the above-mentioned, horizontal evaluation suggests using a series of challenge statements the purpose of which, as illustrated below, is to make certain that dialogue goes beyond the simple clarification of values and prejudgments to the point where issues of appropriateness or rightness can be raised in relation to a mutually recognized normative framework. Is an action or understanding right or appropriate?

Challenge Statement*

Intention ←       →Practice

Consideration of What is Appropriate

*Challenges may be issued by the observer or observed teacher.

For example, if a teacher wants students to obey his or her classroom rules in all circumstances, the observer could raise questions about student and teacher rights or perhaps about the kind of adult authority called for in a democracy. The challenge issued concerns the type of teacher-student relations desired in the classroom and demands justification based upon an articulated normative framework.

Like all horizontal methods, challenge statements are not only initiated by the observer but also by the observed teacher, who should also challenge the evaluation process itself—especially when peer relations are in danger of giving way to hierarchy. A challenge to an emerging expert-practitioner relationship, one reminiscent of administrative supervision, is a call to remember the purposes of horizontal evaluation. Furthermore, challenge statements should reach beyond the classroom context and reflect the interests of others in the educational community. Otherwise, conversation may become distorted if it emanates from a narrow perspective that does not include the diversity of interests that have a stake in schooling.

## THE STUDY

*Methodology*

*Participants.* Twelve of sixteen elementary teachers in an "extended learning" program, Horizons, volunteered to participate in this study. The teachers formed six dyads of their own choosing. Four groups completed the study; two dropped out because of other professional commitments. All of the teachers were female, with between three and fifteen years' teaching experience and an interest in understanding their work better. This group of teachers differed from most others in that they traveled among schools to meet particular gifted and talented student needs, although their overall class size and work load was similar to that of most other teachers in the district.

*Procedure.* In October 1984, participants received four hours of training in horizontal evaluation from the research team. The training consisted of describing methods for conducting postobservation conferences, role-playing using the techniques, and watching a videotape of peer teachers using the horizontal model. After training, the teachers participated in a trial observation and conference in which they used the methods. In order to give feedback to each dyad about the use of horizontal evaluation methods, their trial postobservation conference was audiotaped and discussed.

During the study, each team was asked to conduct two observations and two follow-up conferences (one for each member of the dyad) per month for five months, for a total of ten observations and conferences per dyad. Most dyads followed this plan with only minor variations. The conferences were audiotaped and later transcribed for analysis. The research team was not present in any way.

At the conclusion of the observation/conference period, the twelve participants were interviewed by a member of the research team. A structured interview format was used, which gathered information about the effect of the horizontal evaluation experience on participants' teaching goals, attitudes about evaluation, and the way they viewed their role as teacher.[10]

*Data Analysis.* Audiotape transcriptions of all postobservation conferences were first analyzed by the authors in order to develop categories for data reduction. Three research assistants were then trained to code statements in the transcriptions by category. If a statement did not fit into a category, it was labelled with a question mark; if, on the other hand, it fit two or more categories, it was coded for each. After the training period, the research assistants coded the transcripts independently and then compared results and resolved discrepancies by consensus. The authors then grouped the data by category and compared the frequency of types of statements within and across dyads. The quotes used in this study represent categories with the highest frequency of statements. The transcribed interviews were analyzed by the research team, which came to a consensus on the teachers' dominant positions during the structured interview.

*Limitations.* It is important to note that the limited sample size and type of teachers used in the study make generalizations about the impact of horizontal evaluation impossible. Our intention is to suggest the potential of the model in the hope that additional research will be undertaken to determine its implications for teachers working in other settings.

## DISCUSSION

Analysis of postobservation conference and interview transcripts indicated that three of the four dyads successfully used horizontal evaluation. These dyads evaluated teaching techniques in relation to their articulated ends; they also considered the appropriateness of those ends. Moreover, in the process, understanding of teaching was altered and expanded. Through the horizontal evaluation methods they challenged the perception that teachers are or should be dependent on others for the determination of teaching aims and for evaluation. One dyad, however, stands in stark contrast. This dyad focused only on technical issues and persisted in viewing evaluation as a hierarchical process, something done to teachers by experts.

To understand why horizontal evaluation might be used effectively by some pairs, but not by others, we compared the three dyads empowered by the process to the one that was not. This comparison revealed significant differences in the type and quality of teacher relations obtained through the peer evaluation process. These differences have great bearing on whether peer evaluation is reproductive or transformative. In the sections that follow, we describe the nature of teacher relations and the impact of horizontal evaluation on the commonsense notion of teaching for the three successful dyads and for the dyad that failed to challenge the reproductive influence of evaluation on teaching.

### Successful Use of Horizontal Evaluation: Teacher Relations

When employed properly, horizontal evaluation changed and improved the nature of teacher relations. The most obvious influence was that it softened teacher isolation.

> I think it's [horizontal evaluation] a real important thing for teachers to do with one another. In our position we are terribly isolated . . . and I think that just that sense of trying to find out ways to solve the same problems so that you're not recreating a wheel all the time helps. It's real neat to see that other people are going through the same kinds of issues. And, when you're working with one another you see ways to find solutions that you might not have thought about alone.

Moreover, horizontal evaluation did more than get teachers together to chat; it also gave them the opportunity and means by which to critically consider practice in relationship to their stated intentions.

> "Helen [was able] to point out little holes in my . . . stated intents, [and give me ways of seeing] what I did and how I might evaluate my work. So, . . . I would like that to be an ongoing thing, and I hate for it to stop now."

Some teachers were openly self-critical. One, for example, questioned her contribution to the evaluation process; she doubted her ability to analyze teaching and to give meaningful feedback.

I don't feel like I did a real good job. I feel like it was just a beginning, and that I would like to keep working at it. I think the more I did it, the better I would get at looking at things and being able to track down what's going on and then, being able to share that with another person.

Through sharing perceptions and critically assessing practice non-defensively, the teachers developed a strong sense of collegiality characterized by a clear recognition of weaknesses tempered by an even stronger sense of personal and professional strengths. Teacher collegiality is well-illustrated by one interaction: "I was learning so much when I was [watching] you. It's great." Her partner responded by saying:

I feel the same way about you. It looks much easier when you watch someone else do it. Like when I was watching you do it, I thought, 'How's she doing all this? How's she tap dancing with all those kids around and how's she handling it so well?' I think, 'Do I do that same thing?' The constant comparing [of my performance to yours] is good for me . . . it makes me think, 'How am I in this area?' It's nice to sit down and watch someone else go through it. I learned a lot today.

The development of collegiality appears to be a necessary condition for teachers to transform their technical understanding of teacher role. First, the teachers in the successful dyads were more able to make judgments about one another openly and honestly which, in turn, were attended to seriously. Second, collegiality enabled teachers to be self-critical, to reveal doubts and problems otherwise hidden from view. They discovered, in the process, that usually what troubled them also troubled others. In this way, as will be clearly seen in the sections that follow, they began to understand teaching and evaluation differently.

*Successful Use of Horizontal Evaluation: Challenging the Common View of Teaching*

By using horizontal evaluation, the teachers in the successful dyads began to question the common view of teaching as a technical activity. Instead of assessing the way a particular technique fulfilled an assumed aim, the teachers analyzed aims and means reflexively. Aims and means were changed after being subjected to careful scrutiny. Moreover, the horizontal evaluation process encouraged the teachers to consider the moral and political values underlying intentions and practice and to make changes based upon consideration of the rightness of such values. In the two sections that follow, we describe the results of the teachers' analyses of aims and of the relationship of aims and means.

*Analysis of the Relationship of Aims and Means.* Examples of teachers engaging in ends-means analysis are abundant. In one conference, for example, the observing teacher asked a question about the tests, project reports, and writing samples being used. Traditional evaluation schemes would most likely consider the validity of these student assessment devices and whether they are used as intended. The observing teacher, however, asked a prior question: can using these testing procedures be justified in terms of an agreed-upon aim for the lesson and unit being taught? In asking this question, the observing teacher noted a contradiction between an implicit and explicit aim: "I think," she said, "sometimes we have a disparity between wanting students to get material and our intention to teach [cognitive] prosesses . . . It's certainly a dilemma." The discussion that followed centered on the conflict between the aim to develop cognitive processes and an assignment focusing on student product, suggested by the use of various testing instruments. Both teachers had been unaware of this tension, but once revealed, changes could be made based upon the values inherent in the desired cognitive process approach.

In another conference, the observed teacher noted that no student answered the question "about what problems might [exist] if you have smaller children in the house with [clothing] hangers." The observer posed a challenge to the teacher by commenting that "the students probably didn't respond because the teacher was fishing for the right answer." This challenge prompted the observed teacher to reflect on the way her questioning related to her stated intention of having open-ended discussions where ideas can be related in safety. Realizing that she had undermined her own intention, she commented that students "must pick up on the fact that even though I'm having an open-ended discussion, in all the openess there is a right answer." By analyzing questioning in this way the conversation went beyond technical considerations—how to ask better questions—to consider the appropriateness of the form of questioning. In this way, the teachers revealed a taken-for-granted aspect of the role of teacher, where teachers know right answers and deliver them to students.

Relating means to ends also lead to the discovery of other unintended teaching outcomes. One case revealed that the teacher was inadvertently helping recreate inequality. The observer noted that, "In terms of your intents, the first one [to make students feel worthwhile], you do that really nicely with the verbal kids." While this comment was supportive, it also raised a serious ethical issue. The observed teacher took the hint and asked, "But not with the nonverbal kids?" The discussion that followed revealed that the observed teacher focused attention on the verbal students, who were almost all boys. By analyzing the situation together, a previously hidden practice became apparent, which could then be judged as to its rightness.

At other times, the analysis of intentions and practice threw into doubt commonplace teacher decisions. In the elementary grades, teachers typically assign seats so that the boys sit on one side of the room while the girls sit on the other. Usually, this arrangement is not questioned. When it is questioned, the issue usually raised is whether it encourages misbehavior: A quiet classroom is assumed to be a good classroom. The observer wondered about this practice noting that "there are boys over here and girls over there." Together the teachers then began to explore the issue in relation to the teacher's stated intention for the lesson: to have all students interact and respond to others' comments. Analysis quickly revealed that dividing the class according to gender made interaction between boys and girls difficult. Once the importance of boy/girl interaction was established, recommendations were then made in keeping with the teachers' agreed-upon standard of rightness. In this case, the observer suggested that "you could just sit with a group [of students] in a circle." Through analysis of the decision, deep-seated and unexamined educational values were revealed and changed.

The analysis of the relationship of aims to means frequently touched upon issues beyond the immediate concern of the classroom teacher. For example, several discussions centred on the rightness of the procedures for admission into the Horizons program. Students were selected into the program through teacher recommendations and high standardized achievement test scores. One teacher commented that this procedure constrained her aim "to encourage the abilities of all children in a sort of even-handed way because I can't take as many girls for math because they don't seem to have the interest or the motivation in that area." Analyzing the values inherent in the admission procedures lead to frustration but also renewed dedication to "try to encourage a girl ... when I do have one in class."

*Analysis of Ends.* In order to assess the appropriateness of education aims, teachers used communication analysis, historical perspectives, and challenge statements. Program goals and the value of teacher control were most often addressed.

Extended learning programs typically claim the development of higher-order thinking skills as their most cherished goal. Horizon teachers were no different. Normally, evaluation focuses on a teacher's ability to develop these skills, which is important, but only partially adequate where the aim is to transform instruction. Using horizontal evaluation, the teachers not only assessed their skill in meeting this goal but subjected the goal itself to scrutiny. They wanted to know what higher-level thinking skills were and whether the aim is a desirable one. For example, in one conference, the teacher used communication analysis to explore the meaning of "higher-level thinking": "If we consider knowledge and comprehension lower-level thinking... It seems so easy to define higher-level thinking skills by using Bloom's Taxonomy. But for me, it's just getting beyond the memorization and regurgitation of knowledge." The observer responded: "In that sense, just making choices, even though you don't go through a long, involved process of using criteria and why is it that you chose this, would be a high level." The teachers did not agree on exactly what higher-level thinking skills are but, by trying to clarify their meaning, they had taken an important step toward evaluating the central program aim.

Teachers are generally concerned about class control. Usually, evaluation is concerned with whether a teacher can maintain control. The teachers in the study shared this concern, but also, through using horizontal evaluation methods, subjected it to analysis: They wanted to know what kind of control was being exerted, how it was being exerted, and whether what was being done was right. One teacher, for example, noted that the observed teacher referred to herself in the third person, "you refer to yourself as Mrs. T., rather than saying 'I'. Were you aware of that?" The peer teacher said that she was not, and wondered if it were the result of being a mother. The observer agreed, but challenged the teacher by noting that "it also removes you one step from [the students]; it's real subtle." By exploring the use of language, the observed teacher was able to consider the way distancing herself may be an attempt to increase her control over students. Clearly, this is a realization she would not have made by herself. "I can't believe that [I refer to myself in the third person]. This is why the process [horizontal evaluation] is so beautiful because I would never have picked up on doing that." Once the teacher better understood the subtle way in which she was exerting control over students, discussion then shifted to considering the desirability of gaining student compliance by distancing oneself from students.

The method of historical perspective was also used to shed light on the issue of teacher control. With respect to the issue one teacher commented,

> I have to say that only thing I felt uncomfortable about is I come from an educational system, the Catholic school, where the teacher was in control. When I have independent study going on like that and I don't know what everyone is doing, I get nervous wondering if people are wasting time . . .

After considering the way she had been socialized into believing that teacher control over all classroom interaction is an essential part of the teacher role, she assessed the appropriateness of this aim within her own classroom. While considering the issue, the observer reassured her that "when you left the room they were working very well independently." Although this teacher did not change her view that a teacher must be in control at all times, she was less certain that this ability was a universal characteristic of a good teacher: "Maybe I have to give them credit for being able to work [independently]."

In contrast to most of the more widely used teacher evaluation schemes, the successful use of horizontal evaluation helps teachers to confront the common view of teaching. Three of the four dyads came to see teaching more broadly. Teaching is more than a technical activity; it is an ethical, political act that includes the right and responsibility of teachers to engage in evaluation.

## Reproducing the Common View of Teaching: The Failed Dyad

One dyad failed to develop collegial relations or to challenge the notion that teaching is synonymous with instructing. This dyad bears careful analysis for what it can teach us not only about the way to use the horizontal evaluation model more effectively but, more importantly, about the strength of the common view of teaching.

The first conference of the failed dyad began by the observer mechanically assessing the goals stated by her partner.

> In meeting each one of your goals I just gave you a rating . . . on your first long-term objective, which was to foster joy of learning, I gave you a *superior*. On your second long-term objective, which was to expose students to ideas they might not meet elsewhere, I gave you *excellent*. On mere passive acceptance of information, I gave you a *superior*.

When the roles were reversed, her partner followed the same procedure: objectives were listed, and quick assessments made.

Despite their training in the use of horizontal evaluation, these teachers assumed positions of experts; hierarchy was imposed on the process from the beginning. And, pleasing the expert or hiding or explaining away failure became the task of the observed teacher. Penny's feedback to Samantha is typical: "I was very pleased to see how you were in commending [students]"; at another time she said, "I was so pleased at the way you were having them interpret the pictures." Apparently, if Penny was pleased, then Samantha was doing a good job. On her part, Penny kept Samantha from viewing a risky lesson: "Some days are better than others, that's why I'm not letting you see me on Thursday." So much for collegiality!

Once hierarchy was established, defensiveness followed, and it was virtually impossible for the dyad to appropriately use the methods of horizontal evaluation. The teachers gave up and went through the motions of giving feedback, which was reduced to praise or suggestions of how to do something differently. For Samantha, the situation was worse. She did not consider herself to be Penny's intellectual equal and, as the process continued, she became increasingly insecure and then stopped giving suggestions at all; she could only praise Penny because to give a suggestion was to hint at criticism.

> Now, in my case and Penny's, we are two different kinds of teachers. I'm more of a practitioner, and I think Penny's more of a theoretician. And, she's a very, very intelligent person. I found myself thinking Penny might be getting more out of the experience if she were working with someone her intellectual equal.

By the end of the study, neither teacher was able to break away from the belief that evaluation is expert-driven, involves finding fault, and is something done to teachers.

Not surprisingly, holding to this view of evaluation severely restricted the range of topics discussed by these teachers. Technical questions and issues dominated. Such issues were safe topics for discussion because teachers can talk about them endlessly without having to question any of the educational assumptions they hold. All that matters is that a solution "works." Numerous examples of this kind of talk were found in their postobservation transcripts: "Maybe I tried to do too much in one lesson. Maybe I have too many objectives." "One of my greatest weaknesses is that I bite off more than I can chew. I always do too much at one time." And, "It turned out to be an exciting experience except that it was just too much for one hour." The issue is how to fit more content into less time. Other technical issues included: when is it best to reinforce a student's response; and how to effectively use techniques learned in a workshop. Unfortunately, these topics only help reproduce the common view of teaching.

Where the successful dyads viewed evaluation as a process where peers work together to help one another better understand and improve practice, the failed dyad thought of evaluation as a hierarchial process—one teacher, an expert, tells another teacher what is appropriate. Through our comparison of the failed dyad with the successful ones, we have concluded that if the aim of evaluation is transformation, then the process must empower teachers, while teachers must be able and willing to replace hierarchial relations with colleagueship. Whatever the reasons for the failed dyad—technocratic mindset, lack of trust, or personal dislike—it is important to note that teachers fall back on *some* kind of sensemaking paradigm. In this case, it was the widespread technocratic model.

## CONCLUSION

If evaluation is to improve teaching, then it must attend to the way teachers understand their work. For the successful dyads, the use of horizontal evaluation resulted in a richer understanding of the teacher role. As one teacher remarked, "I began to see the role of evaluator as part of being a teacher." And, to their surprise, evaluation was found to be an interesting and challenging process, one clearly within their reach as professionals. "I was pleasantly surprised how easy it was. I think before [the study] I had somewhat of a stigma about evaluation, but I found . . . when two people want it, when two people are trying to improve their teaching, it's a fascinating experience."

In addition, because evaluation focused on increasing and enriching understanding as well as improving skill (rather than pleasing an expert), the process opened up possibilities for altered teacher relations.

> If teachers used horizontal evaluation, there might be less of the 'I have to protect my little group' [mentality]. I mean, like first, second, and third grade teachers do their thing, and the fourth, fifth, and sixth do their thing. I think there might be some efforts in terms of establishing unity.

The teachers felt more powerful. Those in the successful dyads came to think, for example, that to be part of the evaluation of teaching is more than a responsibility, it is a right.

> "You know that no one really has the right or the knowledge to tell us what to do. I guess the [horizontal evaluation] process would essentially be giving us back the power that we should have . . . and I think that this is the power we deserve [to have] as professionals."

These are promising developments. Clearly, if teacher evaluation is to be part of the solution to the current problems facing American education, then a different approach to evaluation is needed—one that places teachers at the center of the evaluation process and that is based upon a radically different view of teachers and of teaching. Teachers must be perceived as individuals capable of making reasonable decisions not only about the means of education, but also about its aims. And, teaching must come to be seen as an ethical and political act that bears rich fruit only when in the hands of individuals who have thought deeply, carefully, and critically about the decisions they make. No other view of teachers or of teaching is likely to produce, or attract, the kind of people needed to meet the challenges before us.

## NOTES

1. For a critical discussion of administrative supervision, see W. John Smyth, "Teachers as Collaborative Learners in Clinical Supervision: A State-of-the-Art," *Journal of Education for Teaching* 10 (Jan. 1984): pp. 24–38.

2. Florida Coalition for the Development of a Performance Meausrement System, *Domains: Knowledge Base of the Florida Performance Measurement System* (Tallahassee, Florida: Office of Teacher Education and In-Service Staff Development, 1983), p. 1.

3. *Manual for Coding Teacher Performance on the Summative Observation Instrument* (Tallahessee, Florida: Office of Teacher Education and In-Service Staff Developmentt, 1985), p. ii.

4. See Jacob Van Hoven, "Peer Involvement: A Working Model of Staff Development," *Catalyst for Change* 14 (Feb. 1974): pp. 27–30.

5. See Robert Goldhammer, *Clinical Supervision: Special Methods for the Supervision of Teachers* (New York: Holt, Rinehart and Winston, 1969), pp. 57, 61, 63.

6. See Shirley McFaul and James Cooper, "Peer Clinical Supervision in an Urban Elementary School," *Journal of Teacher Education* 34 (Sept. 1983): pp. 34–39.

7. See W. John Smyth, "Peer Clinical Supervision as 'Empowerment' versus 'Delivery of a System,'" paper presented at the annual meeting of the American Educational Research Association, San Francisco, California, April 1986, pp. 18–19.

8. For a description of the original horizontal evaluation model, see Andrew Gitlin, "Horizontal Evaluation: An Approach to Student Teacher Supervision," *Journal of Teacher Education* 32 (Sept. 1981): pp. 47–50.

9. For a description of universal pragmatics, see Jürgen Habermas, *Communication and the Evolution of Society* (Boston: Beacon Press, 1976).

10. Participants were asked the following questions:

1. Has the peer review process changed what you try to achieve as a teacher?
2. Has the peer review process changed how you feel about evaluating a peer?
3. Did the peer review process influence your job satisfaction?
4. Has the peer review process influenced what it means to be a teacher?
5. What are your general reactions?

MARY HAYWOOD METZ

Chapter Twelve

# Teachers' Pride in Craft, School Subcultures, and Societal Pressures

We are hearing much of late about the inadequacies of our schools and about teachers as a national problem. Sometimes teachers are seen as the source of the problem because they are not "the best and the brightest" among college graduates; they are accused of not being imaginative enough, intellectually stimulating enough, or dedicated enough to perform well in the teaching role. Sometimes teachers are seen as suffering the effects of a problem they do not create; they are pictured as victims whose commitment and effort level flag or who leave teaching because they are not paid well enough, are not given raises based on merit, have no career ladder, and are not given opportunities for collegial consultation and planning. While elements of either of these constructions of "the problem" of contemporary public school teachers may have some validity, I want to explore some dimensions of teachers' working lives which receive much less attention in current policy debates.

Much literature has pointed to the importance of intrinsic rewards for teachers.[1] A sense of pride of craft, of efficacy in their chosen work, seems crucial to teachers' occupational identity and to their sense of satisfaction with their work. In a recent ethnographic study of three magnet middle schools,[2] I found teachers' ability to feel a sense of pride in their work central to their attitudes toward it. Teachers' pride in their work was not solely an individual matter, however. For most teachers, it was formed by a collective definition of the nature of teaching and learning, of schools, and of students, which faculties subconsciously and spontaneously developed. In other words, each faculty developed a subculture in which most, but not all, teachers participated.[3] That subculture provided a context for shared interpretation of students', administrators', and teachers' behaviors consonant with common fundamental assumptions. The highly generalized assumptions of the subculture provided a framework of thought within which teachers made sense of daily events and within which they both formed and justified their own actions.

This chapter explores one of these three schools' faculty cultures. It attempts to show the way such a culture can grow up spontaneously without being formally encouraged or even consciously recognized by any of the participants, and yet can have profound effects on teachers' thought and behavior. It also attempts to show the way this particular culture was centered in teachers' attempts to maintain their pride in their abilities as good teachers under difficult circumstances. I suggest, although my data do not establish, that this school was fairly typical, that faculties of schools where teachers find it difficult to experience success in teaching or where others denigrate their efforts—either accurately or inaccurately—will develop faculty cultures which defend their pride in their work. If this is true, then efforts at reform of teaching must take into account both teachers' need for a sense of pride in work, and the collective bases of this pride. Such efforts must approach the development of faculty subcultures as both potential obstacles to, and potential resources for, reform efforts.

This chapter considers the sources of the teachers' subculture, outside as well as inside the school. School faculties construct their subcultures in part from the common societal and occupational culture they bring with them to the school and from regional, class, ethnic, or religious subcultures shared by large subgroups or by all teachers in a given school. They develop a distinctive school suculture in response to their interactions within the school with one another, students, and administrators. This subculture is also based on their interactions with parents, representatives of the school district, and community citizens.

The faculty of the school I discuss experienced a series of disparate pressures undercutting their pride in their ability as teachers. Their faculty culture was constructed around the preservation of that pride. In showing the way in which this faculty constructed a culture in response to the pressures which bore upon it, I am suggesting that other faculties subject to similar pressures will develop similar cultures. At the least, they will face similar problems, to which the cultures they do develop must respond.

## CULTURE AS AN INFLUENCE ON TEACHERS

Most of the strategies for improvement of teachers' working lives have not been informed by close studies of teachers' experience of those lives. We are all social creatures who understand and respond to "objective" rewards or working arrangements in terms of their social meaning. That social meaning is developed and understood through a culture shared by a group of related persons. To understand what kinds of rewards will motivate teachers to work more effectively or at a higher level of effort, we must know something about the cultural milieu in which they participate.

To define culture one must look first to anthropologists' use of the term. Although their definitions are by no means identical and sometimes quite disparate,[4] one can discern some broad themes in most of the anthropological approaches to the concept. Culture is more than a cognitive map or set of rules for communication and behavior; it is also a system of meanings which includes values. It is a broad, diffuse, potentially contradictory body of shared interpretations of the "facts" of the experienced world and of values about what ought to be. Ordinarily, it grows up not only without conscious planning but without conscious recognition that it exists at all.

Cultural understandings are tacit; they are rarely articulated as abstract propositions. They are elements of common sense so well known by persons sharing the culture that sensible adults have no need to mention them. Among initiates, cultural knowledge is too self-evident to be discussed.[5] The tacit quality of culture gives it much of its force. Because its elements are not discussed, they are not debated by either insiders or outsiders. Internal contradictions between cultural elements are not brought to attention.[6]

Culture grows originally from a group's need to make sense out of the circumstances in which its members find themselves. Once developed, a culture provides a set of shared lenses through which changing experience is interpreted. Change in the culture of a group already sharing a common culture will be affected by the way in which the existing culture filters the meaning of the group's continuing or new experiences.

## THE CASE STUDY: HORACE MANN MIDDLE SCHOOL

The case study briefly reported here derives from a larger study of three magnet middle schools. That study attempted to discover the distinctive character which each school developed and to trace the organizational sources of that character. One important source of that organizational character was faculty culture. Readers interested in a full and documented account of the faculty culture briefly outlined here are referred to the report of the full study.[7] Here the faculty culture of the Mann middle school and its sources inside and outside the school are merely sketched for their value in suggesting processes that may be at work in many American schools—although not in the exact configuration found in this single school. The purpose is to raise questions, not to give firm conclusions.

I performed the research on which this account is based alone. During 1979–80, I was present in the school one day a week from September to December, and was present most days of the week from March to June. I attended faculty meetings and parent meetings for one full year. I observed in classes, halls, cafeterias, and playgrounds, and participated in the informal life of the faculty in the lounges, halls, and lunchrooms, as well as attending faculty meetings, meetings of teaching teams, parent organization meetings, and special school events. I conducted open-ended semistructured interviews with most teachers and administrators and with a small stratified sample of students. I took notes on many informal conversations as well. I also studied school documents such as handbooks, curriculum guides, and daily announcements.

The school described here, the Horace Mann Middle School for the Gifted and Talented, was a magnet middle school serving sixth through eighth graders. It was located in the city of "Heartland" (a pseudonym), which has one of the thirty largest school districts in the United States. As a magnet school, it served a student body of volunteers admitted according to racial quotas. Nearly one-half of the students were members of ethnic minorities; almost all of them were black. Horace Mann was the only middle school in the city allowed to use entrance criteria. Its students were nominated by classroom teachers throughout the city as qualifying for the school on the basis of one or more of seven broad criteria ranging from general specific intellectual gifts to psychomotor or leadership ability. On nationally standardized tests of reading and mathematics, one-half of the students scored in the top one-fourth and three-fourths in the top one-half. While the student body was not universally gifted in the narrowly intellectual sense, their academic skills were far above those found in other schools in the city, where only one-third of the students scored in the top one-half on such tests. Furthermore, the weakest students were almost close to the median; there were only a handful of really weak students. In addition, because students had to be chosen by teachers and their transfer requested by parents, the children selected were generally cooperative and pleasant toward adults, and their families were, for the most part, middle class or ambitious members of the working class. As one teacher put it, they were "95 percent nice kids."

Because of an arrangement insisted upon by the Heartland teachers' union, magnet schools retained the faculties who had been serving in the buildings where they were located. The middle school for the gifted and talented was originally located in the Atlantic Avenue Junior High School. It had been a school serving poor black students, with a student body that had a bad reputation in the neighborhood and city for vandalism and violence. In the first year, seventy seventh graders in the gifted and talented program shared the building with neighborhood eighth graders, who were finishing their career at the school. In the second year, three full classes of gifted and talented sixth through eighth grades were accepted; in August, however, the students and faculty were transferred together to share the Horace Mann High School building with a new magnet high school program that had not filled that facility. The study took place during the third year of the gifted and talented program, the second year in the Mann High School building.

Because we hear much discussion of the importance of a student body in determining the effects of a school, I unconsciously anticipated that the faculty of this school, which clearly had the most socially and academically select student body in the city, would have high morale. Consequently, I was surprised to find that the dominant majority of Mann's faculty were angry and bitter and took their feelings out in psychic withdrawal from the school and from their teaching.

They expressed their alienation from the administration of the school and its formal procedures through myriad small actions. They refused to chuckle at administrators' pleasantries in faculty meetings and rushed from the room when they ended. They seemed to take an active delight in telling of administrative mistakes or the snarling of logistical arrangements. They clustered near the exits, ready to leave at the first possible moment at the end of the day. Most maintained that good teaching for a gifted and talented program was simply good teaching of the ordinary kind. There was nothing special to be done. They also maintained both that the student body was so diverse academically that it was impossible to teach them all effectively and—in the next breath—that they were clustered closely around grade level and so not really a gifted group with whom special programs would be possible or appropriate.

They also expressed their alienation in actions that affected their teaching and the introduction of cooperative activities. Most taught in highly routinized patterns of lecture, recitation, and seatwork. While students started homework at their desks almost all teachers sat at the front of the room, working on paperwork, in contrast to teachers at other schools in the study, almost all of whom circulated among the students offering help while they worked at their desks. Only a few teachers were willing to attend the many workshops or courses on gifted and talented education available in the area. Two of the three academic teams were disabled in a number of activities as a result of the unwillingness of several members to participate.

The teachers' resistance to special activities for a gifted and talented program and their contradictory comments about the nature of the student body reflected their school subculture. The traditional methods they used in teaching their moderately heterogeneous classes seemed to have been more reflective of the broader technical culture of secondary education. The other middle schools in the study used a variety of approaches other than lecture, recitation, and seatwork, which made it easier for them to work with heterogeneous groups. These schools were more oriented toward elementary education than Mann, and their magnet specialties encouraged more innovations in teaching methods. It seemed never to occur to most of Mann's teachers, or to the administrators, that classes might be taught with non-traditional methods to deal more effectively with student diversity. They saw variations in classroom pedagogy at other middle schools, if they were aware of them at all, as reflections of special magnet programs or as not having the honorific qualities of secondary education, preparing the students for high school. Patterns of both curriculum and pedagogy are more standardized in secondary than in elementary education; the culture of the occupation takes them as givens. Because of the tacit quality of culture, the common pedagogy of secondary education shaped teachers' practice at Mann, but was taken as inevitable and not experienced as a limitation or constraint.

*Experience at the Old Inner City School and Faculty Culture*

It took quite a while to make sense of this puzzling behavior. Two keys provided the first clues. The first was variation within the faculty in these patterns. Some new teachers who had joined the school after it became a gifted and talented school were much less alienated. In fact, a handful spoke in glowing terms of enjoying working with a student body that was more able and enthusiastic than students they had encountered previously. These teachers also used more varied and innovative methods of instruction in their classes. Some new teachers followed the majority pattern, however, and were even outspoken articulators of it. Although these were teachers who, for various reasons, were unhappy to have been assigned to Mann and who all had close regular contact with old-timers in settings such as carpools. They also used the same distinctive rhetoric as the old-timers, a sign that they had been intensively socialized into the continuing faculty's group and their cultural perspective.

Thus, teachers from the old Atlantic Junior High School seemed to define the terms of the faculty culture. Most of these teachers did not raise the subject of the old Atlantic program. But a few who spoke of it provided a crucial clue to understanding the whole group. One white woman gave a vivid and passionate account:

*Interviewer:* What was Atlantic like before the change [to a magnet program]?
*Mrs. Rohr:* That's a funny thing. This is just like you've died and gone to heaven. I don't understand why a teacher would moan and groan and complain and say that it is such hell here.

I spent ten years at that hellhole, and there is just no describing it unless you've taught in an inner city junior high school with seventh, eighth, and ninth graders. We had ninth graders that were eighteen years old. In its real heydey, we had two and three fires a day, constant false alarms, horrible vandalism, fights. I couldn't count the number of knives and junk that I saw in my classroom in ten years. I mean there's no comparison. Teacher assaults, you know, teachers knocked in the face and the mouth, in the eyes, knifings. Two art teachers I know were knifed. I mean just gross, gross misconduct and horrible, horrible behavior. For a few years there the kids were right off the walls.

Although emotion may have led this teacher to exaggerate, her comments are consistent with the reputation of Atlantic Avenue in the city. It was clearly a school where the kind of opposition that can develop between poorly achieving working-class and minority students and their teachers was in full flower.[8]

One white male teacher who kept to himself and who, like the woman just quoted, was much more positive about the gifted and taltened program than most teachers, described the impact of his experience at Atlantic on his feelings of self-worth as a teacher.

> *Mr. Selig:* At Atlantic I probably didn't smile at all. Maybe until February. And you really almost had to do that for survival.... Teachers didn't have as much authority. *After a while you really lost your sense of self-worth, you really did.*
>
> *Interviewer:* Tell me more about that.
>
> *Mr. Selig:* Well I just simply felt that—I realized I had a family and that they had to be fed. I really hadn't been trained for anything else besides teaching. And I simply went to work every day. Tried to do the best I could and it really didn't bother me whether a student got this or a student got that. It didn't bother me. I'd just go and do my job.... *At Atlantic you almost think that what the kids are doing to you is a personal affront.* You know, you tend to get extremely angry. It takes a long time to get over that, to realize that the kids aren't really angry at you. They really aren't striking out at you as an individual. It takes a long time.... *Cause I'm telling you a lot of times you can go home and start questioning your own values. You start stereotyping. It's really shameful how you lose all that self-respect and idealism. (Emphasis added.)*

Mr. Selig's quick transitions back and forth from feelings of anger and the temptation to stereotype to  loss of self-respect is illuminating. He suggests that a teacher involved in chronic conflict with students tends to lose a sense of his or her own efficaciousness and professional worth.

Another white man from Atlantic Avenue who was active in the core group of teachers and a member of the department that most set the tone of the faculty culture still felt the anger Mr. Selig said it took him so long to get over. He emphasized withdrawal from caring how much the students learned:

> If kids are all the time fighting in class and calling you names and so on, when it's time for your prep period or you go home at night, you don't spend your time thinking up nice little activities for those children. It's sort of as though—well I guess every child deserves a good education—but it's as though, "If you don't respect me and what I have done for you, why should I do this for you?"

All of these teachers suggest that conflict between students and teachers was high at the old Atlantic Avenue school and that teachers responded to feelings of rage and frustration with withdrawal. Of the three teachers, only Mr. Selig saw that the students might have some reason for their behavior. It is certainly likely that teachers' withdrawal and anger contributed to students' hostility. But for our purposes, the important point is that Atlantic faculty members learned to support one another in seeing themselves as good teachers who could not display their abilities because the students were difficult. When they experienced new difficulties at Mann—even though it was a situation other teachers in the city envied—they continued to see themselves as good teachers who could not display their abilities because of the students they were given.

At Atlantic, the teachers had also blamed the principal, in fact a succession of principals, for their own inability to be effective. The Atlantic principal had not been transferred with the program, and the teachers now spoke of him fairly kindly. But the same teacher who said that being at Mann was like having "died and gone to heaven" said with a laugh that she wished she had "had a tape recorder" when teachers who now complained about the Mann administrators had been talking about the Atlantic principal at the old school.

Criticism of administrators served the teachers' image of themselves as capable professionals in impossible circumstances. According to the implicit logic of their claims, the administrators, along with students, created such difficult conditions that no teacher could have displayed his or her strengths. When difficulties developed at Mann, teachers continued to see themselves as competent persons in impossible circumstances, making new administrators and a group of students who were not ideally selected for a gifted and talented program the source of their inability to show their true worth. In both situations they assumed that the locus of control of the situation was not with themselves, a more fundamental assumption and one less easily subject to examination than characterizations of specific groups of students or administrators.

Seen as an attempt to maintain their pride in their professional abilities, the teachers' puzzling behavior becomes understandable and consistent. Their deepest, most tacit assumption was that good teaching is only possible when organizational conditions are favorable. Teachers cannot control these conditions, but they can only practice their craft effectively and demonstrate their own true worth under appropriate conditions. Without such conditions, the best teachers can do is to engage in a holding action, to go through the motions of teaching without much hope of being effective. Their capabilities as teachers cannot be assessed from their performance in such a holding action.

In this context, the teachers' refusal either to cooperate with the administrators or to seek innovative teaching approaches in their classrooms were actions that confirmed their perspective that the school did not provide the conditions for teachers to demonstrate their true capacities. To have tried new approaches would have been to risk their reputations under circumstances that—as they saw them—ensured failure. It is well worth asking whether the great conservatism and reluctance to try new approaches often observed in public school faculties—and especially in those dealing with student bodies considered difficult or lacking in prestige—may not come from similar social psychological dynamics shared and expressed in a common and deeply tacit subculture.

This interpretation of the dynamics of the Mann faculty's stance seems to be confirmed by exceptions to the teachers' usual behavior. In some situations where teachers worked with groups composed only of very able students, in a few classes and in some extracurricular competitive teams with an academic character, teachers worked with a publicly visible energy and enthusiasm that they did not display in their regular classes. Furthermore, they attempted to express their professionalism through their dress. As a group, they dressed extremely well; most of the men wore ties and jackets and the women wore dresses and suits that would have been appropriate in business offices.

## *The New School: Faculty Culture as a Defense Against Mistrust*

The lingering effects of these teachers' experience at Atlantic Avenue confirms the deep scars to professional pride that outwardly disdainful teachers may experience when the dynamics of conflict in schools serving poor minority students with low achievement are at their most negative. Generally, however, cultures do not simply persist untouched when conditions change radically. Why then did these teachers continue to feel helpless, unable to display their abilities in teaching, and why did they see the student body and administration as still undercutting their efforts?

The new situation offered almost as many assaults to their professional pride as had the old. The assaults simply came from new directions. First, it became clear that both the central office and the most vocal parents of the new student body mistrusted the Atlantic teachers' ability to deal effectively with gifted and talented students. This distrust was dramatically expressed during the development of the new program. In its first year, it consisted of only seventy seventh graders at Atlantic Avenue, while the rest of the school served neighborhood eighth graders who had started at the school the year before.

A small group of teachers were chosen to teach the gifted and the talented students. Central office personnel and teachers from an already-established elementary school for the gifted and talented worked intensively with the chosen teachers. Other teachers were literally forbidden to have any contact with the gifted students. They might help a colleague set up a lab or an art room, but they were expected to leave the room when the students entered. The teachers not chosen for the gifted and talented program took serious offense at this treatment. They made barbed jokes about "gifted and talented teachers" in the direction of their chosen colleagues. Always unspoken was the assumption that if some teachers were "gifted and talented" by association with their students, others were "inner city teachers" by association with theirs. When the whole student body was gifted and talented students in the next year, these excluded teachers became part of the gifted and talented faculty, but the stigma of their former students still clung to them.

The assistant principal who functioned as administrator in charge of the middle school at Mann told me that he considered one of his tasks to be "reawakening enthusiasm for teaching" in the teachers who had been at Atlantic Avenue. He spoke of them as all in one category. Some parents were critical of the teachers from Atlantic, also as one category. They assumed that after dealing with a population of inner city students these teachers would be unprepared to work with "gifted and talented" students unless they received considerable special retraining and perhaps not even with such assistance. Both at full Parent Teacher Organization meetings and in committees including staff and parents, some parents openly expressed uneasiness about the Atlantic faculty as a whole and criticized individual teachers vehemently and unselfconsciously. Teachers could do little but silently listen to these attacks. Some parents also approached individual teachers with criticisms of their curriculum, classroom strategy, or grading.

The teachers from Atlantic Avenue thus found their pride assaulted, sometimes with brutal directness, by parents and by administrators. When these teachers maintained that good teaching is the same with all types of students, they were in effect maintaining that they were perfectly qualified to teach gifted and talented students and not tainted or made incompetent by their years of contact with inner city students. When they claimed that they could not teach effectively with students as diverse—or as ordinary—as those in the program or with an administration that behaved as this one did, they were defending their professional competence by saying that they did not control the conditions crucial for optimum performance. The stance that had sheltered their pride in the face of angry students at Atlantic now sheltered it in the face of critical parents and administrators at Mann.

Two important lessons can be learned from this reaction of the Mann faculty. First, the response shows the way a faculty can together develop a subculture that helps it turn an intolerable situation into a tolerable one, through the power of social consensus and support. In so doing, the subculture the members develop may lead them to react in ways that appear irrational to outsiders. If one wants to change the behavior of such a faculty, one cannot simply preach a "rational" perspective. One must change the conditions from which the teachers' perspective springs and which make it sensible to them. At Mann, any attempt at changing the teachers' behavior would have required a component that would support their pride as good teachers.

Second, the response of the parents to the Atlantic teachers in their new role as teachers for the gifted and talented provides dramatic evidence of the ways in which the public judges teachers by the students they teach. Parents whose children were labelled gifted and talented were deeply suspicious of teachers who had been teaching inner city children.

Parents' reactions varied according to their own social background, however. When the school was moved from the Atlantic Avenue Junior High School to the Mann High School in August, preceding its second year, parents organized to resist. They were united and were successful in getting a good deal of media publicity, although not in preventing the move. In the following year, however, a deep schism developed between the most critical parents and others who favored patience and support of the school's staff. This split was partly along social class lines. Working- and lower-middle-class parents, in interviews, compared the school to their children's former schools and were grateful for the new school; they supported the staff. Some upper-middle-class parents with as much as (or more) education as the teachers compared the school to an ideal and became angry at its shortcomings in such a light; they were most critical of the staff. The readiness of upper-middle-class parents to criticize and attempt to direct teachers has been remarked upon by several authors.[9] Teachers who work with the children of such parents must develop protective strategies to defend their autonomy and their sense of competence and worth.

## Teachers' Pride and the Administrative Hierarchy

The situation in which the school found itself led to an unusually forceful use of administrative powers. The high school in the Mann building was also a new magnet school. The logistical problems in launching two new schools in one building were awesome. In addition, both schools were under obligation to offer distinctive and attractive programs to please volunteering parents and students from the moment that they opened. In this situation, little opportunity was found for prolonged staff discussion of alternative options and for democratic development of programs. The administrators felt obligated to make decisions unilaterally and to enforce them strongly. The principal, especially, was formal in his manner with teachers and unshakable in his directives to them.

Teachers varied in their response to this treatment. One set of teachers, all women, spoke directly of the strong administrative structure and direction favored by the principal. They said that the school was run with a strong hierarchical hand. They also mentioned the formalized procedures of the office, and they felt that the middle school teachers were treated "like stepchildren." They said directly that their feelings were hurt by these arrangements—although they were not sure that any insult or belittling implication was intended. These teachers laid little blame on the administrators, however; some said they appreciated the predictability that flowed from strong central direction. Teachers who attempted some informal leadership within the faculty for special activities encouraged by the administration, or who initiated ideas and provided focus in teaching team meetings were in this group. A few also went to outside workshops on gifted and talented education. They seemed to be beginning to move away from the faculty culture.

Another set of teachers, all men except one marginal case, made no mention of the principal's strong use of authority in their interviews. On the contrary, they brought up every piece of evidence of administrative confusion, irrationality, or weakness that they could; stories of incidents that could cast a negative light on either the principal or administrator in charge of the middle school were shared and repeated by different informants.

By failing to acknowledge the strong and pervasive direction used by the principal—which was formally legitimate regardless of how much it might violate *informal* norms for teacher autonomy—and by suggesting that the principals were weak and/or incompetent, they undermined the legitimacy of the principals' claim to obedience. The powers of the office might legitimate pervasive direction of these teachers' efforts, but if the holder of the office were weak or otherwise incompetent, then the legitimacy of his specific commands was undercut. Teachers' obligation to obey was then correspondingly attenuated. This group of teachers ignored many directives and avoided taking voluntary steps consonant with the directions in which the administration wished to move the school.

While these teachers phrased their discussion of the administration in highly personal terms, if this interpretation is correct, the picture they painted was in fact drawn for the purpose of providing a formal justification for disobedience to formally legitimate authority. Teachers elsewhere who resent the encroachment of increased hierarchical direction upon the informal autonomy of their role may similarly phrase their rebellion in terms of personal attacks upon the capabilities of the hierarchical officeholders. Increasingly active hierarchical administration may lead to increased personal criticism of administrators as a strategy of delegitimation of hierarchical powers.

These teachers' resistance to the principal's strong use of authority sprang in part from a wish to protect the traditional informal autonomy of teachers. But it also reflected the more general ambivalence toward authority which observers of American culture have remarked upon repeatedly ever since the days of de Tocqueville.[10] While we accept the legitimacy of authority in principle, we are suspicious of it and often make cultural heroes of persons who ignore or defy it.

Defiance of authority is one strand in our conception of manliness. It is not surprising that the most rebellious teachers were men; they were acting consistently with the ambivalence with which our national culture regards subordination to authority by men, especially by those who have little prospect of eventually taking over the authority to which they are subject. The women could perhaps be said to be following cultural expectations for women in their relative willingness to speak of injury to their pride and in responding with hurt feelings to their subjection to administrative directives and to the office staff's apparently mistrustful limitation of their access to various material resources. The men active on this issue denied the presence of strong directives and dismissed the belittling behavior of the office staff as inefficient and wrong headed. More in keeping with men's culturally prescribed roles, they construed the situation as the setting for a power struggle; their definition of the other side's behavior was a tactic in that struggle.

## LESSONS FROM THE MANN SCHOOL ABOUT TEACHERS' DILEMMAS

The faculty of the Atlantic Junior High School in their transition to becoming the faculty of the Mann Middle School for the Gifted and Talented teaches us three important lessons about current crises in teaching. First, Mann's teachers show us the importance of faculty culture as it can create special meanings for events and practices and as it can provide socially shared solutions to difficulties experienced by a faculty. An understanding of culture provides a key to understanding the Mann faculty's display of puzzling, seemingly irrational behavior and makes it understandable and coherent in the light of the faculty's common history and current dilemmas. A study of the culture that provides a common implicit context for thought and action in other schools may make the teachers' behavior similarly comprehensible. Attempts at reform must be couched in terms which are appealing in the framework of that culture.

In addition, the administrators' strong and pervasive control over the teachers' work elicited a resentment that is hardly surprising to persons familiar with the social science literature describing the relations of school administrators and teachers.[14] Such control abrogates teachers' informal right to determine much of the content of teaching and virtually all of the social relations within the classroom, a right which proves one of the most prized conditions of teaching as an occupation, and a major reward in the experience of teachers.

Despite its importance, teachers' pride is a difficult issue to introduce into public discourse about teaching, let alone to act upon. Teachers are not eager to recognize its importance. To admit that one's pride is hurt is itself to deepen the wound to pride. Public acknowledgement of a hurt to pride makes it more real; such acknowledgement in itself confirms the diminution of one's status. And for teachers collectively either as faculties or as an occupation to speak of these wounds would have the same effect. They can speak of the need to be respected as professionals, to have their expertise and hard work recognized, but these calls for respect do not touch the kinds of daily and yearly experiences to which the Mann faculty was responding.

Similarity, it is difficult to enter into public discourse about the ways in which teachers' experience in schools for poor children and minorities is corrosive of their pride without seeming to blame poor and minority communities or families for the conflict between students and teachers—a conflict to which the teachers in fact contribute as much as do students. These students and their families and communities are themselves subject to worse social pressures than those bearing on teachers. They can hardly be expected to be deeply concerned with white middle-class teachers' problems of pride—or even to give them much credence.

Nor can one expect upper-middle-class families to withdraw their pressure on teachers whom they see as deficient simply because teachers find this attitude condescending and belittling. Such parents are likely to respond that they are simply making realistic assessments of the skills of public servants, who should be answerable to them as

taxpayers. Furthermore, these parents place well-being of their individual children above the feelings of their teachers.

Finally, state legislatures, and administrators at the school system
and school levels have the legitimate right and duty to control events in
schools. They are accountable for teachers' performance and will claim
that teachers' feelings of pride or their enjoyment of autonomy are of
little significance weighed against effective teaching. Teachers who
want to experience pride in their work should simply take care to be
effective—in the administrators' or legislators' terms.

All of these arguments are reasonable and defensible. But none
touches the reality illustrated at Horace Mann. The fact remains that
teachers who feel themselves under attack are likely to pour their energies into self-defense. In doing so, they will often construct a culture
that frees them from responsibility to develop effective teaching and
constructive social relationships with students. All of the reasonable
claims of the groups surrounding teachers are fruitless if their actions
contribute to a condition which, by wounding teachers' pride, leads
them to become entrenched in the poor teaching patterns these groups
hope to alter. Even though pride is virtually a taboo topic, its importance must be acknowledged, implicitly if not explicitly. National and
local policies and practices can be self-defeating if they violate teachers'
pride, regardless of how appealing or reasonable they may seem on
other grounds.

## IMPLICATIONS OF THE MANN FACULTY'S BEHAVIOR
## FOR THE CRISIS IN TEACHING

It is well worth exploring the suggestion that the current perception
of a crisis in teaching is in large part a reflection of conditions that
are making it increasingly hard for teachers to experience pride in their
work. Like the Mann teachers, many faculties across the country may
respond to such conditions by constructing artificial bases of pride that
distract them from the task of teaching. They may simultaneously
withdraw their psychic investment from their daily teaching and seek
their significant experiences elsewhere. In fact, social and economic
changes are now underway that may alter the conditions of teaching in
ways which will increasingly drive teachers to find artificial means of
bolstering their pride or to invest their energies in other activities.

A steadily climbing proportion of children are being raised in
poverty. A growing percentage of school children are minorities; most
of them also poor. Such children are socially stigmatized by the more
affluent and by ethnic majorities; their teachers share their stigma

whatever their own economic, educational, and ethnic status. Second, statistically, poor and minority children do not perform well in school. Teachers in schools for such children quickly find themselves teaching below grade level or teaching to a broad span of achievement, with a heavy concentration at the lower end. In high schools, fewer of the high-prestige, advanced academic classes can be offered and so teachers have little access to the affirmation of their own disciplinary knowledge afforded by teaching such classes. Finally, the large proportion of poor minority students who achieve poorly are more likely than other students to come into conflict with their teachers and peers during the course of daily life in school.[15] Teachers must deal with endemic disruptions of academic activity and contests of will that distract both them and other students from the teaching and learning which are their defined task. Because of the steady increase in poor and minority children as a proportion of those of school age, an increasing proportion of the teaching force will face social stigma, decreased success in transmitting subject matter, and more daily conflict with students. In other words, if nothing else changes demographic changes are presenting increasing proportions of teachers with social opprobrium, instructional failure, and heightened daily stress.

But other things are changing. Foreign economic competition and the current political climate are increasing public emphasis on excellence in education and decreasing emphasis on equality of opportunity. Successful students are drawing public attention and praise, while less successful students—and their teachers—are, in the main, ignored or criticized, A shrinking domestic economy and increasingly tight labor market for educated workers are creating greater parental anxiety about the performance of children and greater selectivity by colleges and employers. The ranking of student's performance, which has long been a part of school life is becoming more marked. In many middle-class schools, those students who perform in the lower part of the student body lose prestige and importance, while the most able compete fiercely for success. Teachers who teach classes designed for the less successful students share in their loss of prestige and importance.[16] There is an intensification of a pattern of social prestige for teaching being given only to those teachers who work with top performers.

Concurrent with the increased emphasis on ranking students is a drive at the national level and by various interest groups to increase students' standardized test scores. This emphasis pushes teachers toward a signifcant narrowing of their curricular objectives and lessens their control over their academic and social agenda with students.

Whole subjects may be made marginal. Also, because testing in this country is predominantly norm referenced, it condemns the half of students who will score below the median by the very logic of the system to an increasingly visible label as "below average," a label from which their teachers will also suffer if such students are clustered in particular schools or particular classes within schools.

At the same time, the sensibilities of both the public and educational professionals are turning increased emphasis upon hierarchy and accountability within the schools. Legislative and judicial regulation of the schools, on the rise since the 1950s,[17] has been increasing at an accelerated rate, especially in the issuance of curricular and procedural guidelines by state legislatures and departments of education, as well as by central offices in school districts. The "strong principal" is becoming an educational folk hero. Such administrative regulation and tight control decreases teachers' actual discretion and their subjective sense of being in charge of the curricular and social aspects of their work with students. Being in charge, free to use one's own judgment within the classroom world, has traditionally been one of the major rewards of teaching.[18] It is also a basis of a feeling that one is a respected person doing significant work.

These changes, which come from the larger society, and which are at least in part independent of one another, converge to undercut the broad social prestige of a large portion of the teaching force, the respect teachers can expect to command from the media, from chance acquaintances, from parents, and from their associates in private life who are not teachers. They also converge to lessen teachers' control over classroom and their ability to feel that they have developed a teaching strategy of their own. Finally, they limit teachers' access to results defined as successful.

The measures currently being discussed as nostrums for a demoralized teaching force hardly touch on these issues. More rigorous selection of teachers will not change these pressures undercutting their efforts and their prestige. Merit pay and career ladders reward some individuals and mitigate their feelings of failure or frustration, but these rewards are by definition scarce goods. They cannot make a whole faculty feel more appreciated. Nor will they make students learn better or be more cooperative. In schools with mixed populations, these rewards will most likely go disproportionately to the teachers who work with the most motivated and successful children and so to increase the demoralization of those who work with the less successful.

Attempts to exert more administrative supervison and to introduce mechanisms for accountability may prevent some abuses but may deepen teachers' sense of having little control over their working lives and so increase alienation. Attempts to give teachers more time for collegial efforts may indeed help, but collegial discussions among discouraged faculties may also lead to the spread of alienation and to social confirmation of the perceived hopelessness of a situation.

As we think about a crisis in teaching, we must think about it as teachers experience it. When large numbers of teachers seem to choose strategies that are not the most effective for learning or are not supportive of students, the reasons for their behavior may not lie in their feelings as individuals but in difficulties lodged in pervasive social patterns confronting teachers. When possible, attempts at reform should seek to change those social patterns. Because many extend well beyond the school, they cannot be changed as easily as can school policy. Where such conditions cannot be changed, at least by persons concerned with education, educational reformers could help teachers' morale simply by candidly acknowledging the difficulties teachers must face. They could then concentrate upon helping the teachers to find ways to cope with difficulties—ways designed to be helpful to the students and also supportive of the teachers' sense of competence.

An earlier version of this paper was presented at the annual meeting of the American Educational Research Association, San Francisco, April 19, 1986. The author gratefully acknowledges partial support for this work under Grant No. G-79-0017, Project No. 8-0640, from the National Institute of Education and partial Support from the Wisconsin Center for Education Research, which was supported in part by a grant from the National Institute of Education (Grant No. NIE-G-84-0008). The paper was prepared at the National Center on Effective Secondary Schools, School of Education, University of Wisconsin-Madison, which is supported in part by a grant from the Office of Educational Research and Improvement (Grant No. OERI-G-86-007). Any opinions, findings, conclusions, or recommendations expressed in this paper are those of the author and do not necessarily reflect the views of NIE, OERI, or the U. S. Department of Education.

## NOTES

1. See, for example, Sari Knopp Biklen, "Teaching as an Occupation for Women: A Case Study of an Elementary School" (Final Report to the National Institute of Education, Grant Number NIE-G-81-0007, 1983); Philip Jackson, *Life in Classrooms* (New York: Holt, 1968); and Dan C. Lortie, *Schoolteacher: A Sociological Study* (Chicago: University of Chicago Press, 1975).

2. Mary Haywood Metz, *Different by Design: The Context and Character of Three Magnet Schools* (New York: Routledge and Kegan Paul, 1986).

3. Some schools, especially larger schools, develop two competing faculty subcultures—although none of the three schools in this particular study did so.

4. See Clifford Geertz, *The Interpretation of Cultures* (New York: Basic Books, 1973); Peggy R. Sandy, "The Ethnographic Paradigm(s)," *Administrative Science Quarterly* 24 (December 1979): 527–38; and Linda Smircich, "Concepts of Culture and Organizational Analysis," *Administrative Science Quarterly* 28 (September 1983): 339–58.

5. See George and Louise Spindler, "Anthropologists View American Culture," *Annual Review of Anthropology* 12 (1983): 49–78.

6. In sociology there is a long tradition of interest in the development of distinctive cultures within organizations, for example: Chester I. Barnard, *The Functions of the Executive* (Cambridge, Mass.: Harvard University Press, 1962 [First published 1938]; Burton R. Clark, *The Distinctive College* (Chicago: Aldine, 1970); and Philip Selznick, *Leadership in Administration* (New York: Harper and Row, 1957). There are also several studies of schools which give rather rich descriptions of distinctive organizational cultures if one reads them with a cultural framework in mind, even though most do not emphasize a cultural perspective. Examples are Philip Cusick, *The Equalitarian Ideal and the American High School* (New York: Longman, 1983); Harry L. Gracey, *Curriculum or Craftsmanship: Elementary School Teachers in a Bureaucratic System* (Chicago: The University of Chicago Press, 1972); Sara L. Lightfoot, *The Good High School: Portraits of Character and Culture* (New York: Basic Books, 1983); Joan Lipsitz, *Successful Schools for Young Adolescents* (New Brunswick, N.J.: Transaction Books, 1984); Linda McNeil, *Contradictions of Control* (New York: Routledge and Kegan Paul, 1986); Gertrude McPherson, *Small Town Teacher* (Cambridge, Mass.: Harvard University Press, 1972); Carl Nordstrom, Edgar Z. Friedenberg, and Hilary A. Gold, *Society's Children* (New York: Random House, 1967); Leila Sussman, *Tales Out of School: Implementing Organizational Change in the Elementary Grades* (Philadelphia: Temple University Press, 1977); and Ann Swidler, *Organization Without Authority* (Cambridge, Mass.: Harvard University Press, 1979). Some systematic theoretical treatments of culture in schools, at least as seen from a managerial perspective, are also emerging, for example the papers in Thomas J. Sergiovanni and J. E. Corbally, eds., *Leadership and Organizational Culture* (Urbana: Universty of llinios Press, 1984).

7. Metz, *Different by Design: The Context and Character of Three Magnet Schools.*

8. For summaries of literature describing these processes, see Frederick Erickson, "Qualitative Methods in Research on Teaching" (Occasional paper no. 81, The Institute for Research on Teaching, Michigan State University, East Lansing, Mich., 1985) and Mary Haywood Metz, "Sources of Constructive So-

cial Relationships in an Urban Magnet School," *American Journal of Education* 91 (February 1983): 202–45.

9. Biklen; McPherson; and Ray Rist, *The Invisible Children: School Integration in American Society* (Cambridge, Mass.: Harvard University Press, 1978).

10. Spindler and Spindler.

11. Erickson; and Metz, "Sources of Constructive Social Relationships."

12. Howard Becker suggested thirty years ago that teachers prefer to teach children at the middle of the social scale because of the pressures placed upon them by children and/or parents who are either poor or affluent. Howard Becker, "The Career of the Chicago Public School Teacher," *American Journal of Sociology* 57 (March 1952): pp. 470–77. Mann's story suggests such pressures are still commonly experienced by teachers when students are from either end of the social scale.

13. Merrilee K. Finley, "Teachers and Tracking in a Comprehensve High School," *Sociology of Education* 57 (October 1984): 233–43; and Reba Page, "Perspectives and Processes: The Negotiation of Educational Meetings in High School Classes for Academically Unsuccessful Students" (Ph.D. diss., University of Wisconsin-Madison, 1984).

14. Charles Bidwell, "The School as a Formal Organization," in *Handbook of Organizations,* James March, ed. (Chicago: Rand McNally, 1965), pp. 972–1022; E. Mark Hanson, "Organizational Control in Educational Systems: A Case Study of Governance in Schools,"in *Organizational Behavior in Schools and School Districts,* Samuel B. Bacharach, ed. (New York: Praeger, 1981), pp. 245–76; Jackson; and Lortie.

15. Erickson; and Metz, "Sources of Constructive Social Relationships."

16. Finley; and Page.

17. Arthur E. Wise, *Legislated Learning: The Bureaucratization of the American Classroom* (Berkeley: University of California Press, 1979).

18. Andrew Hargreaves, "Experience Counts, Theory Doesn't: How Teachers Talk about Their Work," *Sociology of Education* 57 (October 1984): 244–54; Jackson; and Lortie.

MICHAEL W. APPLE

Chapter Thirteen

# Teaching and Technology: The Hidden Effects of Computers on Teachers and Students

## INTRODUCTION

Many of the western industrialized nations are facing severe problems. There is an extensive structural crisis in the economy, authority relations, and values. The symptoms are visible everywhere—in the very high under and unemployment rates now plaguing us, in the fear that the United States, for example, is losing its edge in international competition, in the calls for sacrifices by labor and for greater work discipline, in the seemingly widespread belief that "our" standards are falling. The analyses of this crisis have not limited just to our economic institutions. Commentators and critics have spent a good deal of time focusing on the family and especially on the school. Economically and politically powerful groups have, in fact, been relatively successful in shifting the blame for all of the above-mentioned problems *from* the economy *to* institutions such as schools. That is where the real problem lies, or so it is said. Thus, if we could solve the problems of education, we could solve these other problems as well. Change the "competencies" of our teachers and students, and all else will tend to fall into place naturally.

Documents such as *A Nation at Risk* and others have pointed to a crisis in teaching and in education in general. Among the many recommendations these reports make is greater stress on the "new technology." The crisis in schools and teaching, they admit, is complicated and widespread, but one step toward a solution is the rapid introduction of computers into schools. The emphasis on computers is quite strong. It is singled out for special attention in nearly all of the national documents, especially those that are responding to the larger social and economic problems we are now experiencing. This will give our students new skills, skills that are necessary in the international competition for markets and jobs. It will also necessitate and create a more technically knowledgeable teaching force (hence, the proposals in many states to mandate computer literacy for all students now in teacher education programs). It will also eliminate much of the drudgery of teaching and make the tasks of teaching more interesting and creative. Will it?

## THE POLITICS OF TECHNOLOGY

In our society, technology is seen as an autonomous process. It is set apart and viewed as if it had a life of its own, independent of social intentions, power, privilege. We examine technology as if it was something constantly changing and as something that is constantly changing our lives in schools and elsewhere. This is partly true, of course, and is fine as far as it goes. However, by focusing on what is changing and being changed, we may neglect to ask what relationships are remaining the same. Among the most important of these are the sets of cultural and economic inequalities that dominate even societies like our own.[1]

By thinking of technology in this way, by closely examining whether the changes associated with "technological progress" are really changes in certain relationships after all, we can begin to ask political questions about their causes and especially their multitudinous effects. Whose idea of progress? Progress for what? And fundamentally, who benefits?[2] These questions may seem rather weighty ones to be asking about schools and the curricular and teaching practices that now go on in them or are being proposed. Yet, we are in the midst of one of those many educational bandwagons that governments, industry, and others so like to ride. This wagon is pulled in the direction of a technological workplace, and it carries a heavy load of computers as its cargo.

The growth of the new technology in schools is definitely not what one would call a slow movement. In one recent year, a 56 percent increase was reported in the use of computers in schools in the United

States and even this may be a conservative estimate. Of the 25,642 schools surveyed, more than 15,000 schools reported some computer usage.[3] In the United States alone, it is estimated that in excess of 350,000 microcomputers have been introduced into the public schools in the past four years.[4] This is a trend that shows no sign of abating. Nor is this phenomenon limited to the United States. France, Canada, England, Australia, and many other countries have "recognized the future." At its center seems to sit a machine with a keyboard and a screen.

I say "at its center," because in both governmental agencies and in schools themselves the computer and the new technology have been seen as something of a savior economically and pedagogically. "High tech" will save declining economies and will save our students and teachers in schools. In the latter, it is truly remarkable how wide a path the computer is now cutting.

The expansion of its use, the tendency to see all areas of education as a unified terrain for the growth in the use of new technologies, can be seen in a two-day workshop on integrating the microcomputer into the classroom held at my own university. Among the topics covered were computer applications in writing instruction, in music education, in secondary science and mathematics, in primary language arts, for the handicapped, for teacher recordkeeping and management, in business education, in health occupation training programs, in art, and in social studies. To this is added a series of sessions on the "electronic office," how technology and automation are helping industry, and how we all can "transcend the terror" of technology.[5]

Two things are evident from this list. First, vast areas of school life are now seen to be within the legitimate purview of technological restructuring. Second, a partly hidden but exceptionally close linkage exists between computers in schools and the needs of management for automated industries, electronic offices, and "skilled" personnel. Thus, recognizing both what is happening inside and outside of schools and the connections between these areas is critical to any understanding of what will probably happen with the new technologies, especially the computer, in education.

As I have argued elsewhere, all too often, educational debates are increasingly limited to technical issues. Questions of "how to" have replaced questions of "why."[6] In this chapter, I reverse this tendency. Rather than dealing with what the best way might be to establish closer ties between the technological requirements of the larger society and our formal institutions of education, I step back and raise a different set of questions. I consider a number of rather difficult political, economic, and ethical issues about some of the tendencies in schools and the larger society that may make us want to be very cautious about the current technological bandwagon in education. In so doing, a range of areas must be examined: Behind the slogans of technological progress and high tech industry, what are some of the real effects of the new technology on the future labor market? What may happen to teaching and curriculum if we do not think carefully about the new technology's place in the classroom? Will the growing focus on technological expertise, particularly computer literacy, equalize or further exacerbate the lack of social opportunities for our most disadvantaged students? Of course, many more issues need to be raised. Given limited space, however, I devote the bulk of my attention to those noted above.

At root, my claim will be that the debate about the role of the new technology in society and in schools is not and must not be just about the technical correctness of what computers can and cannot do. These may be the least important kinds of questions in fact. At the very core of the debate instead are the ideological and ethical issues concerning what schools should be about and whose interests they should serve.[7] The question of interests is very important currently because, due to the severe problems besetting economies like our own, a restructuring of what schools are *for* has reached a rather advanced stage.

Thus, while a relatively close connection has always existed between the two, an even closer relationship now exists between the curriculum in our schools and corporate needs.[8] In a number of countries, educational officials and policymakers, legislators, curriculum workers, and others have been subject to immense pressure to make the "needs" of business and industry the primary goals of the school system. Economic and ideological pressures have become rather intense and often very overt. The language of efficiency, production, standards, cost effectiveness, job skills, work discipline, and so on—all defined by powerful groups and always threatening to become the dominant way we think about schooling[9]—has begun to push aside concerns for a democratic curriculum, teacher autonomy, and class, gender, and race equality. Yet, we cannot fully understand the implications of the new technology in this restructuring unless we gain a more complete idea of what industry is now doing not only in the schools but in the economy as well.

## TECHNOLOGICAL MYTHS AND ECONOMIC REALITIES

Let us look at the larger society first. It is claimed that the technological needs of the economy are such that, unless we have a technological literate labor force, we will ultimately become outmoded economically. But what will this labor force actually look like?

A helpful way of thinking about this is to use the concepts of increasing *proletarianization* and *deskilling* of jobs. These concepts signify a complex historical process in which the control of labor has altered, one in which the skills workers have developed over many years are broken down and reduced to their atomistic units, automated, and redefined by management to enhance profit levels, efficiency, and control. In the process, the employee's control of timing, over defining the most appropriate way to do a task, and over criteria that establish acceptable performance are slowly taken over as the preogatives of management personnel who are usually divorced from the place where the actual labor is carried out. Loss of control by the worker is almost the result. Pay is often lowered. And the job itself becomes routinized, boring, and alienating as conception is separated from execution and more and more aspects of jobs are rationalized to bring them into line with management's need for a tighter economic and ideological ship.[10] Finally, and very importantly, many of these jobs may simply disappear.

There is no doubt that the rapid developments in, say, microelectronics, genetic engineering and associated "biological technologies," and other high tech areas are, in fact, partly transforming work in a large number of sectors in the economy. This may lead to economic prosperity in certain sections of our population, but its other effects may be devastating. Thus, as the authors of a recent study that examined the impact of new technologies on the future labor market demonstrate:

> This transformation ... may stimulate economic growth and competition in the world marketplace, but it will displace thousands of workers and could sustain high unemployment for many years. It may provide increased job opportunities for engineers, computer operators, and robot technicians, but it also promises to generate an even greater number of low-level, service jobs such as those of janitors, cashiers, clericals, and food service workers. And while many more workers will be using computers, automated office equipment, and other sophisticated technical devices in their jobs, the increased use of technology may actually reduce the skills and discretion required to perform many jobs.[11]

Let us examine this scenario in greater detail.

Rumberger and Levin make a distinction that is very useful to this discussion. They differentiate between high tech industries and high tech occupations, in essence between what is made and the kinds of jobs these goods require. High tech industries that manufacture technical devices such as computers, electronic components, and the like currently employ less than 15 percent of the the paid work force in the United States and other industrialized nations. Just as importantly, a substantial knowledge of technology is required by *less than one fourth* of all occupations within these industries. On the contrary, the largest share of jobs created by high tech industries are in areas such as clerical and office work or in production and assembly. These actually pay below average wages.[12] Yet this is not all. High tech occupations that do require considerable skill—such as computer specialists and engineers—may indeed expand. However, most of these occupations actually "employ relatively few workers compared to many traditional clerical and service fields."[13] Rumberger and Levin summarize a number of these points by stating that "although the percentage growth rate of occupational employment in such high technology fields as engineering and computer programming was higher than the overall growth rate of jobs, far more jobs would be created in low-skilled clerical and service occupations than in high technology ones."[14]

Some of these claims are supported by the following data. It is estimated that even being generous in one's projections, only 17 percent of new jobs created between now and 1995 will be in high tech industries. (Less generous and more restrictive projections argue that only 3 to 8 percent of future jobs will be in such industries.)[15] As I noted though, such jobs will not be all equal. Clerical workers, secretaries, assemblers, warehouse personnel, etc., these will be the largest occupations within the industry. If we take the electronic components industry as an example here, this is made much clearer. Engineering, science, and computing occupations constituted approximately 15 percent of all workers in this industry. The majority of the rest of the workers were engaged in low-wage assembly work. Thus, in the late 1970s, nearly two-thirds of all workers in the electronic components industry took home hourly wages "that placed them in the bottom one-third of the national distribution."[16] If we take the archetypical high tech industry—computer and data processing—and decompose its labor market, we get similar results. In 1980, technologically oriented and skilled jobs accounted for only 26 percent of the total.[17]

These figures have considerable weight, but they are made even more significant by the fact that many of that 26 percent may themselves experience a deskilling process in the near future. That is, the reduction of jobs down into simpler and atomistic components, the separation of conception from execution, and so on—processes that have had such a major impact on the labor process of blue, pink, and white collar workers in so many other areas—are now advancing into high technology jobs as well. Computer programming provides an excellent example. New developments in software packages and machine language and design have meant that a considerable portion of the job of programming now requires little more than performing "standard, routine, machine-like tasks that require little in-depth knowledge."[18]

What does this mean for the schooling process and the seemingly widespread belief that the future world of work will require increasing technical competence on the part of all students? Consider the occupations that will contribute the most number of jobs not just high tech industries but throughout the society by 1995. Economic forecasts indicate that these will include building custodians, cashiers, secretaries, office clerks, nurses, waiters and waitresses, elementary school teachers, truck drivers, and other health workers, such as nurses aides and orderlies.[19] None of these are directly related to high technology. Excluding teachers and nurses, none of them require any postsecondary education. (Their earnings will be approximately 30 percent below the current average earnings of workers, as well.)[20] If we go further than this and examine an even larger segment of expected new jobs by including the forty job categories that will probably account for about one-half of all the jobs created, it is estimated that only about 25 percent will require people with a college degree.[21]

In many ways, this is strongly related to the effects of the new technonlogy on the job market and the labor process in general. Skill levels will be raised in some areas, but will decline in many others, as will jobs themselves decline. For instance, "a recent study of robotics in the United States suggests that robots will eliminate 100,000 to 200,000 jobs by 1990, while creating 32,000 to 64,000 jobs."[22] My point about declining skill requirements is made nicely by Rumberger and Levin. As they suggest, while it is usually assumed that workers will need computer programming and other sophisticated skills because of the greater use of technology such as computers in their jobs, the ultimate effect of such technology may be somewhat different. "A variety of evidence suggests just the opposite: as machines become more sophisticated, with expanded memories, more computational ability, and sensory capabilities, the knowledge required to use the devices declines."[23] The effect of these trends on the division of labor will be felt for decades. But it will be in the sexual division of labor where it will be even more extreme. Historically, *women's work* has been subject to these processes in very powerful ways; therefore, we will see increased proletarianization and deskilling of women's labor and, undoubtedly, a further increase in the feminization of poverty.[24]

These points clearly have implications for our educational programs. We need to think much more rigorously about what they mean for our transition from school to work programs, especially because many of the "skills" that schools are currently teaching are transitory because the jobs themselves are being transformed (or lost) by new technological developments and new management offensives.

Take office work, for example. In offices, the bulk of the new technology has not been designed to enhance the quality of the job for the largest portion of the employees (usually women clerical workers). Rather, it has usually been designed and implemented in such a way that exactly the opposite will result. Instead of accomodating stimulating and satisfying work, the technology is there to make managers' jobs "easier," to eliminate jobs and cut costs, to divide work into routine and atomized tasks, and to make administrative control more easily accomplished.[25] The vision of the future society seen in the microcosm of the office is inherently undemocratic and perhaps increasingly authoritarian. Is this what we wish to prepare our students for? Surely, our task as educators is neither to accept such a future labor market and labor process uncritically nor to have our students accept such practices uncritically as well. To do so is simply to allow the values of a limited but powerful segment of the population to work through us. It may be good business, but I have my doubts about whether it is ethically correct educational policy.

In summary, then, what we will witness is the creation of enhanced jobs for a relative few and deskilled and boring work for the majority. Furthermore, even those boring and deskilled jobs will be increasingly hard to find. Take office work, again, an area that is rapidly being transformed by the new technology. It is estimated that between one and five jobs will be lost for every new computer terminal that is introduced.[26] Yet this situation will not be limited to office work. Even those low-paying assembly positions noted earlier will not necessarily be found in the industrialized nations with their increasingly service-oriented economies. Given the international division of labor, and what is called "capital flight," a large portion of these jobs will be moved to countries such as the Philippines and Indonesia.[27]

This is exacerbated considerably by the fact that many governments now find "acceptable" those levels of unemployment that would have been considered a crisis a decade ago. "Full employment" in the United States is now often seen as between 7 and 8 percent *measured unemployment.* (The actual figures are much higher, of course, especially among minority groups and workers who can only get part-time jobs.) This is a figure that is *double* that of previous economic periods. Even higher rates are now seen as "normal" in other countries.

The trend is clear. The future will see fewer jobs. Most of those that are created will not necessarily be fulfilling, nor will they pay well. Finally, the level of technical skill will continue to be lowered for a large portion of them.[28]

Because of this, we need convincing answers to some very important questions about our future society and the economy before we turn our schools into the "production plants" for creating new workers. *Where* will these new jobs be? *How many* will be created. Will they *equal* the number of positions lost in offices, factories, and service jobs in retailing, banks, telecommunications, and elsewhere? Are the bulk of the jobs that will be created relatively unskilled, less than meaningful, and themselves subject to the inexorable logics of management so that they too will be likely to be automated out of existence?[29]

These are not inconsequential questions. Before we give the schools over to the requirements of the new technology and the corporation, we must be very certain that it will benefit all of us, not mostly those who already possess economic and cultural power. This requires continued democratic discussion, not a quick decision based on the economic and political pressure now being placed on schools.

Much more could be said about the future labor market. I urge the interested reader to pursue it in greater depth because it will have a profound impact on our school policies and programs, especially in vocational areas, in working-class schools, and among programs for young women. The difficulties with the high tech vision that permeates the beliefs of the proponents of a technological solution will not remains outside the school door, however. Similar disproportionate benefits and dangers await us inside our educational institutions as well and it is to this that we shall now turn.

## INEQUALITY AND THE TECHNOLOGICAL CLASSROOM

Once we go inside the school, a set of questions concerning "who benefits?" also arises. We need to ask about what may be happening to teachers and students given the emphasis now being placed on computers in schools. I do not talk about the individual teacher or student here. Obviously, some teachers will find their jobs enriched by the new technology and some students will find hidden talents and will excel in a computer-oriented classroom. What we need to ask instead (or at least before we deal with the individual) is what may happen to classrooms, teachers, and students differentially. Once again, I seek to raise a set of issues that may not be easy to solve, but cannot be ignored if we are to have a truly democratic educational system in more than name only.

While I have dealt with this in greater detail in *Ideology and Curriculum* and *Education and Power*,[30] let me briefly situate the growth of the technologized classroom into what seems to be occuring to teaching and curriculum in general. Currently, considerable pressure is building to have teaching and school curricula be totally prespecified and tightly controlled for the purposes of "efficiency," "cost effectiveness," and "accountability." In many ways, the deskilling that is affecting jobs in general is now having an impact on teachers as more and more decisions are moving out of their hands and as their jobs become even more difficult to do. This is more advanced in some countries than others, but it is clear that the movement to rationalize and control the act of teaching and the content and evaluation of the curriculum is very real.[31] Even in those countries that have made strides away from centralized examination systems, powerful inspectorates and supervisors, and tightly controlled curricula, an identifiable tendency is found to move back toward state control. Many reforms have only a very tenuous hold currently. This is in part due to economic difficulties and partly due as well to the importing of American styles and techniques of educational management, styles and techniques that have their roots in industrial bureaucracies and have almost never had democratic aims.[32] Even though a number of teachers may support computer-oriented curricula, an emphasis on the new technology needs to be seen in this context of the rationalization of teaching and curricula in general.

Given these pressures, what will happen to teachers if the new technology is accepted uncritically? One of the major effects of the current (over-) emphasis on computers in the classroom may be the deskilling and depowering of a considerable nember of teachers. Given the already heavy workload of planning, teaching, meetings, and paperwork for most teachers, and given the expense, it is probably wise to assume that the largest portion of teachers will not be given more than a very small amount of training in computers, their social effects, programming, and so on. This will be especially the case at the primary and elementary school level where most teachers are already teaching a wide array of subject areas. Research indicates, in fact, that few teachers in any district are actually given substantial information before computer curricula are implemented. Often, only one or two teachers are the "resident experts."[33] Because of this, most teachers have to rely on prepackaged sets of material, existing software, and specially purchased material from any of the scores of software manufacturing firms that are springing up in a largely unregulated way.

The impact of this can be striking. What is happening is the exacerbation of trends we have begun to see in a number of nations. Rather than teachers having the time and the skill to do their own curriculum planning and deliberation, they become isolated executors of someone else's plans, procedures, and evaluative mechanisms. In industrial terms, this is very close to what I noted in my previous discussion of the labor process, the separation of conception from execution.[34] The question of time looms larger here, especially in gender terms. Because of the large amount of time it takes to become a "computer expert" and because of the patriarchal relations that still dominate many families, *men teachers* will often be able to use "computer literacy" to advance their own careers while women teachers will tend to remain the recipients of prepackaged units on computers or "canned" programs over which they have little control.

In her excellent ethnographic study of the effects of the introduction of a districtwide computer literacy program on the lives of techers, Susan Jungck makes exactly this point about what happened in one middle school.

> The conditions of time [needs to] be examined in terms of gender differences because it was the women teachers, not the men, in the Math Department who were unprepared to teach about computers and they were the ones most dependent on the availability of the [canned] Unit. Typically, the source of computer literacy for in-service teachers is either college or university courses, school district courses or independent study, all options that take considerable time outside of school. Both [male teachers] had taken a substantial number of university courses on computers in education. Many [of the ] women, [because of ] child care and household responsibilities . . . , or women who are single parents . . . , have relatively less out of school time to take additional coursework and prepare new curricula. Therefore, when a new curriculum such as computer literacy is required, women teachers may be more dependent on using the ready-made curriculum materials than most men teachers.[35]

The reliance on prepackaged software can have a number of long-term effects. First, it can cause a decided loss of important skills and dispositions on the part of teachers. When the skills of local curriculum planning, individual evaluation, and so on are not used, they atrophy. The tendency to look outside of one's own or one's colleagues' historical experience about curriculum and teaching is lessened as considerably more of the curriculum, and the teaching and evaluative practices that surround it, is viewed as something one purchases. In the process—and this is very important—the school itself is transformed into a lucrative market. The industrialization of the school I talked of previously is complemented, then, by further opening up the classroom to the mass-produced commodities of industry. In many ways, it will be a publisher's and salesperson's delight. Whether students' educational experiences will markedly improve is open to question.

The issue of the relationship of purchased software and hardware to the possible deskilling and depowering of teachers does not end here though. The problem is made even more difficult by the rapidity with which software developers have constructed and marketed their products. There is no guarantee that the mass of such material has any major educational value. Exactly the opposite is often the case. One of the major knowledgeable government officials has put it this way. "High-quality educational software is almost non-existent in our elementary and secondary schools."[36] While perhaps overstating his case to emphasize his points, the director of software evaluation for one of the largest school systems in the United States has concluded that of the more than 10,000 programs currently available, only approximately 200 are educationally significant.[37]

To their credit, the fact that this is a serious problem is recognized by most computer enthusiasts, and reviews and journals have attempted to deal with it. However, the sheer volume of material, the massive amounts of money spent on advertising software in professional publications, at teachers' and administrators' meetings, the utter "puffery" of the claims made about much of this material, and the constant pressure by industry, government, parents, some school personnel, and others to institute computer programs in schools *immediately,* all of this makes it nearly impossible to do more than make a small dent in the problem. As one educator put it, "There's a lot of junk out there."[38] The situation is not made any easier by the fact that teachers simply do not now have the time to thoroughly evaluate the educational strengths and weaknesses of a considerable portion of the *existing* curricular material and texts before they are used. Adding one more element, and a sizable one at that, to be evaluated only increases the load. Teachers' work is increasingly becoming what students of the labor process call *intensified.* Thus, one has little choice but simply to buy ready-made material, in this way continuing a trend in which all of the important curricular elements are not locally produced but purchased from commercial sources whose major aim may be profit, not necessarily educational merit.[40]

A key concept found in Jungck's argument above is essential here: that of gender. As I have demonstrated in considerable detail in *Teachers and Texts,*[41] teaching—especially at the elementary school level—has been defined as "women's work." We cannot ignore the fact that 87 percent of elementary teachers and 67 percent of teachers over all *are* women. Historically, the introduction of prepackaged or standardized curricula and teaching strategies has often been related to the rationalization and attempt to gain external control of the labor process of women workers. Hence, we cannot completely understand what is happening to teachers—the deskilling, the intensification, the separation of conception from execution, the loss of control, and so on—unless we situate these tendencies into this longer history of what has often happened to occupations that are primarily composed of women.[42] Needless to say, this is a critically important point, for only by raisng the question of *who* is most often doing the teaching in many of these schools now introducing prepackaged software can we see the connections between the effects of the curricula and the gendered composition of the teaching force.

A significant consideration here, besides the loss of skill and control, is expense. This is at least a three-pronged issue. First, we must recognize that we may be dealing with something of a "zero-sum game." While dropping, the cost of computers is still comparatively high, although some manufacturers may keep purchase costs from the purchase of software later on or through a home/school connection, something I discuss shortly. This money for the new technology *must come from somewhere.* This is an obvious point but one that is very consequential. In a time of fiscal crisis, where funds are already spread too thinly and necessary programs are being starved in many areas, the addition of computer curricula most often means that money must be drained from one area and given to another. What will be sacrificed? If history is any indication, it may be programs that have benefitted the least advantaged. Little serious attention has been paid to this, but it will become an increasingly serious dilemma.

A second issue of expense concerns staffing patterns, for it is not just the content of teachers' work and the growth of purchased materials that are at stake. Teachers' jobs themselves are on the line here. At a secondary school level in many nations, for example, layoffs of teachers have not been unusual as funding for education is cut. Declining enrollment in some serious regions has meant a loss of position as well. This has caused intense competition over students within the school itself. Social studies, art, music, and other subjects must fight it out with newer, more "glamorous" subject areas. To lose the student numbers game for too long is to lose a job. The effect of the computer in this situation has been to increase competitiveness among staff, often to replace substance with both gloss and attractive packaging of courses, and to threaten many teachers with the loss of their livelihood.[43] Is it really an educationally or socially wise decision tacitly to eliminate a good deal of the choices in these other fields so that we can support the "glamor" of a computer future? These are not only financial decisions, but are ethical decisions about teachers' lives and about what our students are to be educated in. Given the future labor market, do we really want to claim that computers will be more important than further work in humanities and social sciences or, perhaps even more significantly in working-class and ethnically diverse areas, in the students' own cultural, historical, and political heritage and struggles? Such decisions must not be made by only looking at the accountant's bottom line. These too need to be arrived at by the lengthy democratic deliberation of all parties, including the teachers who will be most affected.

Third, given the expense of microcomputers and software in schools, the pressure to introduce such technology may increase the already wide social imbalances that now exist. Private schools to which the affluent send their children and publicly funded schools in more affluent areas will have more ready access to the technology itself.[44] Schools in inner city, rural, and poor areas will largely be priced out of the market, even if the cost of "hardware" continues to decline. After all, in these poorer areas and in many public school systems in general in a number of countries it is already difficult to generate enough money to purchase new textbooks and to cover the costs of teachers' salaries. Thus, the computer and literacy over it will "naturally" generate further inequalities. Because, by and large, it will be the top 20 percent of the population that will have computers in their homes[45] and many of the jobs and institutions of higher education their children will be applying for will either ask for or assume "computer skills" as keys of entry or advancement, the impact can be enormous in the long run.

The role of the relatively affluent parent in this situation does not go unrecognized by computer manufacturers.

> Computer companies ... gear much of their advertising to the educational possibilities of computers. The drive to link particular computers to schools is a frantic competition. Apple, for example, in a highly touted scheme proposed to "donate" an Apple to every school in America. Issues of philanthropy and intent aside, the clear market strategy is to couple particular computer usages to schools where parents—especially middle-class parents with the economic wherewithal and keen motivation [to ensure mobility]—purchase machines compatible with those in schools. The potentially most lucrative part of such a scheme, however, is not in the purchase of hardware (although this is also substantial) but in the sale of proprietary software.[46]

This very coupling of school and home markets, then, cannot fail to further disadvantage large groups of students. Those students who already have computer backgrounds—be it because of their schools or their homes or both—will proceed more rapidly. Their original advantage—one *not* due to "natural ability," but to *wealth*—will be heightened.[47] The social stratification of life chances will increase.

We should not be surprised by this, nor should we think it odd that many parents, especially middle-class parents, will pursue a computer future. Computer skills and "literacy" is having a strategy for the maintenance of middle-class mobility patterns.[48] Having such expertise, in a time of fiscal and economic crisis, is like having an insurance policy. It partly guarantees that certain doors remain open in a rapidly changing labor market. In a time of credential inflation, more credentials mean fewer closed doors.[49]

The credential factor here is of considerable moment. In the past, as gains were made by ethnically different people, working-class groups, women, and others in schooling, one of the latent effects was to raise the credentials required by entire sectors of jobs. Thus, class, race, and gender barriers were partly maintained by an ever increasing credential inflation. Although this was more of a structural than a conscious process, the effect over time has often again been to disqualify entire segments of a population from jobs, resources, and power. This too may be a latent outcome of the computerization of the school curriculum. Even though, as I have shown, the bulk of new jobs will not require "computer literacy," the establishment of computer requirements and mandated programs in schools will condemn many people to even greater economic disenfranchisement. Because the requirements are in many ways artificial—computer knowledge will not be so very necessary and the number of jobs requiring high levels of expertise will be relatively small—we will simply be affixing one more label to these students. "Functional illiteracy" will simply be broadened to include computers.[50]

Thus, blame is not focused on inequalities in the economy or on the lack of meaningful and fulfilling work. Nor is attention paid to the way the new technology for all its benefits is "creating a growing underclass of displaced and marginal workers." Rather, the problem is personalized, and it becomes the students' or workers' fault for not being computer literate. One significant social and ideological outcome of computer requirements in schools, then, is that they can serve as a means "to justify those lost lives by a process of mass disqualification, which throws the blame for disenfranchisement in education and employment back on the victims themselves."[51]

Of course, the process may not be visible to many parents of individual children. However, the point does not revolve around the question of individual mobility, but large scale effects. Parents may see such programs as offering important paths to advancement and some will be correct. However, in a time of severe economic problems, parents tend to overestimate what schools can do for their children.[52] As I documented earlier, there simply will not be sufficient jobs and competition will be intense. The uncritical introducton of an investment in hardware and software will by and large hide the reality of the transformation of the labor market and will support those who are already advantaged unless thought is given to these implications now.

Let us suppose, however, that it was important that everyone become computer literate and that these large investments in time, money, and personnel were indeed so necessary for our economic and educational future. Given all this, what is currently happening in schools? Is inequality in access and outcome now being produced? While many educators are continually struggling against these effects, we are already seeing signs of this disadvantagement being created.

There is evidence of class-, race-, and gender- based differences in computer use. In middle-class schools, for example, the number of computers is considerably more than in working-class or inner-city schools populated by children of color. The ratio of computers to children is also much higher. Moreover, these more economically advantaged schools not only have more contact hours and more technical and teacher support, but they provide a different level of computer instruction than that generally found in less advantaged schools. Programming skills, generalizability, and a sense of the multitudinous things one can do with computers both within and across academic areas, tend to be stressed more[53] (although simply drill- and practice uses are still widespread even here).[54] Compare this to the rote, mechanistic, and relatively low-level uses that tend to dominate the working-class school.[55] These differences are not unimportant, for they signify a ratification of class divisions.

Further evidence to support these claims is now becoming more readily available as researchers dig beneath the glowing claims of a computer future for all the children. The differential impact is made clearer in the following figures. In the United States, while more than two-thirds of the schools in affluent areas have computers, only approximately 41 percent of the poorer public schools have them. What one does with the machine is just as important as having one, of course, and here the differences are again very real. One study of poorer elementary schools found that white children were four-times more likely than black children to use computers for programming. Another found that the children of professionals employed computers for programming and for other "creative" uses. Children of nonprofessionals were more apt to use them for drill- and-practice in mathematics and reading, and for "vocational" work. In general, in fact, "programming has been seen as the purview of the gifted and talented" and of those students who are more affluent. Less affluent students seem to find that the computer is only a tool for drill- and-practice sessions.[56]

Gender differences are also very visible. Two out of every three students currently learning about computers are boys. Even here these data are deceptive because girls "tend to be clustered in the general introductory courses," not the more advanced-level ones.[57] One current analyst summarizes the situation in a very clear manner.

> While stories abound about students who will do just about anything to increase their access to computers, most youngsters working with school computers are [economically advantaged], white and male. The ever-growing number of private computer camps, after-school and weekend programs serve middle-class white boys. Most minority [and poor] parents just can't afford to send their children to participate in these programs.[58]

This class, race, and gendered impact will also occur because of traditional school practices such as tracking or streaming. Thus, vocational and business tracks will learn Operating skills for word processing and will be primarily filled with (working-class) young women.[59] Academic tracks will stress more general programming abilities and uses and will be disproportionately male.[60] Because computer programs have their home bases in mathematics and science in most schools, gender differences can be heightened even more given the often differential treatment of girls in these classes and the ways in which mathematics and science curricula already fulfill "the selective function of the school and contribute to the reproduction of gender differences."[61] While many teachers and curriculum workers have devoted considerable time and effort to equalize both the opportunities and outcomes of female students in mathematics and science (and such efforts are important), the problem still remains a substantive one. It can be worsened by the computerization of these subjects in much the same way as it may have a gendered impact on the teachers themselves.

## TOWARD SOCIAL LITERACY

We have seen some of the possible negative consequences of the new technology in education, including the deskilling and depowering of teachers and the creation of inequalities through expense, credential inflation, and limitations on access. Yet, it is important to realize that the issues surrounding the deskilling process are not limited to teachers. They include the very ways students themselves are taught to think about their education, their future roles in society, and the place of technology in that society. Let me explain what I mean by this.

The new technology is not just an assemblage of machines and their accompanying software. It embodies a *form of thinking* that orients a person to approach the world in a particular way. Computers involve ways of thinking that under current educational conditions are primarily *technical*.[62] The more the new technology transforms the classroom into its own image, the more a technical logic will replace critical, political, and ethical understanding. The discourse of the classroom will center on technique and less on substance. Once again "how to" will replace "why," but this time at the level of the student. This situation requires what I call social, not technical, literacy for all students.

Even if computers make sense technically in all curricular areas and even if all students, not mainly affluent white males, become technically proficient in their use, critical questions of politics and ethics remain to be dealt with in the curriculum. Thus, it is crucial that whenever the new technology is introduced into schools students themselves comprehend the larger social and ethical impacts of computers.

Unfortunately, this is not often the case. One example is provided by a recent proposal for a statewide computer curriculum in one of the larger states in the United States. The objectives that dealt with social questions in the curriculum centered around one particular set of issues. The curriculum states that "the student will be aware of some of the major uses of computers in modern society . . . and the student will be aware of career opportunities related to computers."[63] In most curricula, the technical components of the new technology are stressed. Brief glances are given to the history of computers (occasionally mentioning the role of women in thier development, which is at least one positive sign). Yet in this history, the close relationship between military use and computer development is largely absent. "Benign" uses are pointed to, coupled with a less than realistic description of the content and possibility of computer careers and what Douglas Noble has called "a gee-whiz glance at the marvels of the future." What is nearly never mentioned is job loss or social disenfranchisement. The very real destruction of the lives of unemployed autoworkers, assemblers or clerical workers is marginalized.[64] The ethical dilemmas involved when we choose between, say, "efficiency" and the quality of the work people experience, between profit and someone's job, these too are made invisible.

How would we counterbalance this? By making it clear from the outset that what students need to know about the new technology goes well beyond what we now too easily take for granted. A considerable portion of the curriculum would be organized around questions concerned with social literacy. "Where are computers used? What are they used to do? What do people *actually* need to know in order to use them? Does the computer enhance anyone's life? Whose? Does it hurt anyone's life? Whose? Who decides when and where computers will be used?"[65] Unless these are *fully* integrated in a school program at *all* levels, I would hesitate advocating the use of the new technology in the curriculum. Raising questions of this type is not just important in our elementary and secondary schools. It is even more essential that teachers confront these questions both in their own undergraduate teacher education programs, where courses in educational computing are more and more being mandated, and in the many in-service workshops now springing up throughout the country as school districts frantically seek to keep up with the "computer revolution." Our job as educators involves skilling, not deskilling. Unless teachers and students are able to deal honestly and critically with these complex ethical and social issues, only those now with the power to control technology's uses will have the capacity to act. We cannot afford to let this happen.

## CONCLUSION

I realize that a number of my points in this essay may prove to be rather contentious. But, stressing the negative side can serve to highlight many of the critical issues that are too easily put off given the already heavy work load of school personnel. Decisions made too quickly may come to be regretted later on when forces are set in motion that could have been avoided if the implications of one's actions had been thought through more carefully.

As I noted at the outset of this discussion, there is now something of a mad scramble to employ the computer in every content area. In fact, it is nearly impossible to find a subject that is not being "computerized." Although mathematics and science (and some parts of vocational education) remain the home base for a large portion of proposed computer curricula, other areas are not far behind. If a subject area can be packaged to fit computerized instruction, it will prevail over the methods that teachers have developed after years of hard practical work, even if this is less than sound educationally or economically. Rather than the machine fitting the educational needs and visions of teachers, students, and community, all too often these needs and visions are made to fit the technology itself.

Yet, as I have shown, the new technology does not stand alone. It is linked to real transformations in people's lives, jobs, hopes, and dreams. For some groups, life will be enhanced. For others, dreams will be shattered. Wise choices about the appropriate place of the new technology in education, then, are not only educational decisions. They are, fundamentally, choices about the kind of society we shall have, about the social and ethical responsiveness of our institutions to the majority of our future citizens, and to the teachers who now work in our schools. To understand teaching in this situation requires us to place it into a more complicated nexus of relationships. Only then can choices be made in an ethically justified way.

In the current difficult social and economic setting, it is exceptionally important that educators not allow powerful groups to export their crisis onto the schools. By redefining the serious dilemmas this society faces as being primarily those of the school, and by then convincing the public that many of these problems can simply be solved by an infusion of computers and computer literacy in our educational institutions, dominant groups may create a climate in which the public continues to blame teachers and administrators for economic conditions over which the latter may have little control.[66]

My discussion here has not been aimed at making us all neo-Luddites, people who go out and smash the machines that threaten our jobs or our children. The new technology is here to stay. Our task as educators is to make sure that when it enters the classroom it is there for politically, economically, and educationally wise reasons, not because powerful groups may be redefining our major educational goals in their own image. We should be very clear about whether the future it promises to our teachers and student is real, not fictitious. We need to be certain that it is a future *all* of our students can share in, not just a select few. After all, the new technology is expensive and will take up a good deal of our time and that of our teachers, administrators, and students. It is more than a little important that we question whether the wagon we have been asked to ride on is going in the right direction. It's a long walk back.

This chapter is based on a more extensive analysis in Michael W. Apple, *Teachers and Texts: A Political Economy of Class and Gender Relations in Education* (New York: Routledge and Kegan Paul, 1987).

## NOTES

1. David Noble, *Forces of Production: A Social History of Industrial Automation* (New York: Alfred A. Knopf, 1984), pp. xi-xii. For a more general argument about the relationship between technology and human progress, see Nicholas Rescher, *Unpopular Essays in Technological Progress* (Pittsburgh, Penn.: University of Pittsburgh Press, 1980).

2. Ibid., p. xv.

3. Paul Olsen, "Who Computes? The Politics of Literacy," unpublished paper, Ontario Institute for Studies in Education, Toronto, 1985, p. 6.

4. Patricia B. Campbell, "The Computer Revolution: Guess Who's Left Out?" *Interracial Books for Children Bulletin* 15, no. 3 (1984): 3.

5. "Instructional Strategies for Integrating the Microcomputer Into the Classroom," The Vocational Studies Center, University of Wisconsin-Madison, 1985.

6. Michael W. Apple, *Ideology and Curriculum* (Boston: Routledge and Kegan Paul, 1979).

7. Olsen, "Who Computes?," p. 5.

8. See Michael W. Apple, *Education and Power* (Boston: Routledge and Kegan Paul, 1982).

9. For further discussion of this, see Apple, *Ideology and Curriculum; Apple, Education and Power;* and Ira Shor, *Culture Wars* (Boston: Routledge and Kegan Paul, 1986).

10. This is treated in greater detail in Richard Edwards, *Contested Terrain* (New York: Basic Books, 1979). See also the more extensive discussion of the effect these tendencies are having in education in Apple, *Education and Power*.

11. Russell W. Rumberger and Henry M. Levin, "Forecasting the Impact of New Technologies on the Future Job Market," Project Report No. 84-A4, Institute for Research on Educational Finance and Government, School of Education, Stanford University, February 1984, p. 1.

12. Ibid., p. 2.

13. Ibid., p. 3.

14. Ibid., p. 4.

15. Ibid., p. 18.

16. Ibid., p. 1.

17. Ibid., p. 19.

18. Ibid., pp. 19-20.

19. Ibid., p. 31.

20. Ibid., p. 21.

21. Ibid., p. 1.

22. Ibid., p. 25.

23. Ibid., p. 1.

24. The effects of proletarianization and deskilling on women's labor is analyzed in more detail in Michael W. Apple, "Work, Gender and Teaching," *Teachers College Record* 84 (Spring 1983): 611–628; and Michael W. Apple, "Teaching and 'Woman's Work': A Comparative Historical and Ideological Analysis," *Teachers College Record* 86 (Spring 1985). On the history of women's struggles against proletarianization, see Alice Kessler-Harris, *Out to Work* (New York: Oxford University Press, 1982).

25. Ian Reinecke, *Electronic Illusions* (New York: Penguin Books, 1984), p. 156.

26. See further discussion of the loss of office jobs and the deskilling of many of those that remain in Reinecke, pp. 136–158. The very same process could be a threat to middle and low level management positions as well. After all, if control is further automated, why does one need as many supervisory positions? The implications of this latter point need to be given much more consideration by many middle-class proponents of technology since their jobs may soon be at risk too.

27. Peter Dwyer, Bruce Wilson, and Roger Woock, *Confronting School and Work* (Boston: George Allen and Unwin, 1984), pp. 105–106.

28. The paradigm case is given by the fact that three-times as many people now work in low-paying positions for MacDonalds as for U.S. Steel. See Martin Carnoy, Derek Shearer, and Russell Rumberger, *A New Social Contract* (New York: Harper and Row, 1983), p. 71. As I have argued at greater length elsewhere, however, it may not be important to our company if all students and workers are made technically knowledgable by schools. What is just as important is the production of economically useful knowledge (technical/adminis-

trative knowledge) that can be used by corporations to enhance profits, control labor, and increase efficiency. See Apple, *Education and Power,* especially Chapter 2.

29. Reinecke, *Electronic Illusions,* p. 234. For further analysis of the economic data and the effects on education, see W. Norton Grubb, "The Bandwagon Once More: Vocational Preparation for High-Tech Occupations," *Harvard Educational Review* 54 (November 1984): 429–451.

30. Apple, *Ideology and Curriculum;* and Apple, *Education and Power.* See also Michael W. Apple and Lois Weis, eds., *Ideology and Practice in Schooling* (Philadelphia: Temple University Press, 1983).

31. Ibid. See also Arthur Wise, *Legislated Learning: The Bureaucratization of the American Classroom* (Berkeley: University of California Press, 1970).

32. Apple, *Ideology and Curriculum;* and Apple, *Education and Power.* On the general history of the growth of management techniques, see Richard Edwards, *Contested Terrain.*

33. Douglas Noble, "The Underside of Computer Literacy," *Raritan* 3 (Spring 1984): 45.

34. See the discussion of this in Apple, *Education and Power,* especially Chapter 5.

35. Susan Jungck, "Doing Computer Literacy," (Ph.D. dissertation, University of Wisconsin-Madison, 1985), 236–237.

36. Douglas Noble, "Jumping Off the Computer Bandwagon," *Education Week* (October 3, 1984), p. 24.

37. Ibid.

38. Ibid. See also, Noble, "The Underside of Computer Literacy," p. 45.

39. For further discussion of the intensification of teachers' work, see Apple, "Work, Gender and Teaching."

40. Apple, *Education and Power.* For further analysis of the textbook publishing industry, see Michael W. Apple, "The Culture and Commerce of the Textbook," *Journal of Curriculum Studies* 17, no. 1 (1985).

41. Michael W. Apple, *Teachers and Text: A Political Economy of Class and Gender Relations in Education* (New York: Routledge and Kegan Paul, 1987).

42. Ibid.

43. I am indebted to Susan Jungck for this point. See Jungck, "Doing Computer Literacy."

44. Reinecke, *Electronic Illusions,* p. 176.

45. Ibid, p. 169.

46. Olsen, "Who Computes?" p. 23.

47. Ibid., p. 31. Thus, students' familarity and comfort with computers becomes a form of what has been called the "cultural capital" of advantaged groups. For further analysis of the dynamics of cultural capital, see Apple, *Education and Power* and Pierre Bourdieu and Jean-Claude Passeron, *Reproduction in Education, Society and Culture* (Beverly Hills, Calif.: Sage, 1977).

48. Bourdieu and Passeron, p. 23. See also the discussion of interclass competition over academic qualifications in Pierre Bourdieu, *Distinction* (Cambridge, Mass.: Harvard University Press, 1984), p. 133–168.

49. Once again, I am indebted to Susan Jungck for this argument.

50. Noble, "The Underside of Computer Literacy," p. 54.

51. Douglas Noble, "Computer Literacy and Ideology, *Teachers College Record* 85 (Summer 1984), p. 611. This process of "blaming the victim" has a long history in education. See Apple, *Ideology and Curriculum,* especially Chapter 7.

52. R. W. Connell, *Teachers' Work* (Boston: George Allen and Unwin, 1985), p. 142.

53. Olson, "Who Computes?" p. 22.

54. For an analysis of the emphasis on and pedagogic problems with such limited uses of computers, see Michael Streibel, "A Critical Analysis of the Use of Computers in Education," unpublished paper, University of Wisconsin-Madison, 1984.

55. Olson, "Who Computes?" p. 22.

56. Campbell, "The Computer Revolution," p. 3. Many computer experts, however, are highly critical of the fact that students are primarily taught to program in BASIC, a less than appropriate language for later advanced computer work. Michael Streibel, personal communication.

57. Campbell, "The Computer Revolution," p. 3.

58. Campbell, "The Computer Revolution," p. 3.

59. An interesting analysis of what happens to young women in such business programs and how they respond to both the curricula and their later work experiences can be found in Linda Valli, "Becoming Clerical Workers: Business Education and the Culture of Femininity," in Apple and Weis, eds., *Ideology and Practice in Schooling,* pp. 231–234. See also her more extensive treatment in Linda Valli, *Becoming Clerical Workers* (Boston: Routledge and Kegan Paul, 1986).

60. Jane Gaskell in Olson, "Who Computes?" p. 33.

61. Feodora Fomin, "The Best and the Brightest: The Selective Function of Mathematics in the School Curriculum," in Lesley Johnson and Deborah Tyler, eds., *Cultural Politics: Papers in Contemporary Australian Education, Culture and Politics* (Melbourne: University of Melbourne, Sociology Research Group in Cultural and Educational Studies, 1984), p. 220.

62. Michael Streibel's work on the models of thinking usually incorporated within computers in education is helpful in this regard. See Streibel, "A Critical Analysis." The more general issue of the relationship between technology and the control of culture is important here. A useful overview of this can be found in Kathleen Woodward, ed., *The Myths of Information: Technology and Postindustrial Culture* (Madison, Wisc.: Coda Press, 1980).

63. Quoted in Noble, "The Underside of Computer Literacy," p. 56.

64. Ibid., p. 57. An interesting, but little-known fact is that the largest proportion of computer programmers actually work for the military. See Joseph Weizenbaum, "The Computer in Your Future," *The New York Review of Books,* October 27, 1983, pp. 58–62.

65. Noble, "The Underside of Computer Literacy," p. 40. For students in vocational curricula especially, these questions would be given more power if they were developed within a larger program that would seek to provide these young women and men with extensive experience in and understanding of *all* aspects of operating an entire industry, not simply those "skills" that reproduce workplace stratification. See Center for Law and Education, "Key Provisions in New Law Reforms Vocational Education: Focus is on Broader Knowledge and Experience for Students/Workers," *Center for Law and Education, Inc., D.C. Report,* December 28, 1984, pp. 1–6.

66. See, especially, Marcus Raskin, *The Common Good* (New York: Routledge and Kegan Paul, 1987). This does not mean that schools have no place in helping to solve these problems, simply that: (1) it is insufficient and naive to search for mostly educational solutions; and (2) that the solutions must be considerably more democratic in process *and* effects than those being proposed currently.

Chapter Fourteen

# Teaching and Professionalism:
# A Cautionary Perspective

## INTRODUCTION

Professionalism is an animating theme in the current educational reform movement, so some reflections on its history, meaning, and consequence are in order. The term *professional* has become an honorific in our society today, covering a multitude of uses (e.g., the oldest *profession* in the world; the *professional* housecleaner.[1] Implicit or explicit in this term are comparisons with the elite professions whose stature and status many other lines of work covet and aspire to. As the reform of teaching proceeds under this banner, it is worth taking a look at some aspects of professionalism, then appraising teaching in their light.

We enter an era when teaching renews its efforts to professionalize. *Renew* is the proper term because in the post-World War II era, the dominant trend was the turn to unionization as the collective advancement strategy for teaching. This was, arguably, a necessary and effective move by a weak and often abused occupation, but unionism is in a consolidation phase and appears to have run its course in securing gains for teaching.

Salary increases attributed to bargaining have levelled, teacher rights to due process have been established, and teacher strikes today as often provoke public disapproval as support. Furthermore, the collective bargaining framework for labor-management relations tends to preclude innovation by either side, and to support the status quo in the schools. Bargaining strategies for the most part focus on preserving what has been gained and on minimizing risk. Leaders in both teacher organizations are just beginning to explore new avenues for advancement, and the rallying point is professionalism.

Why this should be so is no mystery:

> Professionalism weaves into a strong braid of ideology our political culture's most potent values. The scientific and technological base of professional practice provides ground for the mystery and efficacy of expertise. Status and wealth accrue to professionals yet the service ideal provides an altruistic motive for their work. Access to the professions is achieved through a public educational system; all may apply, many may be chosen, merit and effort make the difference. Professionals work in organizations and in solo practice, but enjoy considerable autonomy. Expertise is shared within a community, but practice has a strong individual component. Indeed, individualism is an enduring theme in American culture. Self-reliance, that Emersonian virtue, and its cultivation in good judgment are hallmarks of professional work.
>
> That teachers and many other human service workers seek the professional mantle is no surprise. How irresistible is an occupation swathed in science, altruism, democracy, and individualism that pays well to boot. So powerful is the lure of professionalism and so limited the alternatives that occupations in pursuit of status, income, autonomy, and competence will naturally seek to professionalize.[2]

But to what ends and with what results? Two accounts bracket the promises and the dangers.

## Professionalism as Progress

Professionalism represents an effort to establish practice in the human services on a sound footing, to capitalize on and incorporate into practice a base of codified knowledge that progressively improves the work of the professional; and to represent in partnership with the modern state a regulatory framework of shared standards that protect public safety and welfare while advancing society's collective interest in material and spiritual well being.

As the market in a free enterprise system came to organize the production and distribution of goods, so the rise of professions came to rationalize the production and distribution of human services in a manner unparalleled in human history. With the rise of science and technology as the driving force in Western civilization, *profession* came to be synonymous with *progress.* Arguably, the near simultaneous invention of democracy and its keystone, a free, public educational system, of capitalism and the market as efficient organizer of the economy, and of professions with their appropriation of central cultural values, constitute essential elements in this grand, continuing experiment the world knows as—AMERICA.

## Professionalism as Pursuit of Privilege

Such hyperbole rings grandly, but consider the alternative account of the meaning of professionalism. The political-cultural dynamic known as professionalism was the successful effort of certain interests to insinuate themselves into the occupational and status structure in order to secure comparative advantage in the struggle for cultural valuables.[3] The elite occupations constructed and pressed an ideology allowing them to mask what was a blatantly racist, sexist, classist, and nativist drive to cleanse their field of "undesirables" in order to elevate status and income. Behind the skillfully constructed myths of altruism, public welfare, scientific efficacy, and meritocratic access lies the seedy truth: a special interest power grab unparalleled in audacity and effectiveness. Professionalism has degraded caring and compassion in human services, has reinforced gross inequities, and has unnaturally aggrandized a small minority of favored individuals who sought, above all, to establish and perpetuate a new basis for the social transmission of privilege.

These portraits—caricatures, really—etch the lines of analysis too dramatically, but various kinds of historical evidence support each interpretation. Indeed, it would be surprising if any important trend in worldly affairs did not produce a mix of benefits and costs for the human condition. One has only to contemplate the atrocities perpetrated throughout history in the name of noble ideals.

We now seek to professionalize teaching. A closer look at this matter may be instructive. Four topics compose the analysis:

1. the development of standards in the professions;
2. the relation of quality to quantity in the supply of professionals;
3. the relation of excellence to equity in the production of professionals and the distribution of services; and,
4. the role of the professional school in the rise of professions.

## A CLOSER LOOK AT PROFESSIONALISM

### Standards in the Professions

Standards evolved slowly and unevenly across the professions, with the rise of science and of the modern university deeply influencing the evolution from apprentice arrangements modelled on the guild organization of crafts to formal education within a professional school. Reading the law was gradually replaced by attendance at law school; working in an apothecary's shop was replaced with degree programs in pharmacy; attending a variety of quack proprietary medical schools was replaced with university-based scientific training.

The rise of the university was critical, for without it, no alternative to apprentice-based training was found.[4] The university professional school became the funnel through which poured an eager new class of professionals and, with the rise of graduate business schools in the 1940s and 1950s, of managers.

The evolution proceeded in stages. First came the effort to establish a model professional school—Johns Hopkins University in medicine and nursing; Harvard University in law. Then came efforts to require more years of schooling both for entry to the professional school and in the profession itself. Finally came efforts to close down inferior schools and so restrict the supply of professionals while raising standards. Medicine served as both prototype and exception.[5] The phenomenal success of the Flexner report (which accelerated moves already underway by state licensing boards) became the envy of other professions. Lawyers in particular attempted to emulate the doctors, right down to their own Carnegie-funded Flexner-style inquiry, but it took them decades longer to accomplish what the doctors managed in a single decade.[6]

What was the desired end state, the *summum bonum* of the movement? A four-part standard most securely enshrined in medicine:

1. a set of preprofessional courses taken within the undergraduate curriculum, together with a difficult entry examination to medical school;
2. graduation from an accredited medical school;
3. completion of a rigorous professional examination; and,
4. completion of an accredited residency.

This became the most fully elaborated model in all the professions, guaranteeing a very select clientele for the profession. The academic rigor, the years of schooling, the high costs and deferred rewards, all contributed to elite selection.

Other professions aspired to such standards, but none gained the necessary legitimacy. Other fields involve a variety of departures from this austere ideal. The law has never worked out satisfactory procedures for clinical training. Law school students may clerk in courts or work in law offices during the summers, but no professionwide arrangements encourage this. And, in several states, unaccredited law schools continue to exist.

Vestiges of the old apprentice model remain to this day in architecture. In many states one may substitute a certain number of years work in an architect's office for graduation from a school of architecture. In this field too, the clinical or practice component has not been institutionalized. Leaders in the field refer to "the gap" as the two- to three-year period between graduation and examination, when budding architects simply disappear into offices. Just recently have architects begun to establish formal intern programs.[7]

Nor do the architects have a single model for their professional school. There are four-, five-, and six-year programs, articulated in various ways with the undergraduate curriculum, featuring a number of terminal degrees. The move today is toward a five-year program integrated with the undergraduate curriculum, but this is by no means the only route into architecture.

Similarly unstandardized are the feminized, subordinate fields of nursing and social work. The nurses have no strong professional school. Rather, hospital-based two- or three-year programs compete with two-year associate degree programs in junior colleges and with four-year baccalaureate programs in universities. For years, nurse traning in hospitals was a thinly disguised expedient to supply cheap labor. Only in the post-World War II era have registered nurses staffed the hospitals, rather than nurses-in-training.[8]

Social work likewise features a chaos of standards, positions, degrees, and training programs, with much variation among states with regard to regulation.[9] The movement to license social workers began only twenty years ago and has not spread far. Currently, only seventeen states require a license, and little reciprocity exists across states.[10] Some states offer an entry examination for bachelor's degree recipients, others for master's degree holders. Others require the Licensed Clinical Social Worker credential, which includes one to two years of supervised practice in addition to a master's degree. But little enforcement is typically found, and the field of private psychotherapy is crowded with unlicensed practitioners.

Teaching's standards appear inadequate to many today, and "the professions" are often invoked as the proper model. In fact, no single standard is found across the professions, although there has been a historical dynamic associated with development of university-based professional schools. Standards for the professions took definitive shape during the Progressive Era in the United States, but continue to evolve in all fields. Teaching is not the exception but the rule as it seeks professional standards in keeping with its own history, traditions, and unique circumstances.

## Quality and Quantity in Standard-Setting

A second common concern among professions is to raise standards, yet provide enough practitioners to meet demand. Teaching is so much larger than other professions that this problem seems unique to teaching, but in fact all human service occupations face this tension. Responses to supply-and-demand imbalances across the professions have taken a number of forms worth examining.

In medicine, the doctor or physician is synonymous with the M.D., but a variety of so-called "irregular" practitioners have resisted mainstream medicine's efforts to drive them out of the field, and continue to serve communities overlooked by elite, specialized medicine. These include osteopaths, with their own colleges and specialties, chiropractors, midwives, and Christian Science faith healers, among others. If elite medicine had successfully eliminated these varieties of practice, then today many communities across the country would be seriously underserved.

Over the years, other expedients took shape as well. In many publicly supported hospitals, residents and interns help with staffing needs, and during past periods of shortage, foreign-trained residents, often of dubious quality, filled up urban hospitals in New York City, Philadelphia, and elsewhere.[11] The medical establishment has since cracked down on this weak point in medical standard-setting. There now exists a special council to set standards for foreign-trained doctors wishing to practice in this country, including U.S. citizens who train off-shore at nonselective medical schools. (Recall, for example, the U.S. justification for the invasion of Grenada: there was a medical school there.)

Another common move in the professions has been the elaboration of new roles within the field. Following the return of many medicorps men and women from Vietnam, a new position, the physician's assistant, was created to take advantage of the medic's expertise and to help meet demand for medical care in underserved areas. Physician's assistants now have their own university-based training program, licensing examination, and professional organization. Their numbers are growing.

Nurses made a similar move in response to shortages during World War II. A new position in nursing, the practical or licensed vocational nurse arose, to supplement the registered nurse. Today both kinds of nurse serve in private care, hospitals, and nursing homes throughout the country. Again, practical nurses have their own training programs and requirements, licensure examinations, state practice laws, and professional organizations.

Other fields made related moves. In accounting, architecture, and engineering, there are considerably more practitioners than fully licensed professionals. In these fields, state law protects the title not the practice itself. This wrinkle on licensure means that one can practice accounting, architecture, or engineering without obtaining a license, but cannot call oneself a certified public accountant, a registered architect, or a certified engineer.

In architecture, for example, some 200,000 individuals practice in the field, of whom only 75,000 are registered. State law places restrictions on the kind of work and amount of responsibility that less than fully licensed individuals may undertake, but many still practice these professons in subordinate roles.

Of the major professions, law and teaching are somewhat unusual for evolving neither specialties nor new positions within the field. The law profession is informally bifurcated between those serving corporate interests—business, government, unions, etc., and those lawyers serving individual clients in private practice. But this division touches on the status system and the nature of the work, not formal distinctions within the profession.

In teaching, instructional aides work in many schools, but are not considered part of the teaching profession, and the role has not become formalized either as a widely recognized position (such as the practical nurse), or as a professional of lesser qualifications (such as an accountant who has not taken the certification examination).

Every profession had to create flexible means to meet demand. In most professions, however, the means did not threaten the status of the core professional. Either subqualified individuals were allowed restricted practice, or subordinate roles were created and institutionalized. In teaching, however, the expedients used to meet demand—emergency credentials, misassignment of teachers, and increased class sizes—have genuinely damaged the profession in at least three ways.

First, resorting to emergency credentials during times of shortage has allowed the unqualified to enter and stay in the profession. In the past, when large shortages occurred, entire cohorts of unqualified teachers have filled the ranks. Staying on, such teachers convey incompetence to an increasingly educated public, and contribute to teaching's image problems.

Second, increases in class size make teaching more difficult and less rewarding for teachers. Classes of thirty-five or more—not uncommon in recent years—prevent teachers from attending to individual needs, and make teaching an exercise in crowd control rather than education.

Finally, the heedless resorting to unqualified teachers undermines teaching's claim to professional status. It is relatively easy to enact the outer forms of commomplace teaching—lecturing, checking seatwork, keeping order—in many classrooms, without in fact teaching well. But to the casual and uninformed eye, all is well in such classrooms. Consequently, it appears that "anyone can teach," that no special knowledge or skill is required. Despite, or perhaps because of, teaching's ubiquity, detecting quality in teaching is a complex matter. Teaching has not been able to insist on quality when so many in the ranks have been underqualified.

## Excellence and Equity in the Professions

In the formative years of profession-building, the elite professions were able to insist on the quality of the individual practitioner as the most important factor, to the complete disregard of equity. Despite the egalitarian myth of open access to the professions, in contrast to the class-based system that had arisen in Europe, the standards movement helped exclude women, minorities, and immigrants from the professions, and this was quite intentional.[12]

As speeches, correspondence, conference proceedings, and journals of the era make clear, the elite professions sought not only to eliminate "overcrowding" in their fields—a euphemism for reducing supply to drive up fees—but to exclude certain "undesirables" from their ranks. To elevate the status of law, or medicine, or architecture meant association with the right sort of person—white, upper-middle-class, Anglo Saxon males.[13]

Informal policies simply excluded women and minorities. For example, medical schools had quotas on the number of women admitted, and the majority of hospitals in the country refused residencies to women.[14] And when, in 1912, the executive committee of the American Bar Association (ABA) inadvertently admitted two blacks they quickly asked them to resign and thereafter required all members to state their race, a practice not discontinued until 1943.[15]

Standard-setting abetted such tendencies. In the law, the profession's most fervent desire was to drive the urban night schools out of business, because those institutions catered to an ambitious immigrant clientele. The very thought of Jews, Italians, Poles, and other eastern

Europeans pouring into the law, made the elite corporate lawyers and law professors of the ABA and American Association of Law Schools (AALS) shudder in horror. Program accreditation standards became their weapon of choice in cleansing the bar, because the new immigrants has a disconcerting habit of passing the state bar examinations. Likewise, the Flexner report's effect in driving the proprietary medical schools out of business is well-known.

Standard-raising in the professions had an unintentional equity effect as well on the distributon and availability of services. Most clearly in medicine, the demise of the proprietary schools together with the growing specializaton of medicine meant that elite doctors would locate where practice was most lucrative. Rural and inner-city areas came to be underserved, a consequence of reform poignantly reckoned in 1910 by a doctor from a medical school in Chatanooga, Tennessee:

> True, our entrance requirements are not the same as those of the University of Pennsylvania or Harvard; nor do we pretend to turn out the same sort of finished product. Yet we prepare worthy, ambitious men who have striven hard with small opportunities and risen above their surroundings to become family doctors to the farmers of the south, and to the smaller towns of the mining districts . . . . Would you say that such people should be denied physicians? Can the wealthy who are in a minority say to the poor majority, you shall not have a doctor?[16]

Not until the 1960s and the Civil Rights movement was there sufficient public awareness of and concern for these problems. Then commenced in all professions a combination of government programs and professional reforms aimed at equity. These have had some modest successes, and gains have been registered. Today, considerably more women are enrolling in all the professional schools. Minorities have also made gains, although not as dramatically as women. And some reforms have aimed at a better distribution of medical, legal, and other human services. But the exclusionary legacy lives on, and initiatives aiming at redress are politically, fiscally vulnerable and subject to tokenism (witness, for example, attacks on the Legal Services Corporation by government and profession alike).

Teaching cannot afford to trade equity for excellence via an exclusionary strategy. Demand for teachers is too great. Taxpayer dollars cover teacher salaries, so their services must be distributed equitably as a matter of public policy. And times have changed. The expansion of individual rights attendant with the rise of the liberal state, and cultural shifts in the position of women and minorities rule out a return to the prejudices of an earlier era. The task for teaching is unprecedented: to create a mass profession dedicated to providing quality services without sacrificing equity.

## The Pivotal Role of the Professional School

Any reading of the rise of professionalism strongly suggests the centrality of the professional school. Professions took shape in America along with the modern university and this was no accident.

Professions rest on two claims—to knowledge and to trust. To profess means to know and to do what is right for the client. Professionals claim to possess special knowledge and to abide by an ethical code emphasizing the welfare of the client who typically comes before the professional with a serious problem. Our society has given professionals great authority to deal with such problems. A deed of trust has been granted that entails grave obligations.

How will professionals acquire this knowledge and this ethical code: by acquiring the special ways of knowing, judging, valuing, and acting that constitute the professional ethos? The answer begins with formal induction in a professional school. Only a strong initial set of experiences can properly launch a professional career. Beyond the school lies the community of practice and the company of fellows that constitute the reference group for professional behavior. Only in a professional school can one properly commence cultivating the knowledge, skills, and dispositions necessary to effective, ethical practice.

Such rhetoric captures the ideology of professionalism, but the professional school came to serve a variety of purposes. Most important, the school is critical to the generation and transmission of the knowledge base. Scientific medicine had its advent before the rise of the medical schools, but the growth of scientific medicine thereafter took place largely within the schools that served also to transmit the accumulating knowledge to future generations of physicians.

Likewise, the modern law school took shape at Harvard University under the deanship of Christopher Columbus Langdell from 1870 to 1895. Langdell championed the case method and sought to establish a fixed, formal course of study for all lawyers. "If law be not a science", he argued, "a university will best consult its own dignity in declining to teach it. If it be not a science, it is a species of handicraft, and may best be learned by serving an apprenticeship to one who practices."[17] Thus, did the law appropriate a scientific justification for a university-based school. Most other professions have attempted to follow suit.

But the professional school served a latent social function as well:

to screen out undesirables more effectively than tests or academic requirements. In the formative years, the elite professions sought to elevate their status through exclusive association with a certain class of individual. The ideology stressed meritocratic access, but in fact, as accreditation strategies drove out weaker institutions catering to immigrants and the working class, the social composition of the profession was altered as intended. The call for standards, for rigor, for public protection served twin purposes: to elevate the quality of professional preparation and to tramsform law and medicine into elite occupations.

The pursuit of status and competence proceeded hand in hand, with the professional school playing a pivotal role. Education, however, cannot afford an exclusionary strategy as it seeks to ground competence in science. A genuine professional school has yet to emerge in education, and no exemplars exist to rival the impact of Johns Hopkins in medicine or Harvard in law. Rather, the common view is to celebrate diversity in the preparation of teachers, acknowledging the wide range of institutions and programs suited to local conditions.

This view has much to recommend it, but, in terms of professionalization, poses a problem. In other fields. the professional school came to represent the claim for a knowledge base that was standardized. If the curriculum and experiences of teacher education varies among programs, then no core of knowledge appears necessary to effective practice, and the rationale for a profession is undercut. The "true" professions successfully negotiated a consensus on the knowledge base as part of the advancement strategy. The educational field must seek the grounds for such a consensus while respecting the need for diversity and sensitivity to local conditions. This, too, is an unprecedented challenge.


## TEACHING'S CIRCUMSTANCES

If other professions supply lessons for teaching, it is equally the case that teaching is distinctive in a number of respects. Teachers may yearn for the status and wages obtained by doctors and lawyers, but they are properly leery of inappropriate analogues and of professionalism's costs. Any effort to learn from the professions must begin with an appreciation of teaching's circumstances.

Teaching is a public monopoly featuring conscripted clients. Whereas other professions had to secure a market for their services teaching has a captive market based on compulsory education laws.

But this means teaching cannot establish governance arrangements akin to other fields. Tensions will exist between public and professional claims on governance. Policy based on claims of expertise will vie for legitimacy with policy based on representations of the public will. Policy to render teaching accountable will vie with policy to support sound professional judgment. Absent consumer choice, external regulation of teaching will enjoy a strong rationale.

Teaching is a mass profession. No other field, even nursing, approaches the teaching occupation in sheer size, in the numbers needed to keep school. Some 1,300 institutions currently prepare teachers as compared with 174 professional schools in law, 127 in medicine, 92 in architecture, and 383 baccalaureate degree programs in nursing. In the twentieth century, the need to supply enough teachers for a rapidly expanding system dominated the effort to set standards. This pressure persists, prompting calls for new staffing patterns, new roles and positions in the schools that might differentiate salaries and so relieve fiscal burdens while supplying the requisite numbers.

As already indicated, teaching today is heavily unionized. Other semiprofessions, notable nursing and social work, have flirted with unionism over the years, but only in teaching did their strategy take hold on a widespread basis. The organizations that represent teachers contain a large cadre of individuals committed to collective bargaining, to grievance and other due process procedures, to strikes and job actions, to political action at state and national levels, and to adversarialism in response to administrators and school boards.

The union posture is ill-fitted to the pursuit of professionalism. The operating style, underlying assumptions, strategies employed, and the issues agenda, do not square. Professionals, for example, seek control over standards of work as essential to their autonomy. Unions seek highly specified rules and contract requirements that delimit the responsibility of workers. Unions owe protection to their members. This legally binding obligation conflicts with injunctions to rid teaching of incompetents.

From a union perspective, then, incompetence is management's responsibility. Principals serving as agents of the school board evaluate teachers. From a professional perspective, however, incompetence is the profession's responsibility. Peer evaluation, however imperfectly it works in practice, is the professional norm.[18]

Can a heavily unionized occupation professionalize? No precedent exists for such an evolution, no guidelines on how to blend these orientations into a consistent advancement strategy. If the "professional union" is to be more than a contradiction in terms, the grounds for *rapprochement* have yet to emerge.

Another point. A triple whammy plagues teaching's status prospects. It is a feminized occupation involving service to low-status clients—the young—coupled with an equivocal mission in a competitive, materialistic society. Education stands for the American Dream, for hopes of the future, yet as Frances Fitzgerald discovered anew in her recent study of contemporary utopian communities, a strain of anti-intellectualism continues to pervade American life.[19] The citizenry regards teachers with what Lortie termed *reverence and disdain.* We honor teachers in our ideals and ignore them in practice. This mixed regard for the work will continue to case its shadow over efforts to professionalize teaching.

Historically, teaching has also suffered a stereotypical image as "women's work," as a default career for "unsaleable men and unmarriageable women," in Willard Waller's phrase.[20] The high-status, high-paying professions filled with men, the low-status, low-paying semiprofessions with women, who were managed by men. Today, only one-half this equation appears to be changing. In increasing numbers, women are entering the elite professions, but this movement has not served to benefit the semiprofessions. Rather, it appears that the cream is being skimmed among talented women. Perhaps we should update Waller by noting that teaching is becoming the refuge for unsaleable *women* as well as men.

Undoubtedly, this is too harsh and time-bound an assessment. Teaching as work and career is far more resilient than current recruitment trends suggest. The Women's Movement will continue to have potent effects in our society, with the trend toward greater equity. The social meaning of teaching may lose its gender-linked stigma, but this probably will occur slowly and fitfully. For the near term, the mixed regard for teaching will continue to cast a shadow over efforts to elevate its status.

Coupled with teaching's shadowed status is its sheer ubiquity. As Philip Jackson most recently reminds,[21] teaching is omnipresent in our culture. It occurs on television, at the YMCA, in private schools, in universities, in summer camps. Does teaching really require arcane, special knowledge? Appearances suggest otherwise. In other professions, the mysteries of practice contribute to the mastery of professionals. The public has little direct access to practice and so stands in some awe before the professional. The public sees so much of teaching that to sustain claims for a special knowledge base is much more difficult.

Closely related is the perception that teaching requires a fusion of ordinary with special knowledge. To the man in the street, much that a teacher does appears as related to personality dispositions and interpersonal skills as to the employment of technical knowledge. To an extent, every profession blends ordinary with special knowledge, but in teaching the balance appears tipped toward the commonplace. The formula "subject matter plus learning from experience" seems to capture what teachers must know. For at least the foreseeable future, teachers will have difficulty convincing the public otherwise.

Yet, a third issue distinguishes teaching's knowledge base. Most professions possess means for accumulating and transmitting knowledge useful for practice. The concept of a *codified* knowledge base implies not only a system of organization and verification, but of representation and transmission. For certain professions, science and technology compose the code.

In engineering and medicine, for example, the knowledge base for practice is represented in instruments, in written protocols, in compendia such as the Merck manual. In the law, the wisdom of practice is collected and transmitted via legal briefs, court decisions, laws and regulations, and commentaries such as Blackstone's. Carefully crafted cases compromise the curriculum of law school and many business schools. In architecture, the wisdom of the past is handed down via artifacts, plans, and drawings. Budding architects can visit the buildings of the great masters.

But in teaching, as in other human service fields (e.g., nursing, social work, and the ministry), the practitioner deals primarily in utterances, not texts or artifacts.[22] The accumulated experience of the practitioner, who works in isolation. Great teachers leave their marks on students, but not on teaching itself. Social science has begun to contribute precepts and principles useful in teaching, but much of what a good teachers knows may elude science's net.

In Gage's phrase,[23] there may be a scientific base for the art of teaching, but the science itself is probabilistic, requiring judgment in application, and the art remains. Teaching possesses no case knowledge, no method through which to capture, test, and transmit the craft knowledge of the effective teacher. Consequently, one source of wisdom about teaching—what the good teacher has learned and can do—remains untapped. Can social science alone provide the basis for codifying knowledge of teaching? This seems unlikely, but the search for supplementary, complementary, or alternative methods barely has begun.

Finally, teaching stands in a unique relation to the liberal arts. In other professions, the liberal arts form a noninstrumental basis for the profession. All professions seek well-educated men and women, but not for any direct connection to competence on the job. Rather, the liberal arts constitute what Lee Shulman calls an *entitlement,* rather than a *performance* standard.[24] To be entitled to serve as a doctor or lawyer in our society, one must first be an educated person. But this accepted standard allows a clear-cut separation of liberal arts and professional education, a clean distinction in the rationale for each (premedical requirements blur the distinction somewhat in medicine). In teaching, however, this relation is indistinct. The liberal arts serve as *both* entitlement and performance base for practice, making their combination into a course of study a deeply problematic matter.

## TEACHING'S PROSPECTS

The conclusion from even this brief and unsystematic analysis of teaching is inescapable. Teaching cannot in any crude way emulate other fields. Too much about teaching is unique; its special circumstances are fundamental not peripheral. No swift stroke can cut through the social knot binding together teaching's circumstances. What might be some starting points, though, for collective advancement in teaching?

Salary increases provide the most direct, policy manipulable factor, but as historical research has shown,[25] wages in teaching closely parallel fluctuations in demand for teachers. The specter of shortages impels salary increases but teaching's relative position in occupational rankings by average wage has changed little over the years. Teacher organizations must press continuously for higher salaries, but no dramatic breakthrough is likely.

To advance teaching, the tendency is to identify one or more prominent aspects of professionalism, then develop parallels in education. Three examples illustrate the trend: the effort to create standards controlled by the profession; to establish a postbaccalaureate professional school; and to introduce advanced positions into teaching.

The first strategy rises out of recommendations in *A Nation Prepared,* the report of the Carnegie Task Force on Teaching as a Profession.[26] This task force composed of the education coalition of the eighties—business leaders, elected public officials, and teacher organizations—recommended creation of a National Board of Professional Teaching Standards, and are taking steps to implement the recommendation. Research is underway on a new set of assessments for teaching, and a national board will be constituted.

A number of hopes rest on this development. Advocates of teacher professionalism hope that the effort to set standards will encourage emergence of a consensus on teaching's knowledge base, and will provide ground for teacher authority in the schools. If the board's certificate gains legitimacy, this will help undergird claims to expert knowledge in teaching, and will bolster teacher authority in the schools. Assessment procedures should also have a salutary effect on the curriculum of teacher education providing a more powerful conception of teaching around which to organize teacher preparation. And, if the standard includes residency requirements in the schools, then the process should encourage collegiality and involvement of teachers.

Teacher organizations hope that standard-setting will help increase teacher autonomy and control, shifting the balance from external regulation and accountability to professional responsibility. Furthermore, board certification may provide the basis for salary increases. One scenario proposes that districts and perhaps states might add increments to their salary schedules for certified teachers. In this manner, attention to standards will provide a basis for additional status and income.

For their part, elected officials view standard-setting as a desirable public posture. Board standards may provide an objective means for evaluating the quality of teachers, and may exert influence on state licensure standards. Certification may also provide a way to reward excellent teaching, and to identify talent for advanced positions in teaching. Standards connote rigor and scrutiny of teaching. If the public can be guaranteed of improvements in teaching, then they may be willing to allocate additional funds to education. According to these calculations, standards play a pivotal role in creating conditions for advancement.

A second starting point is the creation of a genuine professional school for teachers. This is the approach taken by the Holmes Group as advocated in their report, *Tomorrow's Teachers.*[27] Like the Carnegie report, this reform effort lays out an interconnected set of recommendations, urging that they be implemented in concert. The heart of this reform, however, is to establish a graduate-level professional school that joins a research-based curriculum with a solid liberal arts education, and extends teacher preparation into "professional development schools" that serve as analogs to teaching hospitals.

The Holmes Group also hopes to develop the knowledge base of teaching, as represented not in an assessment, but in a curriculum, hopes to strengthen ties between the university and the schools, and hopes to elevate teaching's status by providing advanced degree preparation for teachers. Part of the stigma that for years has attached to teachers derives from the low prestige associated with schools of education. If teaching is to become professional work, then teacher preparation must be strengthened and must secure greater status and resources on university campuses.

In every other profession, the rise of the professional school was critical to establishment of the profession. The professional school serves a number of indispensable functions, including conduct of research to expand the knowledge base, transmission of professional knowledge to the practitioner, initial socialization of the professional, and gatekeeping for entry. The Holmes Group represents a necessary attempt to establish professional education on a sound footing, to elevate the status of the enterprise, and to enlist the university as ally for the teaching profession.

Both the Holmes Group and The Carnegie Task Force endorse the third strategy, which is to introduce advanced positions into teaching. Teaching has always featured easy entry, high turnover, and reentry, especially among women who drop out to start families then return. Occupational commitment, at least as conceived in terms of the typical male career,[28] has been low in teaching.

A two-tier structure would allow many young people to enter teaching for several years at modest wage levels, then move on to other work. Those who wished to stay on could look forward to advanced positions, higher pay, and expanded responsibilities. This scheme would generate sufficient supply by drawing on the altruism of the young who wished to be "short termers," but would lay the groundwork for professionalism by creating a leadership cadre in teaching, who would be responsible for such advanced responsibilities as supervision and mentoring of neophytes, staff development, curriculum development, and schoolwide decisionmaking. Career teachers would have the option of working ten-to-twelve-month periods. The prospect of advancement into lead positions would help retain the best teachers, who otherwise may leave education entirely or move into administration.

This strategy has strong adherents in the policy community, and many states and localities have already initiated moves in this direction. However, the introduction of status distinctions into teaching has provoked skepticism and opposition from teachers.

From the union perspective, this reform is meddlesome because it undermines solidarity and complicates bargaining (e.g., are teachers who supervise other teachers actually quasiadministrators?). But teachers themselves are also suspicious. Creating advanced positions appears to introduce competition into the teaching ranks, where cooperation is called for; it subtly depreciates regular classroom teaching by rewarding responsibilities outside the classroom; and it threatens to create yet a new layer of bureaucracy in the schools composed of lead or master teachers who oversee the work of regular teachers. Teachers also fear that such plans are in reality disguised merit pay that will reward the few but do little to improve the quality of teaching.[29]

Each of these strategies holds promise, but entails risks. The technical, logistic, and political problems associated with standard-setting are formidable. The effort to establish a genuine professional school for teachers requires some heroic assumption about the capacity and willingness to change in universities dominated by an academic status system and a tradition of faculty control. And the move to create new positions in teaching meets strong resistance from teachers themselves and runs the risks outlined above.

Professionalism is a powerful and beguiling theme with which to rationalize the reform of teaching. However, as this analysis has illustrated, serious social costs have been associated with professionalism as well. Teaching is different from other professions in many respects, but even if similarities outweighed differences, there would be good reason to avoid wholehearted embrace of professionalism modelled on medicine and the law.

As teaching seeks to elevate its status and prospects, it must attend to a broader set of concerns. Professionalism alone is not enough. There must be a social vision animating reform that encompasses but is not limited to the interests of teachers. Educational reform must embrace equity goals, must honor the rights of parents and communities, must promote tolerance for diversity and responsiveness to clients.

In the current historical moment, the rallying cry is "Excellence!" and the dominant rationale is economic competitiveness. Teacher professionalism fits comfortably with these themes. "Fewer and better schools" was Flexner's rallying cry when he made his visits to medical schools. The posture led to fewer and better doctors as well, a single-minded emphasis on the technical excellence of the individual practitioner.

Teachers cannot strike such a narrow, socially impoverished bargain. Improving the technical adequacy of teaching and enhancing the prospects of the profession via higher standards, better professional education, and career ladders must be coupled with a broader social vision of teaching and of education. Concern with instrumental aspects of reform must now be matched with attention to the ideals of reform.

To what ends should we pursue professionalism in teaching? This is the question we must now ask.

## NOTES

1. For an ordinary language analysis of the concept *professionalism,* see J. Moline, "Teachers and Professionalism", in C. E. Finn, D. Ravitch, and R. T. Fancher, eds., *Against Mediocrity. The Humanities in America's High Schools* (New York: Holmes & Meier, 1984), pp. 197–213.

2. G. Sykes, "The Social Consequences of Standard-Setting in the Professions," paper prepared for the Carnegie Task Force on Teaching as a Profession (New York: Carnegie Forum, November 1986), p. 3.

3. This account of professionalism is well-represented in the sociological literature on the professions. The standard reference is M. S. Larson, *The Rise of Professionalism* (Berkeley: University of California Press, 1977).

4. On various aspects in the relationship between the university and the professions, see L. Veysey, *The Emergence of the American University* (Chicago: University of Chicago Press, 1965), for the definitive history; B. Bledstein, *The Culture of Professionalism* (New York: W. W. Norton & Co., 1976), for the early evolution of the relationship; and C. Jencks and D. Reisman, *The Academic Revolution* (Garden City, N.Y.: Doubleday, 1968), for an analysis of strains in the relationship.

5. The rise of the medical profession is treated exhaustively in P. Starr, *The Social Transformation of American Medicine* (New York: Basic Books, 1982); and with special emphasis on the development of medical school in K. Ludmerer, *Learning to Heal: The Development of American Medical Education* (New York: Basic Books, 1985).

6. The definitive history of the development of the legal profession, the law school, and standards for the law is R. Stevens, *Law School. Legal Education in America from the 1850s to the 1980s* (Chapel Hill, N.C: University of North Carolina Press, 1983). For a parallel account emphasizing development of the legal profession outside the elite eastern establishment, see W. R. Johnson, *Schooled Lawyers: A Study in the Clash of Professional Cultures* (New York University Press, 1978).

7. See National Council of Architectural Registration Boards, *Architect Registration Examination Handbook, Volume 1.* (Washington, D.C.: NCARB, 1985). For a thoughtful discussion of trends and controversies in architectural education, see R. Gutman, "Educating Architects: Pedagogy and the Pendulum," *The Public Interest,* 80 (Summer 1985): 67–91.

8. For a standard source on nursing history, see P. A. Kalisch and B. J. Kalisch, *The Advance of American Nursing* (2nd edition) (Boston: Little, Brown,

1982). For the recent revisionist history, see the study by B. Melosh, *"The Physician's Hand". Work Culture and Conflict in American Nursing* (Philadelphia: Temple University Press, 1982); and a collection of essays by E. C. Lagemann, ed., *Nursing History: New Perspectives, New Possibilities* (New York: Teacher's College Press, 1983).

9. A recent interpretative history of the rise of American social work, including attention to strains associated with professionalization efforts is J. H. Ehrenreich, *The Altruistic Imagination. A History of Social Work and Social Policy in the United States* (Ithaca, N.Y.: Cornell University Press, 1985).

10. A. Lareau, "A Comparison of Professional Examinations in Six Fields: Implications for the Teaching Profession" Occasional Paper. (Stanford: October 1985).

11. R. Shryock, *Medical Licensing in America. 1650–1965* (Baltimore, Md.: Johns Hopkins Press, 1967).

12. The case is most clear in the law. See J. S. Auerbach, *Unequal Justice: Lawyers and Social Change in Modern America* (New York: Oxford University Press, 1976). Recent scholarship has traced efforts of women and minorities who persevered in entering the elite professions despite the barriers. See, for example, R. M. Morantz-Sanchez, *Sympathy and Science: Women Physicians in American Medicine* (New York: Oxford University Press, 1985); K. B. Morello, *The Invisible Bar. The Woman Lawyer in America: 1638 to the Present* (New York: Random House, 1986); and G. R. Segal, *Blacks in the Law* (Philadelphia: University of Pennsylvania Press., 1983).

13. See Auerbach; and G. Markowitz and D. Rosner, "Doctors in Crisis," in S. Reverby and D. Rosner, *Health Care in America: Essays in Social History* (Philadelphia: Temple University Press, 1979), pp. 185–205.

14. See M. Walsh, *"Doctors Wanted: No Women Need Apply": Sexual Barriers in the Medical Profession, 1835–1975* (New Haven, Conn.: Yale University Press, 1977).

15. Segal, pp. 18ff.

16. Qouted in Starr, p. 125.

17. Quoted in Stevens, p. 52.

18. For an exploration of these issues, compare E. M. Bridges, *The Incompetent Teacher* (Philadelphia: Falmer Press, 1986), with L. Darling-Hammond, "A Proposal for Evaluation in the Teaching Profession," *Elementary School Journal*, Vol. 86 4 (March 1986): 531–52.

19. F. Fitzgerald, *Cities on a Hill* (New York: Simon and Schuster, 1986).

20. W. Waller, *The Sociology of Teaching* (New York: John Wiley and Sons, 1932), p. 61.

21. P. W. Jackson, *The Practice of Teaching* (New York: Teachers College Press, 1986).

22. This distinction derives from D. R. Olson, "From Utterance to Text," *Harvard Education Review,* Vol. 47 3 (August 1977): 257–81.

23. N. L. Gage, *The Scientific Basis of the Art of Teaching* (New York: Teacher's College Press, 1978).

24. L. Shulman, personal communication.

25. See M. Sedlak and S. Schlossman, "Who Will Teach? Historical Perspectives on the Changing Appeal of Teaching as a Profession," (R-3472-CSTP) (Santa Monica, Calif.: The Rand Corporation, November 1986).

26. Carnegie Forum on Education and the Economy, *A Nation Prepared: Teachers for the 21st Century.* (New York: Carnegie Forum, 1986).

27. The Holmes Group, *Tomorrow's Teachers: A Report of the Holmes Group* (East Lansing, Mich.: The Holmes Group, 1986). See also the collection of articles critiquing this report in *Teachers College Record,* 88 (3), Spring 1987).

28. For a critique of male-centered conceptions of the teaching career, see S. K. Biklen, "I Have Always Worked': Elementary Schoolteaching as a Career," *Phi Delta Kappan,* Vol. 67 7 (March 1986): 504–8.

29. Career ladder schemes in teaching have received considerable scrutiny. For criticisms of the idea, see S. Rosenholtz, "Political Myths About Educational Reform: Lessons From Research on Teaching", *Phi Delta Kappan,* Vol. 66 5 (January 1985): 349–55; and S. Rosenholtz, "Career Ladders and Merit Pay: Capricious Fads or Fundamental Reforms," *Elementary School Journal,* Vol. 86 4 (March 1986): 513–30. For a thoughtful article supporting the introduction of new positions into teaching, see K. Devaney, "The Lead Teacher: Ways to Begin," paper prepared for the Carnegie Task Force on Teaching as a Profession (Washington, D.C.:Carnegie Forum, March 1987).

# Contributors

Michael W. Apple is Professor of Curriculum and Instruction and Educational Policy Studies at the University of Wisconsin, Madison.

Robert V. Bullough Jr. is Associate Professor of Educational Studies and Chair, Division of Secondary Education, University of Utah in Salt Lake City.

Robert Calfee is Professor of Education and Psychology at Stanford University.

Charles W. Case is Dean of the School of Education, University of Connecticut at Storrs.

Catherine Cornbleth is Professor of Social Studies Education at the State University of New York at Buffalo.

Hendrick D. Gideonse is University Professor of Education and Policy Science at the University of Cincinnati.

Andrew Gitlin is Associate Professor in the Educational Studies Department at the University of Utah in Salt Lake City.

Stephen Jacobson is Assistant Professor of Educational Administration and Policy at the State University of New York at Buffalo.

Susan Moore Johnson is Assistant Professor of Administration, Planning, and Social Policy at the Harvard Graduate School of Education in Cambridge.

Mary Haywood Metz is Professor of Educational Policy Studies at the University of Wisconsin, Madison.

Linda M. McNeil is Associate Professor of Education at Rice University in Houston.

Niall C. W. Nelson is Head of the International School of Tanganyika in Tanzania.

Hugh G. Petrie is Dean of the Faculty of Educational Studies at the State University of New York at Buffalo.

Albert Shanker is President of the American Federation of Teachers, AFL–CIO.

R. Jerrald Shive is Associate Dean of the College of Education, University of Iowa in Iowa City.

Gary Sykes is Associate Professor in the Department of Teacher Education at Michigan State University in East Lansing.

Alan R. Tom is Professor and Chair of the Department of Education, Washington University in St. Louis.

Lois Weis is Associate Professor and Associate Dean in the Faculty of Educational Studies at the State University of New York at Buffalo.

# About the Editors

*Lois Weis* is Associate Professor and Associate Dean in the Faculty of Educational Studies, State University of New York at Buffalo.

*Philip G. Altbach* is Professor of Education and Director of the Comparative Education Center, State University of New York at Buffalo.

*Gail P. Kelly* is Professor in and Chair of the Department of Educational Organization, Administration and Policy, State University of New York at Buffalo.

*Hugh G. Petrie* is Dean of the Faculty of Educational Studies, State University of New York at Buffalo.

*Sheila Slaughter* is Associate Professor in the Faculty of Education, University of Arizona.

# Index

279

[